Practical Music Theory

New Insights for Students, Teachers and Working Musicians

Jon P. Nicholson and Robert Greiff

ISBN: 979-8-80-549157-4 (Paperback)
ISBN: 979-8-81-317522-0 (Hardback)
First printing edition 2022

Website: www.practical-music-theory.com
Computer Exercises: www.practical-music-theory.com/Download.aspx

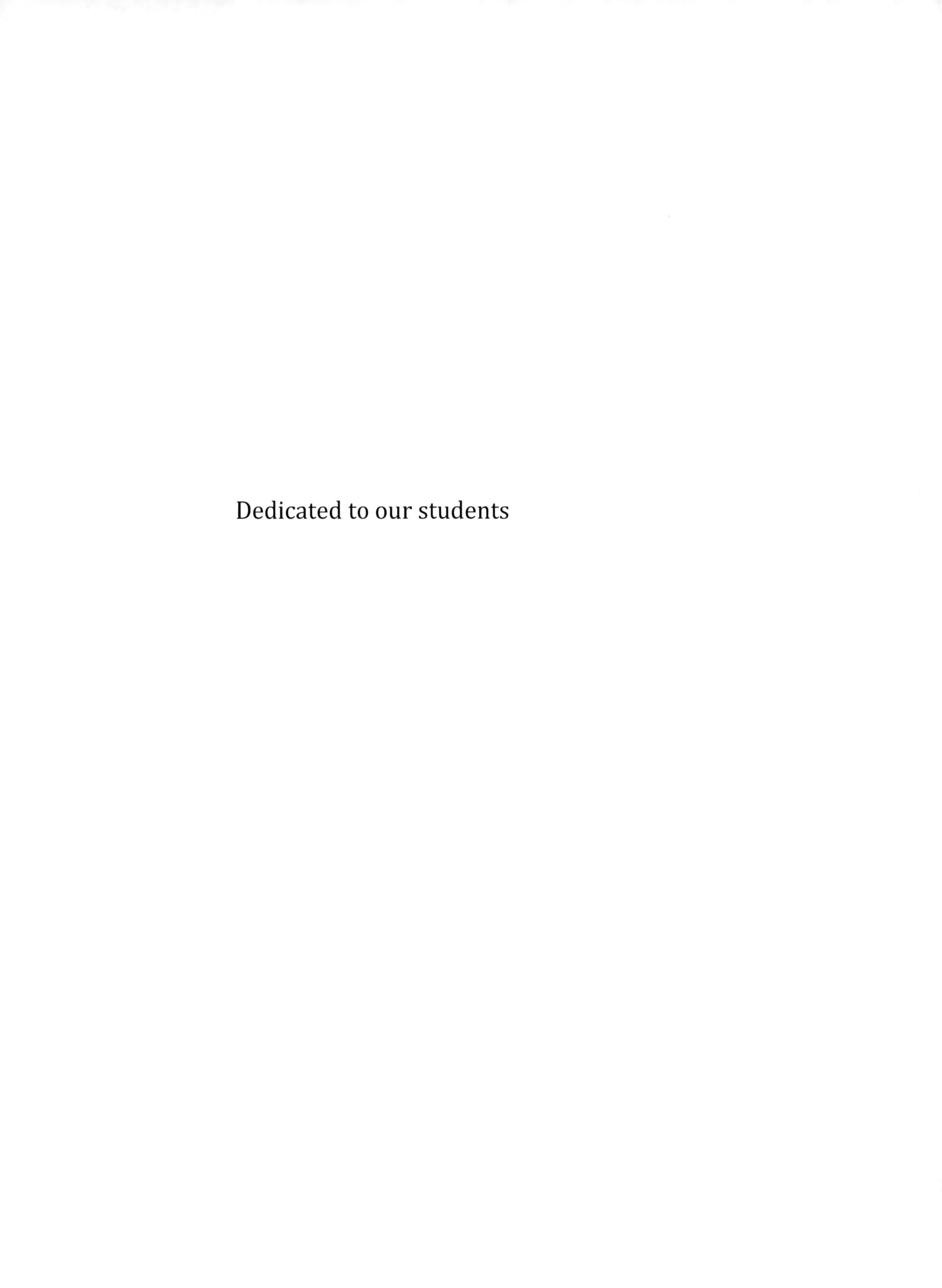

Dedicated to our students

Table of Contents

Preface

"You don't have to be a genius to study music, but if you study music long enough you will become one." (Rekrap Noj)

Music is a serious challenge to the brain. It is also a very enjoyable and fulfilling experience. These two together make music one of the most effective tools available for brain development in young children or for anyone else with a brain. It has also proven to be a very effective therapy for mental health. There are several parts of the brain involved in creating or even listening to music. Consequently the study of music theory is not an easy endeavor, and any teacher who claims to have created an "easy" method of learning music theory is a teacher to be avoided. If it's easy you won't be learning much about music.

That being said, there are some overly difficult ways to teach music theory and then there's this book. Many years of teaching hundreds of students have revealed a lot of barriers to learning music theory due to ambiguous definitions, conflicting opinions, and just plain laborious and useless "rules" that are supposed to be memorized but serve no purpose. Such unrewarding exercises make music study frustrating and take away the joy and fulfillment inherent in music so that only the most determined and/or masochistic students will survive to the rewarding life of a working musician.

This book is a second opinion. There are many publications out there that explain how to read key signatures, how to construct minor triads, plagal cadences, German augmented sixth chords, proper voice leading and avoiding parallel octaves or fifths. These are all important aspects of reading music but they are often presented in terms that make music study more difficult than it needs to be.

Case in point: solfeggio. This is a system whereby students are taught to label each of the 7 notes of the diatonic scale with a one-syllable name – Do, Re, Mi etc. But we already know how to count to 7! The only advantage to solfege is that the names are easy to sing and they're all only one syllable. I have yet to find a student that couldn't manage to sing numbers. And "fixed Do" is absurd. You won't have to learn these systems here.

Almost as useless is the identification of scale degrees by functional names – Tonic, Supertonic, Mediant, etc. Once again, we already know how to count to 7. However, because of the common use of these terms among musicians, (I had to learn it so you must also) in order to converse intelligently with other musicians you will need to know them. (See Chapter 5.)

This book is for musicians, teachers, and students who are thinking about becoming teachers. You may be a total beginner starting from square 1, in which case this book, as a supplement to a graded course for your instrument, will guide you step by step from that clean slate through at least the first semester of college music theory. Or, you may be a teacher who already knows a lot of music theory stuff but you would like a fresh look from perhaps a new angle and perhaps a more logical way to explain how music works. We still start from the beginning, not because you don't already know how to find middle C but because middle D might be a better place to start. (See Chapter 2.)

Another emphasis in this book is the application of what you will learn in music theory to musical performance. There are not many musicians with a college degree that can remember, *e. g.,* how to construct and resolve a French augmented 6th chord. They had to learn it in order to pass the exam in 3rd semester theory, but forgot it the day after the exam, which is really sad because recognizing a chord progression with a French augmented 6th chord offers the performer an opportunity to really tap into the expressiveness of the great masters' works. There is a much simpler way to analyze, understand, and use the augmented 6th chords in compositions and improvisations than the traditional explanations found in every theory text that I have read. (Except this one. See Chapter 25.)

In this book a lot of emphasis is placed on rhythm. (See Chapters 1, 15, 18, and 20.) Pretty much everything about music is rhythm. A musical pitch is a regular pulsating rhythm faster than *ca.* 20 cycles per second (cps). An irregular pulsation is called noise. When one hears regular rhythmic pulses slower than 20 cps, one can distinguish the individual clicks or whatever type of sound is pulsating. Above 20 cps the regular pulsations are interpreted by the human brain as a musical pitch, *ergo,* a musical pitch is rhythm. Beyond *ca.*

20,000 cps you hear nothing (unless you're a dog). Somewhere between *ca.* 20 and 20,000 cps is what we humans recognize as musical pitches.

The faster the pulsation rate the "higher" the pitch. The explosions inside the cylinders of a car engine are considerably faster than 20 cps, and therefore produce a musical pitch. As the engine accelerates you can hear the pitch rising. It would be more accurate to compare pitches as "faster" or "slower" rather than "higher" or "lower." However, for this text the more common terms will be used.

Rhythm is also the element that makes music such a difficult art. The musician must not only play the correct pitches, she/he must play them at exactly the right split instant. Because of this inherent difficulty I tell my students they must learn to live with mistakes because it is impossible to play the hundreds or thousands of pitches in a composition at precisely the right moment at just the right dynamic level with exactly the right articulation and expect to get them all correct. No matter how well you perform a piece, it could have been better. That's why we practice, practice, practice, to make each performance the best possible.

To help us live with our mistakes we concentrate on all the right tones we produce. Yes, I missed the A-sharp, but the other chord tones around it were gorgeous. Also, my finger knew it didn't feel quite right and it hardly even sounded. I tell my students that they will have many decades of playing before they make as many mistakes as I have. Even so, I've had a pretty good income as a working musician and in spite of all my mistakes I still love to play and sing for an audience.

The information given in this text is for the purpose of understanding the commonly accepted methods of creating music today. There are composers who experiment with new sound patterns that cannot be expressed with the usual methods of writing music. This text is not concerned with those types of experimental music. In order to avoid loading the text with a bunch of "usually"s the reader should assume that the comments are addressing only the "commonly accepted methods of writing and playing music today."

Each student has his/her own unique way of learning and each class of students takes on a group dynamic that requires a unique approach for teaching that particular class. The purpose of this book is to present information in a succinct and unambiguous way so as to avoid the confusion found among many books, musicians, teachers, and students of music. This confusion has grown from inaccuracies in training based not necessarily on lack of intelligence in the teacher, student, or author but frequently on ambiguous terminology. The teacher or author may assume meanings that are not the same as in the students' unique experiences. When these students become teachers and authors themselves, these misinterpreted meanings get passed on as mistakes. I hope this writing gives you a more logical and more understandable approach to the study of music theory.

A very important and very helpful aspect of music theory is the patterns that become apparent as we learn the different concepts. Be on the lookout for patterns that apply to more than one item. To the new student, the major scales may appear to have nothing in common with each other. Each scale has a unique set of sharps, flats, and naturals, a unique set of pitches, a unique set of notes on the page, and on the keyboard a unique set of black and white keys. But they must have something in common to all be lumped together as "major scales." What does major scale mean? The most important thing about a major scale is its sound! The sound of a major scale is the relationship of its various pitches to each other. That relationship is produced by playing (in ascending order) whole step, whole step, half step, whole step, whole step, whole step, half step. That pattern of whole and half steps is common to all major scales. All the rest of scale study – black and white keys, fingering, key signatures, functional names – are for the purpose of producing that *sounding* relationship of the pitches of a major scale to each other. Major scales are just one example. Look for the patterns in every item presented in these pages. It will help you to understand, to remember, and to give more meaning to what you are learning.

It is well known that an excellent way to learn something is to teach it. If a student considers how to explain the concepts of music theory to another student, a deeper and more permanent understanding of the material can be gained. As you study this book think of how you would explain each concept to someone else. Even better, find yourself some students to teach

I rarely answer questions from students except as another question. My questions are designed to help the students figure out answers for themselves. The concept is then more permanently fixed in their minds than when merely answering the initial questions. Often the question will be addressed to the rest of the class so they can all work out the answer. Students should be encouraged to ask other students for help with their difficulties. Every student involved will benefit. Classroom discussion is a powerful learning tool.

Another powerful learning tool was employed by the late, great composer, conductor, and professor, Dr. Grant Fletcher at Arizona State University. It is quite simple and useful for students from pre-school to the end of life. If one wants to set something permanently in the memory, the more different ways one can express that concept the more firmly it will be stored in the memory. In Dr. Fletcher's classes, when the students were instructed to write something they were also expected to say out loud what they were writing. If the class was asked to write the key signature of E-major on a grand staff, the students would say out loud every detail of the exercise as they wrote it: "Grand staff, G-clef, F-clef, E-major, four sharps, F♯, C♯, G♯, D♯." If it was a speed drill the students would raise their pencils when they were finished. When 2/3 of the pencils were raised the next challenge was given. It was quite a fun experience and we really learned the stuff. Even when studying alone, saying or especially singing, what you are doing will help you retain new ideas.

In the discussions on rhythm, dissonance, and other elements of music, coefficients are sometimes used. You have probably encountered this concept in math and algebra. Just as a reminder, the coefficients, or powers, of 2 refer to the number sequence of 2^1, 2^2, 2^3, 2^4, etc., which is equivalent to 2, 4, 8, 16, etc. The coefficients or powers of 3 would be 3^1, 3^2, 3^3, 3^4, etc. which is equivalent to 3, 9, 27, 71, etc. As an example of the application to music study, a power of 2 would be the only number used as the bottom number of a meter/time signature.

There are many signs and terms in music notation with more than one name. Some of these differences are because of the different languages used in music. Others are just different terms for the same symbol that are in common use among musicians. A few examples are:

beats also known as (aka) counts

treble clef aka G-clef

bass clef aka F-clef

meter aka time signature

bar aka measure.

A musician needs to be familiar with all these terms since they are in common use. They may be used interchangeably throughout this text. After the initial presentation I will probably choose the term most accurately descriptive of the symbol, *e, g.* F clef instead of bass clef. After that I will probably choose the term that requires the least amount of ink on the page or is the easiest to pronounce, *e. g.* meter instead of time signature and bar instead of measure.

The following definitions of terms will be used in this text:

Pitch: The auditory sensation of a musical sound produced by a steady vibration rate between *ca.* 20 and 20,000 cps.

Note: A written symbol on a music staff indicating the letter name and rhythmic value of a pitch (as in notation).

Key: 1. A key on a music keyboard, such as a piano. 2. The tonal center of a composition.

PNK: From time to time you will find comments in this book which are equally applicable to a pitch, a note, and a key on a music keyboard. The acronym PNK (pronounced "pink") will then be used. For example, the 3 PNKs of a C major triad are C, E, and G, meaning the notes on a score, the keys on a piano, and the pitches that you hear with a C major triad are C, E, and G.

There is a set of interactive computer exercises on the CD attached to this text. They are at least equally important as the text itself for mastering musical skills. This symbol: .

Computer exercise 1.1

---

will appear at the appropriate place to stop reading, open the exercise identified, and practice it. The more thoroughly these skills are mastered the more readily you will be able to understand what comes next. Other written exercises are given in the text but the computer interactive exercises are more fun and very effective.

This book is **not** an "easy" approach to learning music theory. Such an approach doesn't exist. But if you stay with it to the end of the book and learn to play the computer exercises you will be amply rewarded for your efforts and you won't waste time with stuff you don't need. Applying the information and techniques to your keyboard and/or other instrument will enable you to join us in the happiest and smartest group of people on the planet – the musicians.

Chapter 1 – Rhythm I

Rhythm
Meters aka Time Signatures
Beat Values of Notes
Rests
Ties
Dots

Rhythm

The first thing to learn about rhythm is how to spell it. It has no vowel in the second syllable, and only a "substitute" vowel in the first.

The importance of rhythm in music cannot be overemphasized. Listen to the following melody and see if you can recognize it.

Example 1-A

Now listen to that same sequence of notes played with a different rhythm:

Example 1-B

You hear the same exact sequence of pitches but an entirely different song when the rhythm is changed. Any piece of music that you know can become unrecognizable if the rhythm is changed. This means that if you play incorrect rhythm you are playing a different composition from the one written. So let's learn how to read rhythm notation correctly.

Meters aka Time Signatures

Music is notated on a staff of five lines. On the left end of the staff is a clef sign (discussed later) followed by a key signature (discussed later) followed by the **meter,** also known as (aka) the **time signature.** A meter consists of two numbers, one above the other.

Example 1-C

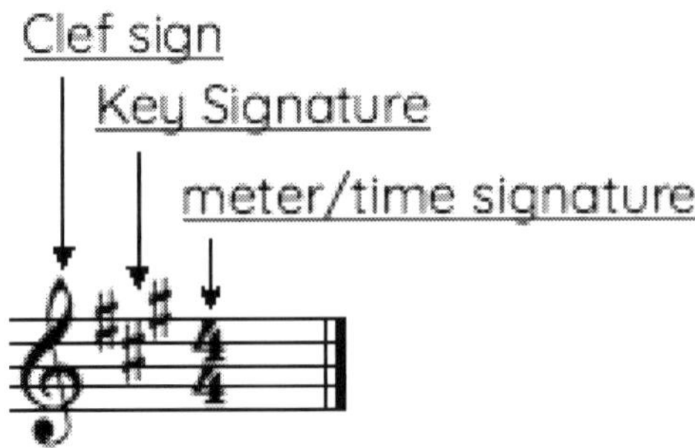

The clef sign and key signature appear at the beginning of every staff of the music. The meter appears only at the beginning of the first staff, unless the composer changes to a different meter later in the piece.

The staff is divided by **bar lines** into sections called **measures** aka **bars**. There is a **double bar** at the end of a composition. Find and identify the clef signs, key signatures, meters, bar lines, measures, and double bars in Examples 1-A and 1-B above.

Music is performed within a system of even beats like the ticking of a clock. The top number of a meter indicates how many of these beats occur in each bar. A metronome can be very helpful. Set the speed as slowly as necessary for you to maintain even beats.

The time signature in Example 1-A indicates that the music is to be played with 4 beats per bar and Example 1-B has three beats per bar. The first beat of each bar is felt as the strongest beat, which defines the group.

Musicians know the value of counting the beats out loud, or tapping the beats with their foot while playing or singing, even while using the metronome. This helps to assure that the notes are played at the proper time and held for the proper duration. With your metronome set at 100 beats per minute (bpm), count out loud an even "**1** – 2 – 3" for each bar in Example1-D below, emphasizing the **1**s.

Example 1-D

Some music moves fast and some moves slowly. Whether the beats are fast or slow they must be even. For Example 1-D above set the metronome at 120bpm and count, then set it at 80bpm and count. Set the metronome at different speeds for all the counting exercises that follow.

The top number of a meter may be any whole number, but is usually within the range of 2 to 12. The most common of these top numbers are 2, 3,

4, or 6. The first beat of each bar is always the strongest beat, but any time the top number is 4 or more, there can be more than one strong beat in each bar. Count the beats out loud in the two examples below, emphasizing the strong beats, which are underlined.

Example 1-E

Example 1-F

Beat Values of Notes

A note on a music staff may consist of three different parts – the note head, the stem, and one or more flags or beams. In combination with the meter this tells the musician when to play a Pitch/Note/Key (PNK) and how long to sustain it.

Example 1-G

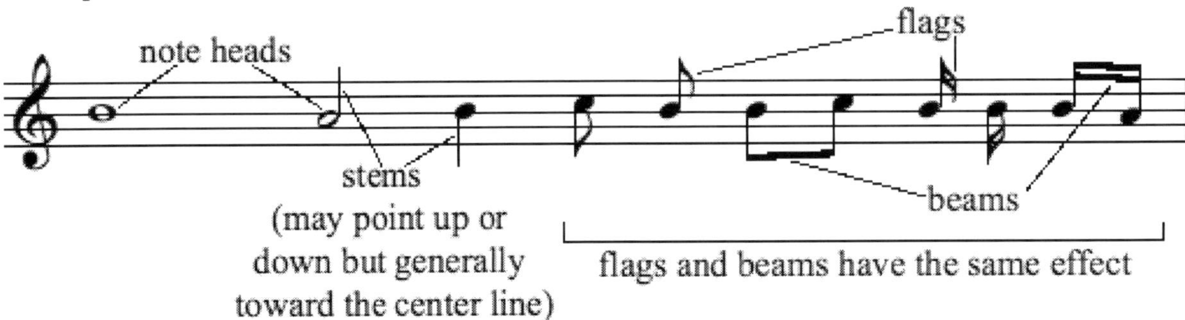

The longest note value in Example 1-G above is the first one on the left, a hollow circle. Every time something is added to the circle it cuts its time value in half. With a stem added to the circle it would take two of the second note to equal one of the first. With the circle filled in it would take two of the third note to equal one of the second. A flag or beam cuts it in half again as does each additional flag or beam. These elements of a note tell us it's time duration compared to other notes.

Note values are identified by different names in different countries. The British and U. S. names for some of these notes are shown in Example 1-H below.

Example 1-H

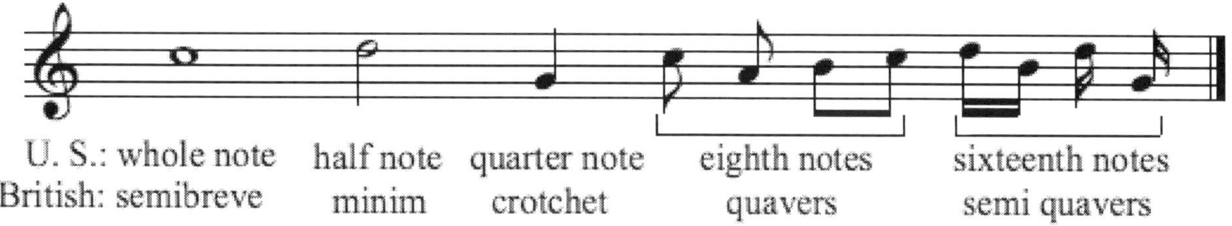

The American frational names of notes sometimes confuse students because they think the fractional name of the note is its time value. Seems logical to me that a note called a half note should get a half beat. Unfortunately, the fractional namc of a note would be it's actual time value only if the bottom number of the meter was 1, which rarely if ever occurs.

Every note in Example 1-I below has a fractional name different from its beat value. I much prefer the British names for that reason. However, I don't live in the British empire and you're learning from this American book so we're stuck with the American system. Musicians are smarter than the average bear so most likely you will overcome this anomaly. When a meter assigns beat/partial beat values to the notes the confusion can be avoided if we use those values to identify the notes, *e. g.* calling a half note a 2-count note, an eighth note a half-count note, etc. These count-value names will be determined by the bottom number of the meter. The count-value is what you need to know to perform the music.

The bottom number of a meter will always be a power of 2. The most common are 2, 4, and 8, but 16 and 32 are not unknown. The bottom number indicates how many beats a whole note receives. In Example 1-I below, the bottom number of the meter is 4. Therefore the whole note is a four-beat note. The half notes have a stem added to the circle, which cuts their time value in half. In 4/4 meter a half note is a two-beat note. The quarter notes, in addition to stems, have the circles filled in. In 4/4 meter they are 1 beat notes. The eighth notes, with one flag, are 1/2 beat notes. It takes 2 of them to make 1 beat. The sixteenth notes, with two flags, are 1/4 beat notes, 4 to a beat.

Example 1-I

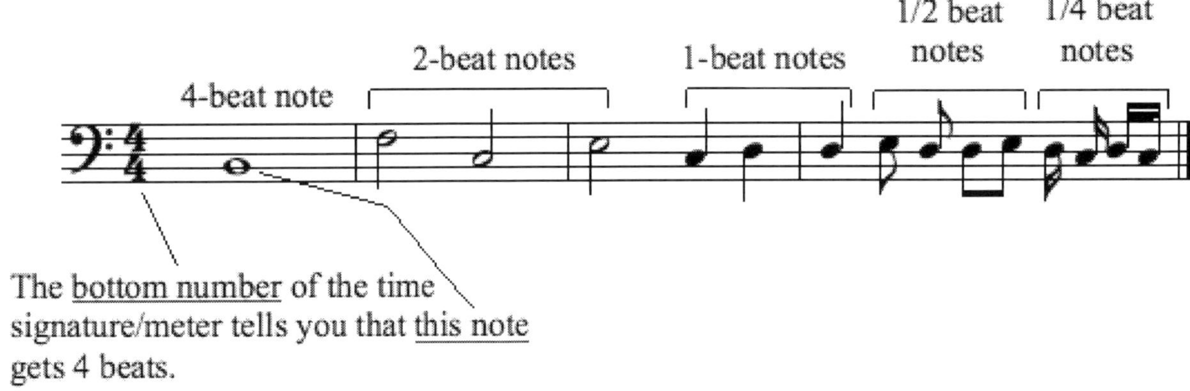

Example 1-J below shows meters with different powers of 2 for the bottom number. The top number indicates the number of beats in each bar.

Example 1-J

A meter is similar to a fraction. If the bottom number of a fraction is larger than the top number, the fraction is < 1. In the case of the meter, if the bottom number is larger than the top number there would be insufficient beats in a bar to accommodate the largest note value – the whole note. The determination of the time values of the other notes would still be their fractional relation to the whole note.

The total time value of the beats in each bar must equal the top number of the meter. In Example 1-K below, each bar contains four beats (indicated by the top number of the meter) and a whole note would receive eight beats (indicated by the bottom number). The fraction 4/8 < 1, and an eight-beat note won't fit in one bar. You cannot squeeze an 8-beat note into a 4-beat bar.

Example 1-K

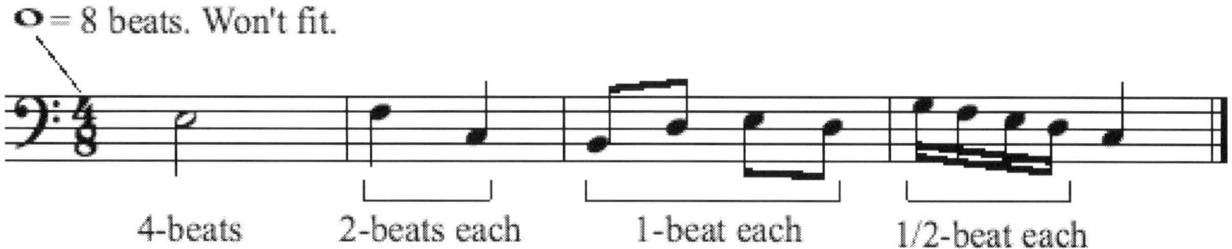

As mentioned earlier, an excellent way to assure that you are playing the correct rhythm is to count out loud while playing. It is helpful to use a counting system that accommodates the <u>shortest note value in the piece</u>. If there are half-count notes in the music you can count "1 and 2 and 3 and 4 and." The "and"s are the second half of each beat and are represented by & in Example 1-L below. When counting, be sure that the numbers and the &s are evenly spaced in time so that both halves of every beat get the same amount of time.

Notice that even for the bars with no half-count notes, the half counts are still given. This is to avoid the very common mistake of giving whole-count PNKs the same amount of time as half-count PNKs when the half counts are not spoken. In the example below, tap one tap for each note while counting out loud. Practice it until you can do it with even counts and properly uneven PNKs. (Think about it. This will be your goal for every piece you perform.)

Example 1-L

What about a piece with one-fourth count (or shorter) notes? For a piece in 4/4 meter, the note with two flags or two beams gets 1/4 beat, or 4

notes to one beat. They can be accommodated by counting as in Example 1-M below. Count out loud and tap the notes as you did in the above example.

Example 1-M

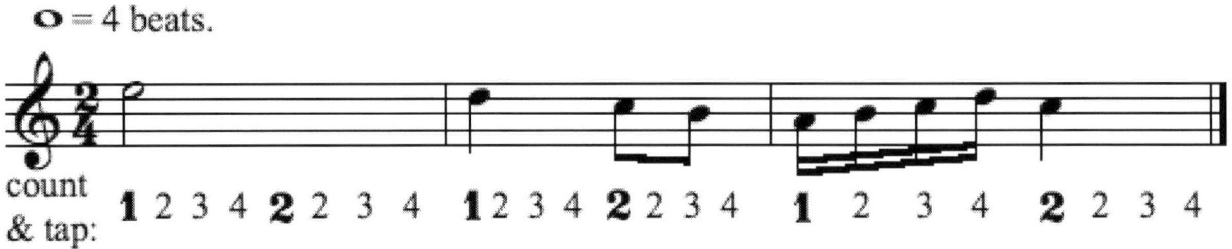

Notice in these examples, and in published music, that the horizontal spacing of the note heads on the staff most often does *not* correspond exactly to the beat value relationships of the notes. This is especially true with vocal music where the note spacing has to accommodate the lyrics. The notes have to align with the syllables being sung and there is a wide variation in the lengths of syllables. The musician must know well the rhythmic values and relationships of the notes and not be distracted by their horizontal spacing on the staff.

Rests

Sometimes a composer wants to include beats or partial beats of silence, where no sound is being played or sung. Musical signs called **rests** are used to indicate beats or partial beats of silence. Each type of note has a corresponding rest. Except for the whole rest all rests have the same beat value as the corresponding notes. See Example 1-N below.

Example 1-N

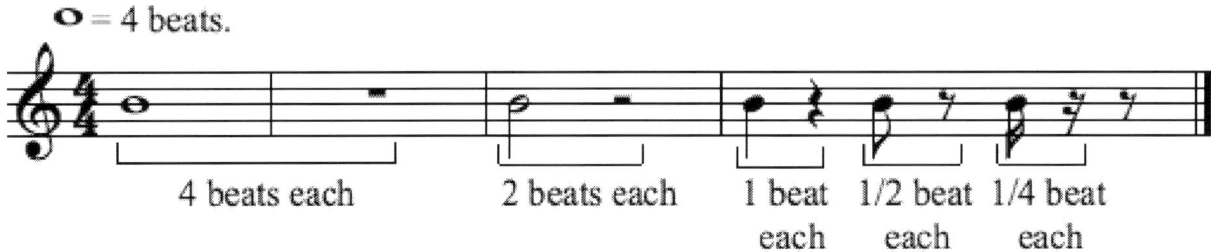

In the above example, the whole rest in the second bar receives four beats. This rest (the black box hanging below the line) is often used to indicate a *whole bar of rest, regardless of the number of beats in that bar.* This means that its beat value will be equal to the top number of the meter. It is the only rest which can have a beat value different from its corresponding note.

Ties

Two more things you need to know about rhythm (for now) - the tie and the dot.

What if the composer wants a 4-beat note in 3/4 meter? You cannot fit a 4-beat note into a 3-beat measure but you can "tie" 2 notes together. In the example below, a 2-beat note is placed on the second beat of the first bar and is connected to another 2-beat note *on the same staff line* (i. e., it's the same note) in the second bar by a curved line. The curved line is called a tie.

The performer will play the first note on beat 2 of the first bar, hold it for 2 beats through beat 3, and continue to hold it for the two additional beats of the next note through beat two of bar 2. Tap and count Example 1-0 below. *N.B.*, there will be one tap for the second note, none for the tied note.

Example 1-0

Another musical symbol called a **slur** is a curved line that looks exactly like a tie. It means to play the notes smoothly connected. The slur may extend over two notes or over many notes, whereas the tie will only connect two notes *of the same pitch with no notes or rests between the two.* The slur always affects *different* pitches. Just remember that the tie connects two notes of the same pitch with no intervening notes or rests.

Example 1-P

Dots

What if the composer wants a note held for 1½ counts? It could be done with a tie, connecting a one-count note to a half-count note. However, there is another way.

Introducing the dot. (Drum roll!) A dot placed just to the right of a note head or a rest increases its time value by one-half. *E.G.*, a dot added to a one-count note or a one-count rest increases its value to 1½ counts.

Example 1-Q

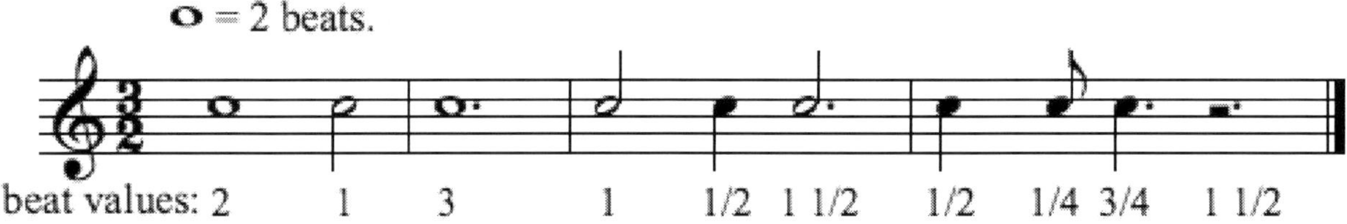

Instead of using dotted rests, composers and/or their publishers oftentimes prefer to add another rest with half the value of the first rest. The effect is the same.

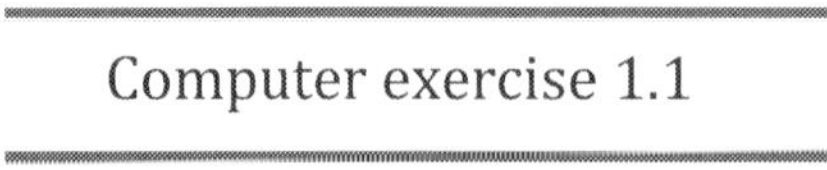

Exercises

For each of the four exercises below write the value of the whole note and draw a note that gets one beat. Write the counts below the notes as indicated in the first bar. Be sure your counts accommodate the shortest note or rest in the example.

Count out loud and tap one tap for each note (except for the second of two tied notes). No taps for the rests. Count with steady, even beats so that the notes/taps are properly uneven. Use a metronome to guarantee even beats.

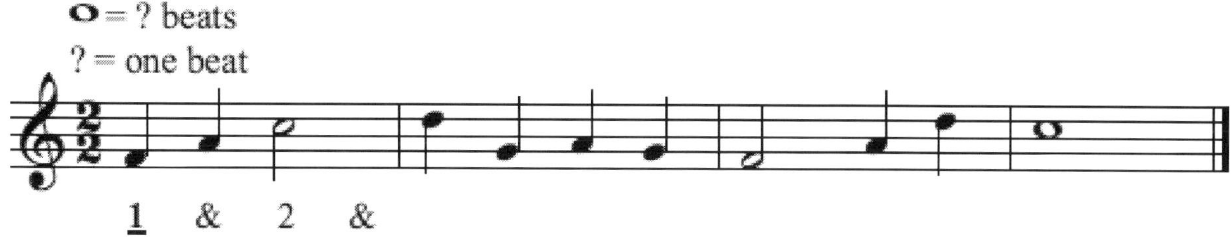

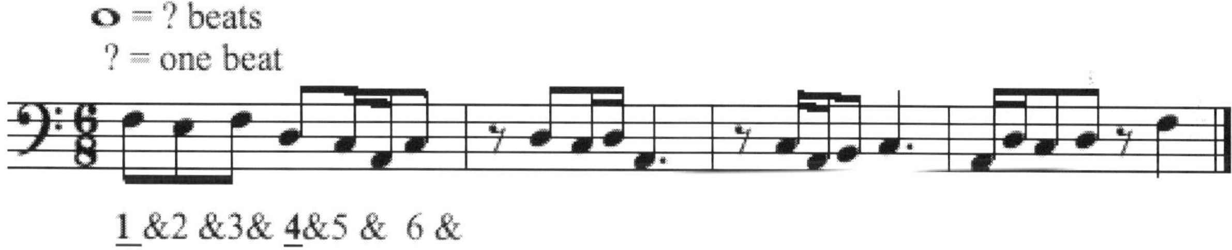

In your Bach Chorales, a hymn book, or some other publication write in the counts and count out loud while you tap the notes. Practice until it's easy and you can do it without writing in the counts.

Chapter 2

The Music Alphabet-Middle D
The Music Keyboard-Middle D
Half Steps and Whole Steps

The Music Alphabet-Middle D

The musical Pitches you hear, the Notes on the lines and spaces of the music staff, and the Keys of a piano – *i. e.* all PNKs - are named with letters of the music alphabet. The music alphabet consists of the first seven letters of the English alphabet: ABCDEFG. A musician needs to know these seven letters backward as well as forward, because sometimes PNKs go up and sometimes they go down.

It's easy to learn the music alphabet backward.

G
F
E
D
C
B
A

In the column above, the middle letter - D - is bigger. We'll refer to this as "middle D." (Middle D will also help identify the keys on the music keyboard later.) Practice saying out loud the top three letters backward – "G, F, E" - several times (without looking at them), then the bottom three letters – "C, B, A" - several times. After that it should not be difficult to say the top three backward, followed by D in the middle, then the bottom three backward and you will have the whole music alphabet backward. Stop reading now and practice this until you can say the music alphabet backward without looking at it, as smoothly and evenly as you can say it forward.

The Music Keyboard-Middle D

The piano, the harpsichord, the pipe organ, and many different types of electronic music keyboards have the same arrangement of black and white keys. Other musical instruments (trumpets, violins, flutes, guitars) have different techniques for selecting specific pitches, but the relationship of musical pitches and notation apply to them all.

The music keyboard is by far the instrument most commonly used for the study of music theory. Familiarity with the keyboard is usually required for theory study. It will be the instrument most used in this course. A thorough understanding of it will be very beneficial. The student should have a music keyboard available for use while studying this book.

Example 2-A

Notice that the fronts of all the white keys are the same width and evenly spaced. The black keys are shorter and are in groups of 2 and 3 throughout the length of the keyboard. The black and white keys alternate except that the black key groups are separated by 2 adjacent white keys.

The white keys are all named with letters of the music alphabet. There are a lot more than seven white keys so the seven letter names are repeated several times. For this reason it is good to think of the music alphabet as a circle with no beginning and no end. After G comes A and you go around again. Since you now know the music alphabet backward as well as forward you can go around the circle in either direction without looking at it.

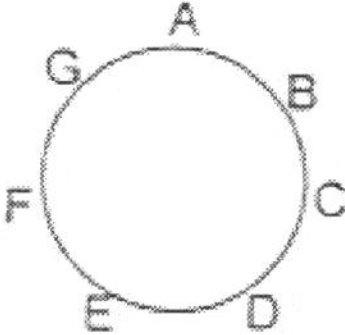

Middle D helps identify the keys of the keyboard. The white key in the middle of the two black keys is named D. Every set of 2 black keys on the music keyboard has a D in the middle between them.

The three white keys to the left of middle D are C, B, and A. From the right of middle D are E, F and G which completes the music alphabet. After you get to G to the right of middle D you start over again with A, followed by B & C which takes you to the next higher middle D in the middle of the next set of two black keys.

Example 2-B

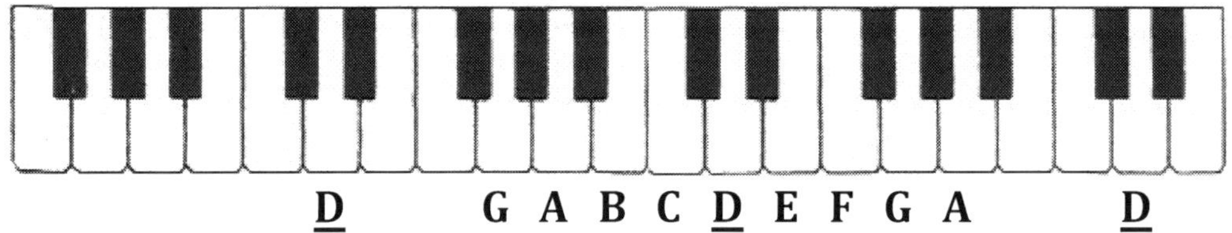

D G A B C D E F G A D

Two more good landmark keys are A (the beginning of the music alphabet) and G (the end of the music alphabet) which are the two white keys in the middle of the 3-black-key group. With middle D, A, and G as landmarks you have keys next to all the other white keys.

Stop reading now and practice playing and saying the letter names of the white keys on your keyboard. Play all the Ds, then all the Cs and Es, then all the As and Bs, then all the Gs and Fs.

DO NOT EVER PUT LETTER NAMES ON THE KEYS! That would greatly slow your learning of their names. With middle D in the middle of each set of 2 black keys and G and A in the 3 black key group you don't need letter names on the keys.

Half Steps and Whole Steps

The smallest interval on the keyboard, from one key to the very next (regardless of color or shape), is called a "half step." Two half steps equal one "whole step." A whole step is two keys with one key between, regardless of the color or shape of the keys.

Example 2-C

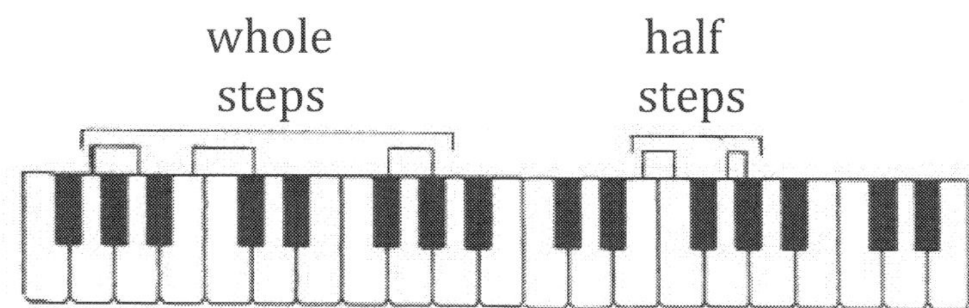

From one **white** key to the next is sometimes a half step, with no black key between (B to C and E to F) and sometimes a whole step, with one black key between (C to D, D to E, F to G, G to A, and A to B). If you play all the white keys from one middle D to the next, you will play some whole steps and some half steps. You can't play a half step with two black keys. So what do all whole steps have in common and what do all half steps have in common? The answer is in the comparison of their sounds. The distance between the *sounds* of a half step is half the distance between the *sounds* of a whole step.

Computer exercise 2.1

Exercises

Say out loud and write the music alphabet backward until you know it backward as well as forward.

Play and sing the names of the white keys, somewhere in the middle of the music keyboard in your comfortable vocal range, until you know them well. Play and sing them in this order: **B E A D G C F.** Then reverse that order: **F C G D A E B.** Play them in different areas of the keyboard to become familiar with the whole keyboard. Play them in the above orders moving always to the right, then always to the left, then alternating left and right.

You will want to know the difference in sound between a half step and a whole step. You can close your eyes and play a series of white keys and learn to hear which are whole steps and which are half steps. If you sing the pitches you hear you will learn to recognize them more quickly.

With your eyes open, play a key at random, black or white, and sing a whole step and half step above and below that pitch. Play the pitches after you sing them to check yourself.

Keep in mind why we study music theory. Music is sound, not notes on a page. The notes on the page represent sounds. We want to learn to recognize, to hear in our minds, what those sounds are. A real understanding of music will give you the ability to hear in your mind what you see on a music score and, conversely, being able to write what you hear. The best way to learn this is to sing. Sing everything you write. You can study music theory anywhere and any time by singing, humming, or just thinking sounds. It also makes the time go faster while waiting in a doctor's office.

Chapter 3

The Music Staff and Clef Signs
Note Heads
Octave
Ledger Lines
Grand Staff
Intervals and Chords
Mnemonics

Music Staff and Clef Signs

Much information is shown to the musician on the music staff. A music staff consists of five horizontal parallel lines. At the beginning of the staff there will be a **clef** sign which identifies one of the lines with a letter of the music alphabet. Unlike the meter, the clef sign appears at the beginning of every staff in the piece. The three different clef signs shown below are the G-clef/aka treble clef, the C-clef, and the F-clef/aka bass clef.

Example 3-A

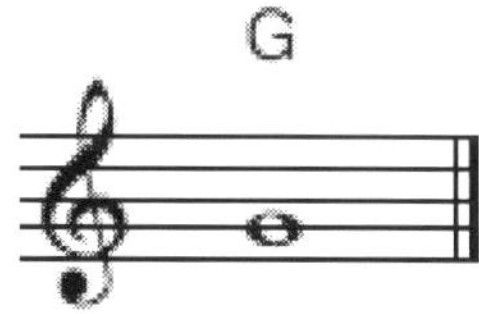

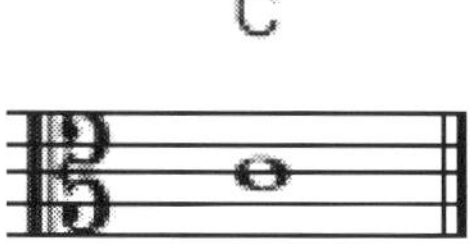

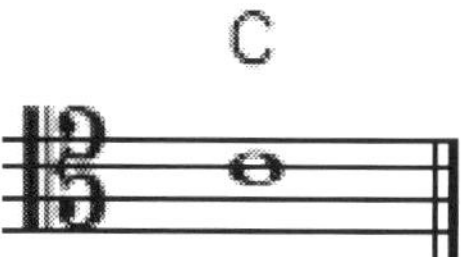

Notice that the G-clef circles around the second line from the bottom of the staff identifying that line as G. The C-clef can be placed with its center on any line, identifying that line as C. It is most often found on the third or fourth line as in the example above. The F-clef begins with a heavy dot on the second line from the top with two dots on each side of that line, identifying the second line from the top as F.

Only the G clef and F clef are commonly used for the keyboard. The C clef is used for certain orchestral instruments like the cello and viola. Since we will be using the keyboard for this theory study we will be showing examples and exercises only with the G-clef and F-clef.

Note Heads

The pitches that are to be played or sung appear on the 5-line staff as small circles. These small circles are called "note heads" and may be centered on any line or on any space between two lines. The diameter of a note head is the same as the width of a space on the staff.

The letter names of these notes are unknown without a clef sign. Once a clef sign identifies one of the lines, all the other lines and spaces can be identified. The notes moving up through the staff are in the same order as moving clockwise around the music alphabet circle.

Example 3-B

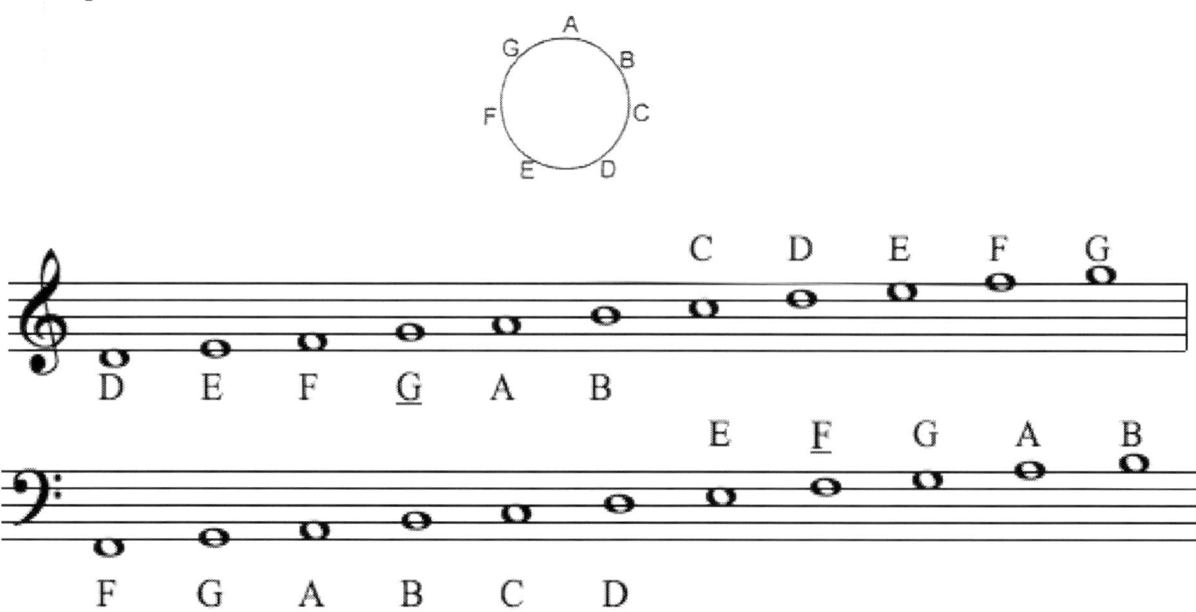

Notice the **G** for the G-clef line and the **F** for the F-clef line.

As we learned in chapter 2, two adjacent white keys on the keyboard are sometimes a whole step (*e.g.*, D to E, separated by a black key) and sometimes a half step (*e.g.*, E to F, with no black key between.) Likewise on the music staff, a note on a space and a note on an adjacent line will sometimes be a whole step and sometimes a half step.

Example 3-C

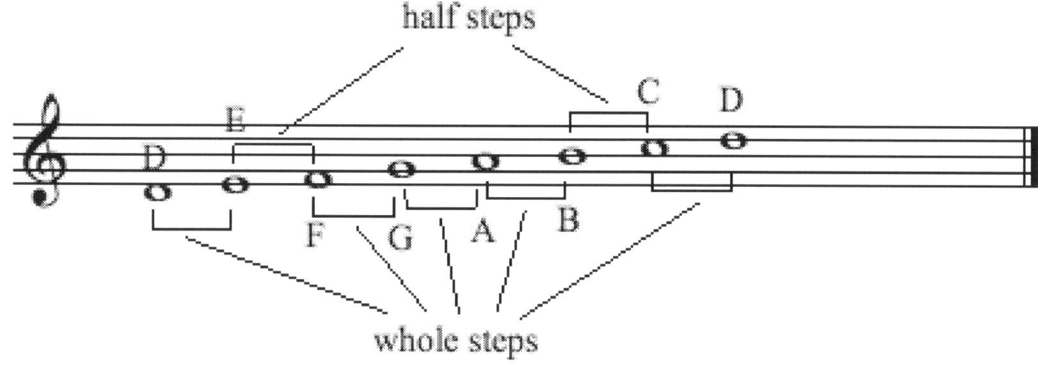

Octave

The term "octave" is very useful in music . Like the words octagon and octopus, octave is going to be eight of something. An octave is the interval from one pitch/note/key (PNK) to the next PNK which has the same letter name. Since there are seven letter names in the music alphabet circle, as you progress clockwise around the circle or to the right on the white keys of the keyboard, the **eighth** letter name will be the same as where you started. If one starts at D on the circle or on the keyboard, the **eighth** letter name or key will also be D, one octave higher.

The vibration rate of a musical pitch is double that of a pitch one octave lower, with the ratio 2:1. The octave is probably the easiest interval to recognize by sound. Play some octaves on the keyboard and then just one key less or more than an octave and listen to the difference.

Ledger Lines

Pitches are sometimes higher or lower than the music staff allows. These notes can be accommodated by the use of **ledger lines** added above or below the staff. The ledger lines and the spaces between function the same as the lines and spaces of a staff and represent an extension of the music alphabet ascending or descending. The only limit to the number of ledger lines that can be added is the pitch range of the instrument.

Example 3-D

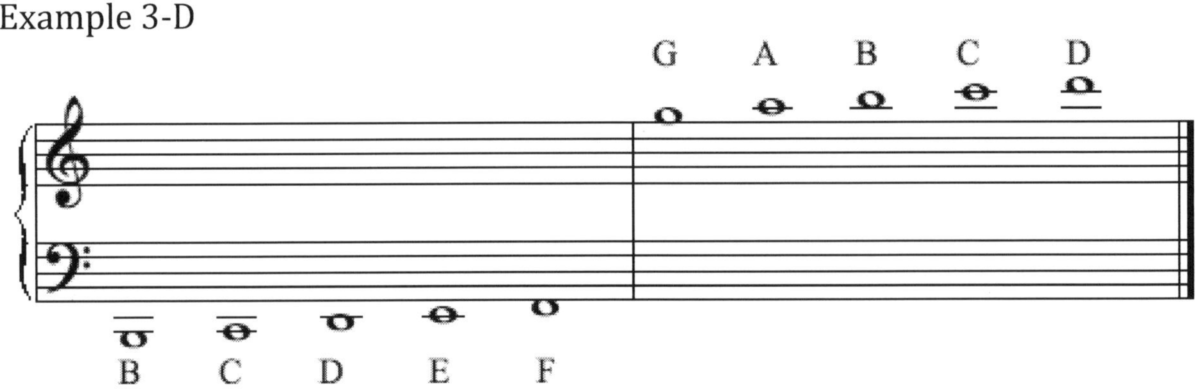

Composers may also use the octave sign – *8va* or *8vb* – to indicate to the performer that the pitches are to be played **one octave higher** or **one octave lower** than written. It is usually easier to read notes an octave higher or lower than written in the staff than to read a pot full of ledger lines.

Example 3-E

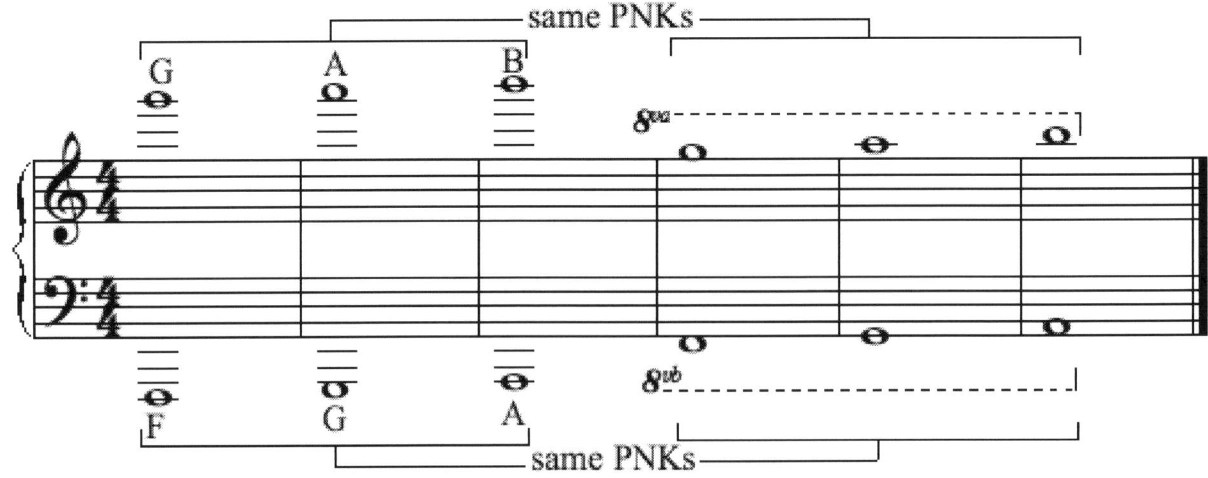

The term "interval" refers to the distance from one PNK to another. It involves some rather illogical mathematics. It will be discussed in more detail in Chapter 9. In the meantime you can ponder why *15va* or *15vb* indicates an interval 2 octaves higher or 2 octaves lower than written.

Grand Staff

Keyboard instruments often have such a wide range of pitches that two music staves may be joined together, with a G-clef on the upper staff and an F-clef on the lower staff. This combination is called a **grand staff** and is quite common for keyboard instruments. By adding one leger line for C between the two staves, the grand staff provides a range of over three octaves with only the one leger line for C in the middle. This C is often referred to as "middle C" because of its location between the 2 staves, although with the two staves moved apart as they usually are, middle C is not really in the middle. See Example 3-F below.

Example 3-F

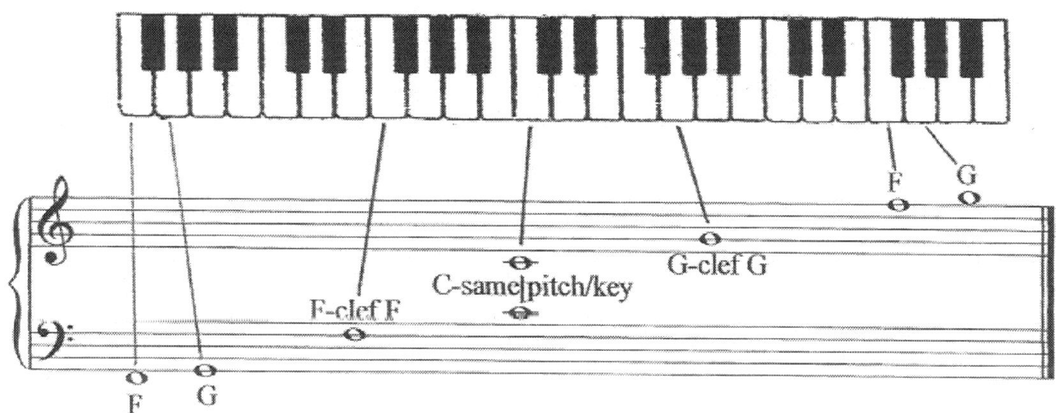

The lowest, left-most C on an 88-key piano keyboard is identified as C-1. As you move up to the right the subsequent C's are identified as C-2, C-3, C-4 (which is middle C), C-5, etc. to C-8 as the top right-most C. The white keys from C-1 to C-2 are identified as D-1, E-1, F-1, G-1, etc. The keys between C-2 and C-3 are then specified with a "2," from C-3 to C-4 with a "3," and so on to C-8. This is a good system to remember because it provides a simple method of identifying the specific octave for any given PNK. See Example 3-G below.

Example 3-G

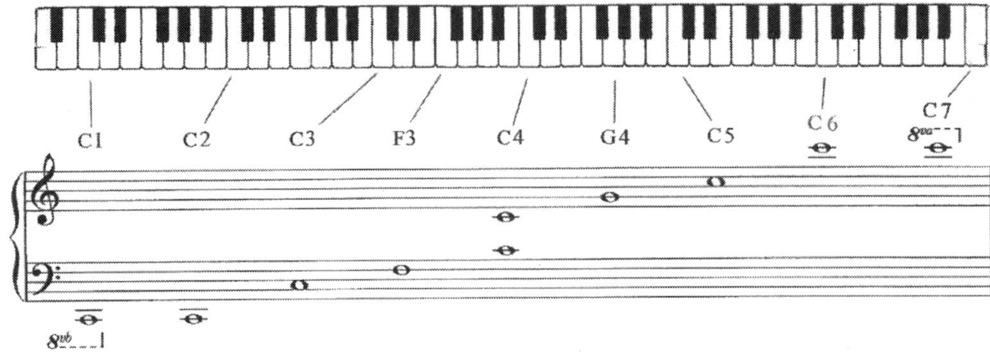

"What if I want C an octave below C-1?" Not to worry. You wouldn't hear it as a musical pitch because its vibration rate is less than 20 cps. The lowest PNK on the piano keyboard (A-zero) vibrates 27.5 cps.

Intervals and Chords

Two pitches sounded at the same time are called a **harmonic interval**. Two pitches sounded sequentially are called a **melodic interval.** Three or more pitches sounded at the same time are called a **chord.** (Experts sometimes disagree on the exact number required for a chord but 3 pitches will be the number for this book.)

If a composer wants more than one pitch to sound at the same time (*e.g.,* a harmonic interval or a chord) the notes will be written vertically on the staff. If the note heads have a stem added and they have the same rhythmic value, they may share the same stem. If two or more notes sounding at the same time are adjacent – one on a line and the other on an adjacent space – the note heads will be offset from each other rather than overlapped, as in the F-clef in bar 2, and in the G-clef in bar 3 of Example 3-H below.

Example 3-H

Exercises

On a blank manuscript practice drawing the three different clef signs, paying close attention to the details. The G-clef starts with a vertical line extending above and below the staff. A curved line then starts from the top of the vertical line curving to the right across the top line and back to the left crossing the vertical line at its juncture with the fourth staff line, then makes a wider curve to the left and back crossing the vertical line at the bottom staff line, then curves up to the right and back crossing the vertical line at the third line. The most important detail is centering the lower wider curve around the second line from the bottom, indicating that it is the G line.

For the C-clef. start with two vertical lines centered on whichever line is to be C. Next draw a line starting from the vertical line at the C line moving up to the right and then back to the left. Then mirror that with a curved line moving down, starting from the C line. The important detail is the centering of the clef on the line which is to be C. This is the only clef sign which can be placed on *any* of the five lines, but the third and fourth lines are the most common. (If a composer chose to do so the C-clef could be placed on a space, but I have never seen one. Also, there is nothing to stop a composer from placing a G-clef or F-clef on other lines or spaces but so far I haven't seen that either.)

For the F-clef, start with a heavy black dot on the second line from the top. From the dot draw a curved line up to the right to touch the top line, then down and back to the left until it crosses the second line from the bottom. Add two smaller dots to the right in the third and fourth spaces. The important details are the heavy dot centered on the fourth line and the two smaller dots on each side the fourth line, indicating the fourth line as F. See Example 3-I below.

Example 3-I

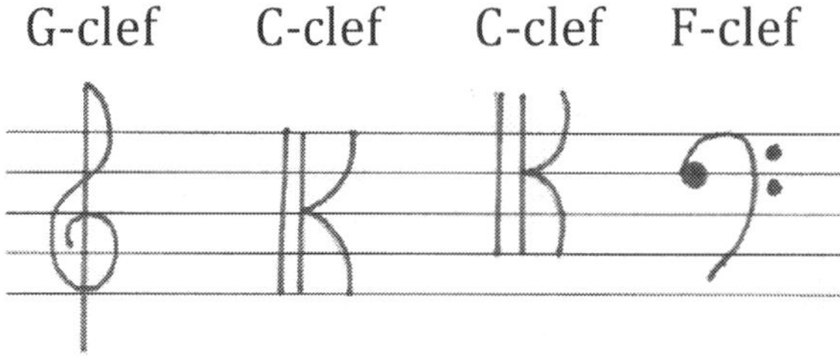

Mnemonics

Example 3-J

<u>landmark notes</u>

Five Cs:
in the middle (sort of)
3 spaces up & 3 spaces down,
2 ledger lines up & 2 ledger lines down

Fs and Gs:
F on the F-clef line and the top line of the G-clef
G on the G-clef line and the bottom line of the F-clef

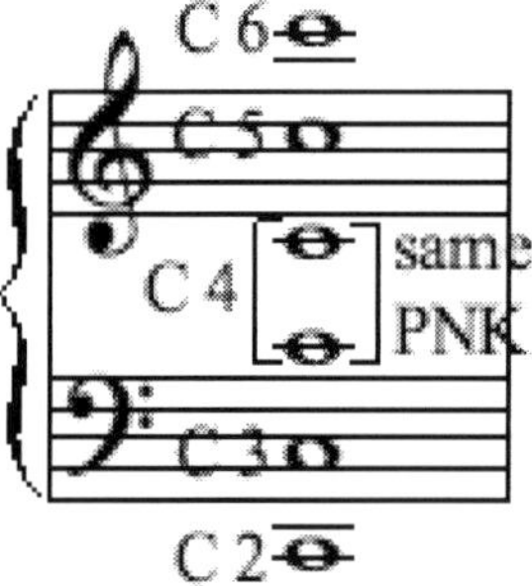

Computer exercises 3.1 & 3.2

Flash Cards

There are flash cards readily available from most music stores and on line. Or you can photocopy the "flash cards" printed on the following pages. Each card has a note printed on a grand staff. As you read each card say the name of the note and play its key on the keyboard. Be sure you play the keys in the correct octave.

For the beginning student a good way to practice with the flash cards is to start with the above landmark notes in Example 3-J first. Once these are thoroughly learned you will know a note on or next to every line and space in the grand staff except the four in Example 3-K below.

Example 3-K

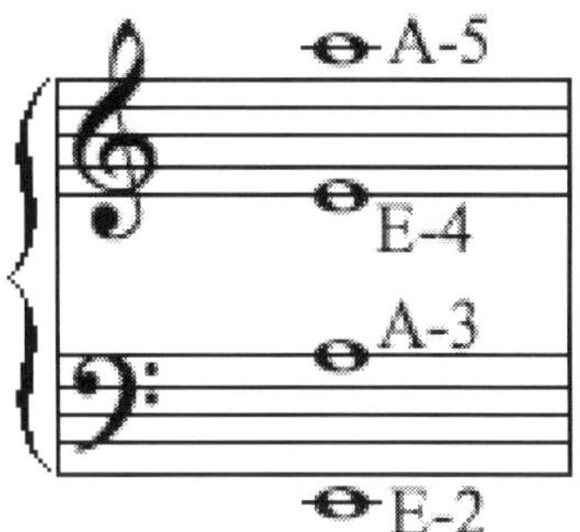

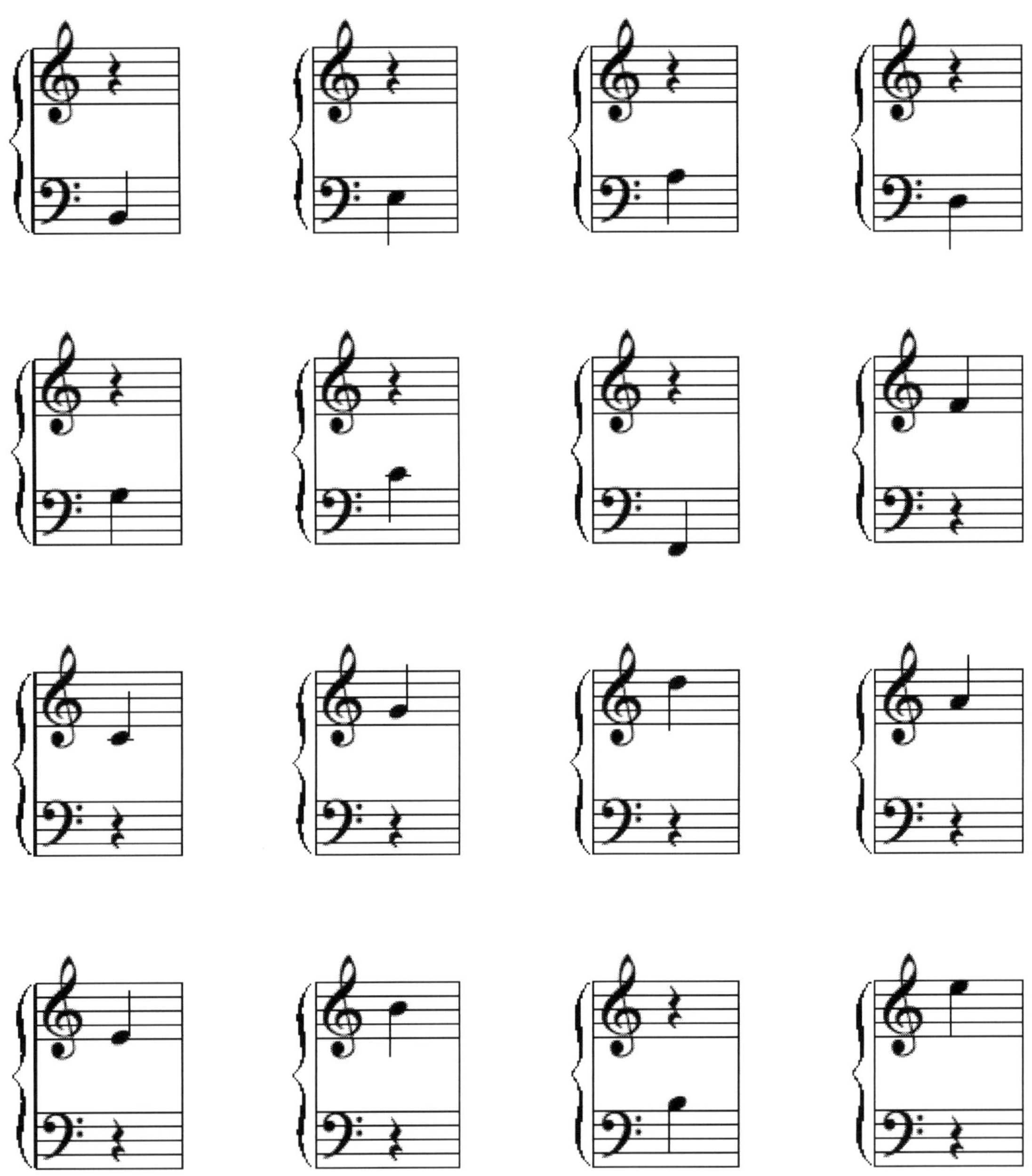

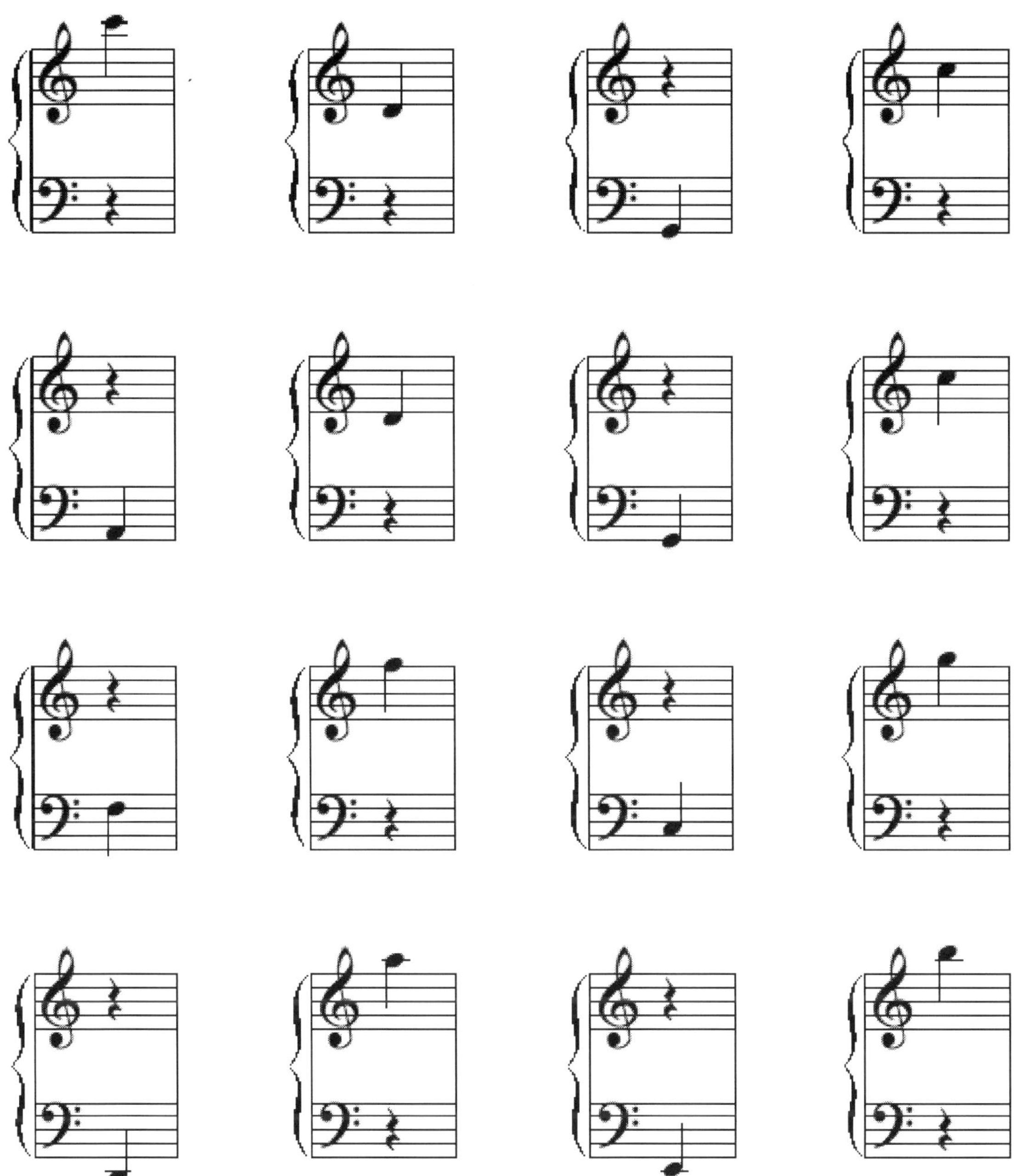

Chapter 4
Sharps and Flats – The Black Keys

Sharps And Flats -The Black Keys

The letter name of a black key is the same as the letter name of the adjacent white key with the term "sharp" or "flat" added. The first key (a half step) to the right of a white key is called a sharp. The first key (a half step) to the left of a white key is called a flat. *E.g.,* the first key to the right of D (a black key) is called "D-sharp", while the first key to the left of E (a black key) is called "E-flat". This is the same key with two different names. All black keys have more than one letter name. This principle in music is called **enharmonic**. D-sharp is enharmonic with E-flat.

Example 4 A

The enharmonic names of the black keys.

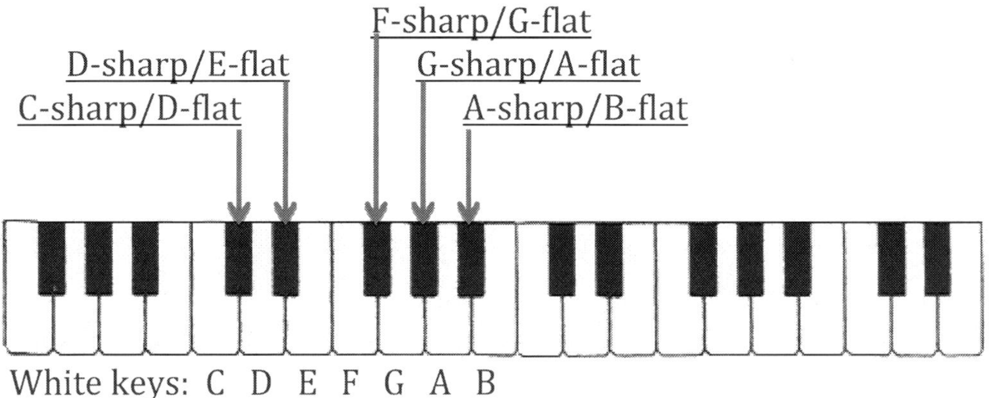

Sharps and flats are not always black keys. The first *key* (not just the first *black* key) to the right of a white key is called a sharp. Likewise the first *key* to the left of a white key is called a flat. This means that on the keyboard there are two *white key sharps* and two *white key flats.* B-sharp (aka C), E-sharp (aka F), F-flat (aka E), and C-flat (aka B) are white keys. These PNKs are enharmonic. You'll just have to trust me that this will eventually make sense and will be useful.

Sometimes a composer wants to cancel a sharp or flat appended to a note or perhaps remind the performer that a note is not sharped or flatted. The sign for this is called a "natural." A note not sharped or flatted may be called by its music alphabet name with the term "natural" added, *e. g.*, D-natural. Although "D" and "D-natural" technically mean the same thing, the "D-natural" can be a useful reminder if it has just been preceded by a D-sharp or D-flat.

The music notation for sharps, flats, and naturals are called "chromatic signs." They are shown below in Example 4-B.

Example 4-B

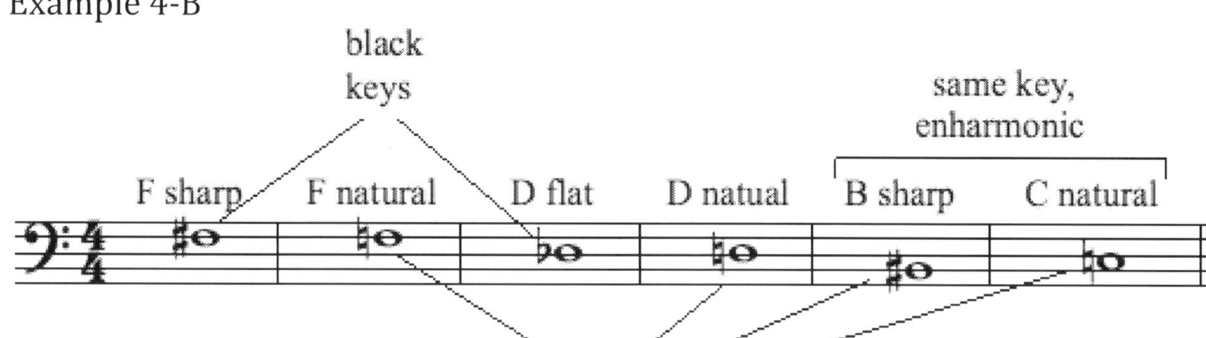

A chromatic sign affects the note head immediately to its right and *every note head on the same line or space which <u>follows</u> it in the <u>same</u> bar.*

Example 4-C

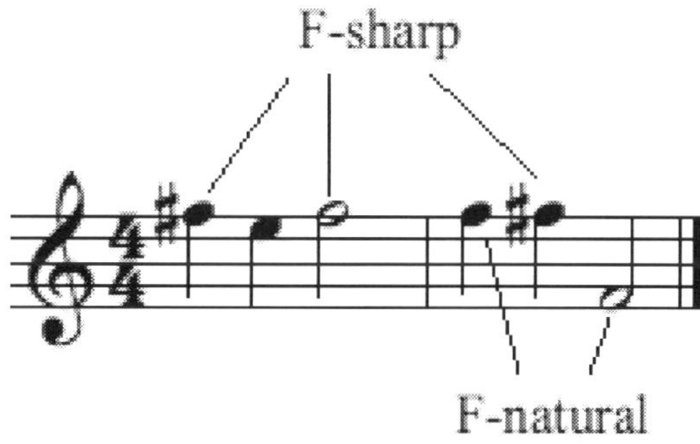

Exercises

On staff paper practice drawing sharp, flat and natural signs. Just as in drawing note heads, it is important to draw chromatic signs correctly so there can be no mistake which line or space the sign refers to. Notice that each symbol has an enclosed portion – at the bottom of the flat sign and in the center of the sharp and natural signs. This enclosed space is centered on the line or space to be indicated and is the width of one staff space, just as is a note head. Check the correct and incorrect examples below.

Example 4-B

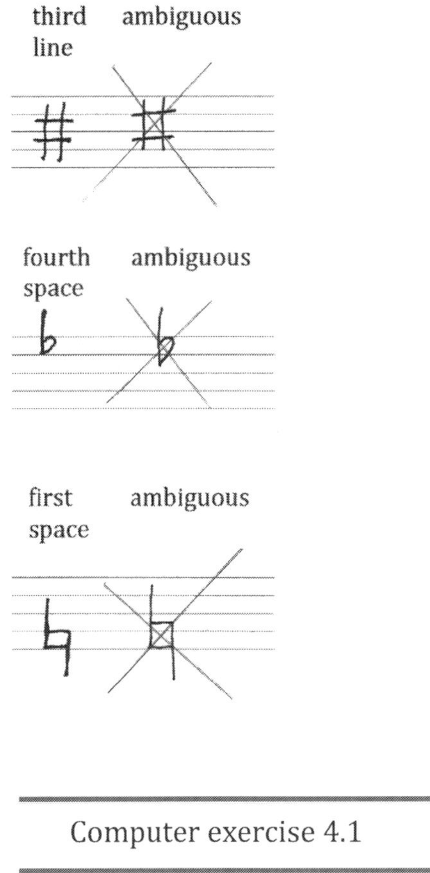

Computer exercise 4.1

On your keyboard play and sing the *two enharmonic* names of each of the black keys. Play and sing them in this order: **B-flat/A-sharp, E-flat/D-sharp, A-flat/G-sharp, D-flat/C-sharp, G-flat/F-sharp**. Then reverse that order: **F-sharp/G-flat, C-sharp/D-flat, G-sharp/A-flat, D-sharp/E-flat, A-sharp/B-flat**.

Chapter 5
Major Scales
Tonal Center
Functional Names

From this chapter on you will need a music keyboard to understand and apply the concepts presented in this book. If your ultimate ambition is to play the piano you will want to get a keyboard with 88 full-size keys and a weighted action similar to a piano. I have dealt with three brands that I can recommend – Roland, Yamaha, and Casio. My preference has always been Roland but I have owned and used all three. All three companies make quite good **and** quite rinky dink models, the differences reflected in their prices. If piano technique is not a goal, you have a wider choice of cheaper brands and models and fewer than 88 keys is O. K.

Major Scales

A **diatonic** scale is a progression of PNK s, either ascending or descending, (clockwise or counter-clockwise around the music alphabet circle) which neither skip nor repeat any letters of the music alphabet within an octave.

In Chapter 2 a half step was identified as the smallest interval in our music system. From one key on the keyboard to the very next key, black or white, is a half step. A whole step is equal to two half steps, or two keys with one key between.

A **major** scale is a diatonic scale with the following ascending whole-step (W) half-step (H) progression: W W H W W W H. This is a **very important/very useful tool**, so this pattern of whole-steps and half-steps should be memorized. It is helpful to recite this when you're first learning to play the major scales on the keyboard. A frequent mistake students make is to say "Whole step" when they play the first key. The first whole step doesn't occur until the *second* key is played. The whole step occurs *between* the first and second PNKs of the scale.

The C major scale is the only major scale that requires no black keys. (Confirm that.) A major scale beginning on any other PNK requires one or more sharps or flats/black keys to effect this pattern. Example 5-A which follows shows the application of the W W H W W W H pattern for two different major scales.

Example 5-A

C major scale
ws
ws
hs
ws
ws
ws
hs

D major scale
ws
ws
hs
ws
ws
ws
hs

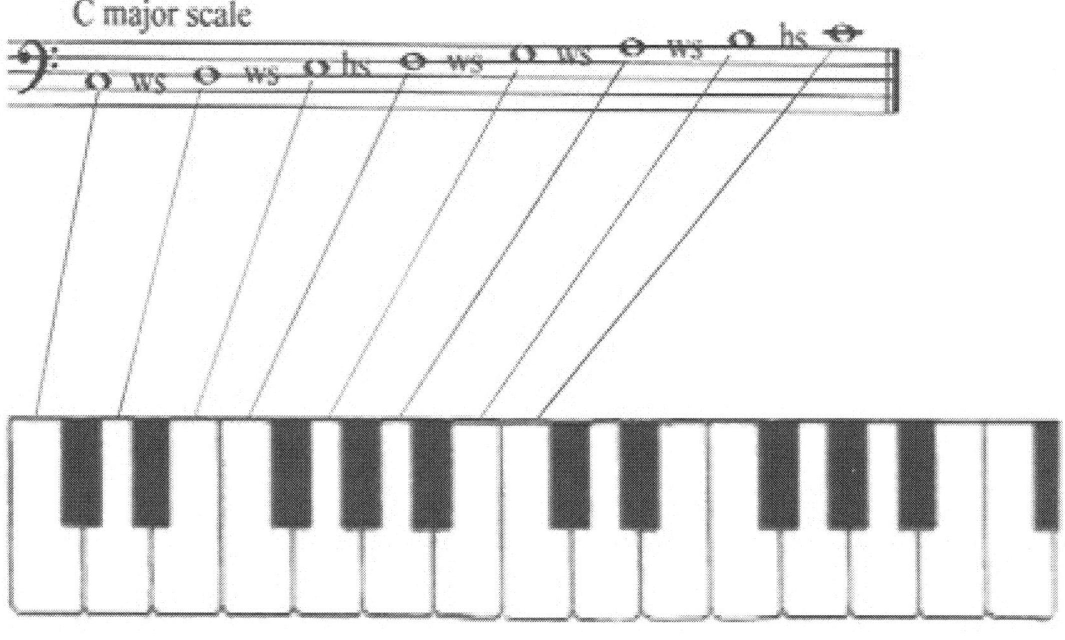

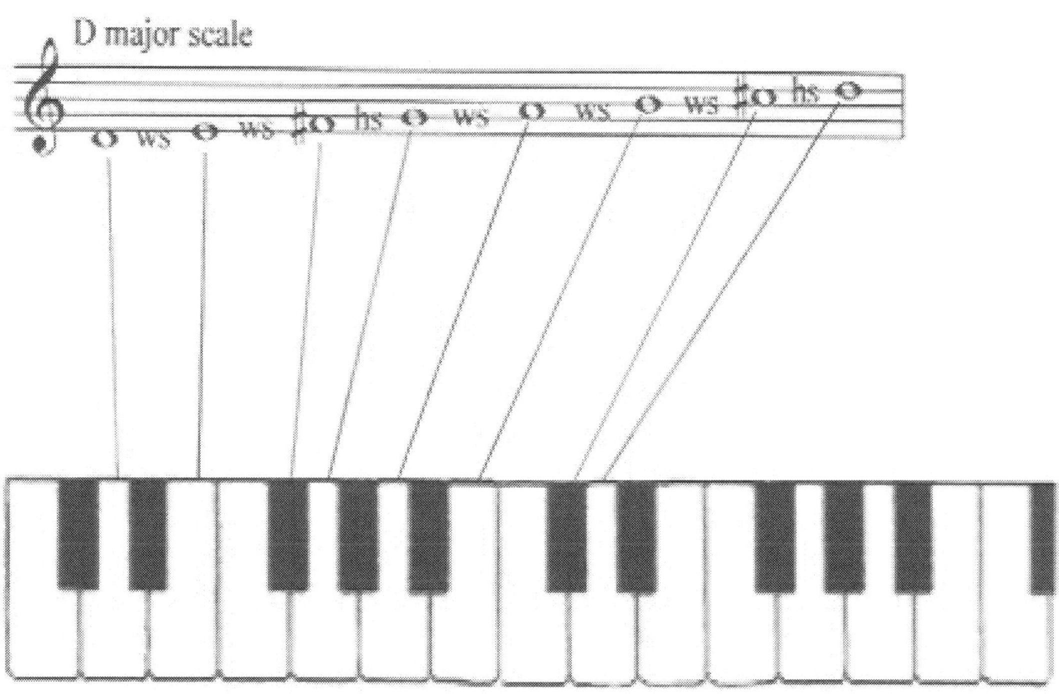

If you intend to be a professional musician, you will want to learn to play scales very rapidly and smoothly. The fingering you use to play the keys is extremely important to effect this. Since proper scale fingering for the keyboard is based on the key signature, scale fingering will have to wait until Chapters 6 and 7. (If you're curious it's OK to look ahead.)

Tonal Center

The first PNK of the major scale is called the "keynote." A major scale is named after the keynote, *e.g.*, the G major scale begins on G followed by the whole-step half-step pattern above. A composition based on the PNKs of a G major scale is said to be in the "key of G". G would be the tonal center of that composition. All other PNKs are identified according to their relationship to that tonal center. A composition in the key of G will come to a satisfying end only on the tonal center G.

Functional Names

Each of the 7 PNK's of a major scale are referred to as scale degree number such-and-such, *e. g.* scale degree number 1 is the keynote. Each of the 7 scale degrees also has a functional name. See the following list:

1-tonic
7-leading tone – a half step below and leading into tonic
6-sub mediant – midway between sub dominant and tonic
5-dominant – second in importance to tonic
4-sub dominant – below dominant
3-mediant – midway between tonic and dominant
2-super tonic – the PNK above tonic
1-tonic – the tonal center

You will often hear musicians referring to the PNKs by these names. It's not so much that the descriptions in the list are all characteristically accurate. Just as the name Mary means nothing about Mary until you get to know her, these functional names won't necessarily help you understand their function. They will take on more meaning as you relate the name to the *sounding* function of the PNK.

Perhaps we should clarify what we mean by the "function" of a scale degree. When a PNK has been established as the tonal center and keynote of a major key, we would say that it is functioning as the tonic PNK, which of course is saying it is the keynote and scale degree #1. All other PNKs derive their functions from their relative position to the tonal center. If E is the tonal center, then B functions as the dominant. If A is the tonal center, B functions as super tonic. The function of B depends on what PNK is tonic. An essential skill for professional musicians is the ability to identify by *sound* every PNK's functional relationship to tonic and thereby also to all other PNKs. This is called **relative pitch**, *not* perfect pitch.

Some of the names are more accurately descriptive than others. Tonic really is the tonal center. Dominant is really a very important PNK. And the leading tone really does lead into the tonal center. I, personally, don't recognize the sound of mediant because it is midway between tonic and dominant any more than that it's the next scale degree above supertonic. What I'm saying is that you don't need to try to justify the functional names of these PNKs. You do need to know them to keep up with the conversation around other musicians. Or to pass the exams in a music theory class. Or to fully understand the rest of this book. Its part of the official language of music.

Exercises

Practice playing major scales beginning on each of the twelve black and white keys of the keyboard. Recite the whole-step/half-step pattern as you play. If you've played it correctly the eighth key will be one octave above the first key and will have the same letter name. <u>Don't concern yourself with speed until you've read chapter 7</u>. We're not working on technique here. We just want a thorough understanding of what is a major scale, including what a major scale *sounds* like.

Practice them until you can hear your mistakes. After you are familiar with the sounds of a major scale, practice them by listening for the WSs and HSs instead of reciting the pattern. Maintain a steady rhythm while you play. (Yes, using a metronome is an excellent idea.)

Recite the PNK names as you play the scales and notice that the black keys are either *all sharps* or *all flats*. You will never have both sharps and flats in the same major scale. Remember that you are playing *diatonic* scales. That means using letters of the music alphabet in alphabetical order and *not skipping nor repeating* any letters.

For example when you play the F-major scale you will play the black key between A and B. The keys immediately preceding that black key are F, G, A. Therefore that black key will be named B-flat, not A-sharp. If you called it A-sharp, you would use the letter-name A twice and skip the letter-name B, which would bring down the curse of the catacombs at your next recital.

For the scales with a black key tonic, for now identify the keynote as a flat and not a sharp. This will avoid getting into double sharps, which you may not know about yet.

As you become more familiar with the scales, sing the functional names of the scale degrees as you play. To practice learning the functional *sounds* of the scale degrees:

1. Establish tonic by playing a major scale.

2. *Sing* a functional name.

3. Play that scale degree to confirm that you sang the correct pitch.

When you become more secure with this you can practice it anywhere without the need for a piano. It's a great way to be productive while walking to class or driving to school. We're not asking for perfect pitch here. <u>Don't sing the letter names of the PNKs.</u> Just work on functional relationships. Choose any pitch as your tonal center and sing the functional names and/or numbers of the other 6 scale degrees at random. Then start from a different tonal center and repeat.

Chapter 6
Major Key Signatures
The Circle of Major Keys
Orders of Sharps and Flats
KS Patterns on the Keyboard
Accidentals

Major Key Signatures

A key signature (KS) is one or more sharps or flats placed on the left end of the music staff immediately following the clef sign. Like the clef sign, the KS is placed on each staff, whereas the time signature only appears on the first staff unless it changes.

A KS of sharps *or* flats tells the performer that all PNKs with the alphabetical letter names of those sharps or flats are to be played sharp or flat throughout the composition **unless** the KS is changed somewhere along the way, **or** a different chromatic sign is placed beside a note head.

Example 6 – A

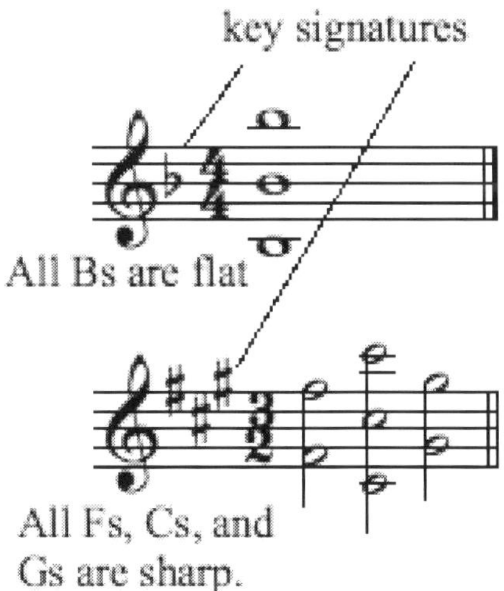

As we discovered in Chapter 5, each major scale has a unique set of black and white keys depending on the keynote you started on. When a composition is based on one of the major scales, we refer to that composition as being in the "key of" the keynote of that major scale. The keynote is the "tonal center" of the music. Tonal center is a very important concept in our study of "western European music." It will be discussed further in Chapter 13.

The first KS in Example 6-A above is one flat – B-flat. The F major scale must have a B-flat with the other 6 PNKs naturals. A composition based on the F major scale would have a KS of one flat on B. It would be in the key of F major. F would be the keynote and F would be the tonal center of the composition.

"So any time I see the KS of one flat – B-flat - I know the piece is in the key of F-major, right." Actually it could be in 7 other keys, but this is only Chapter 6. The good news: Once you have the major keys for a reference, the other 7 are much less difficult.

The Circle of Major Keys

The Circle of Major Keys in Example 6-B below will be an essential tool for understanding everything else that follows in this text. It is very important for understanding music.

Example 6-B

Circle of Major Keys

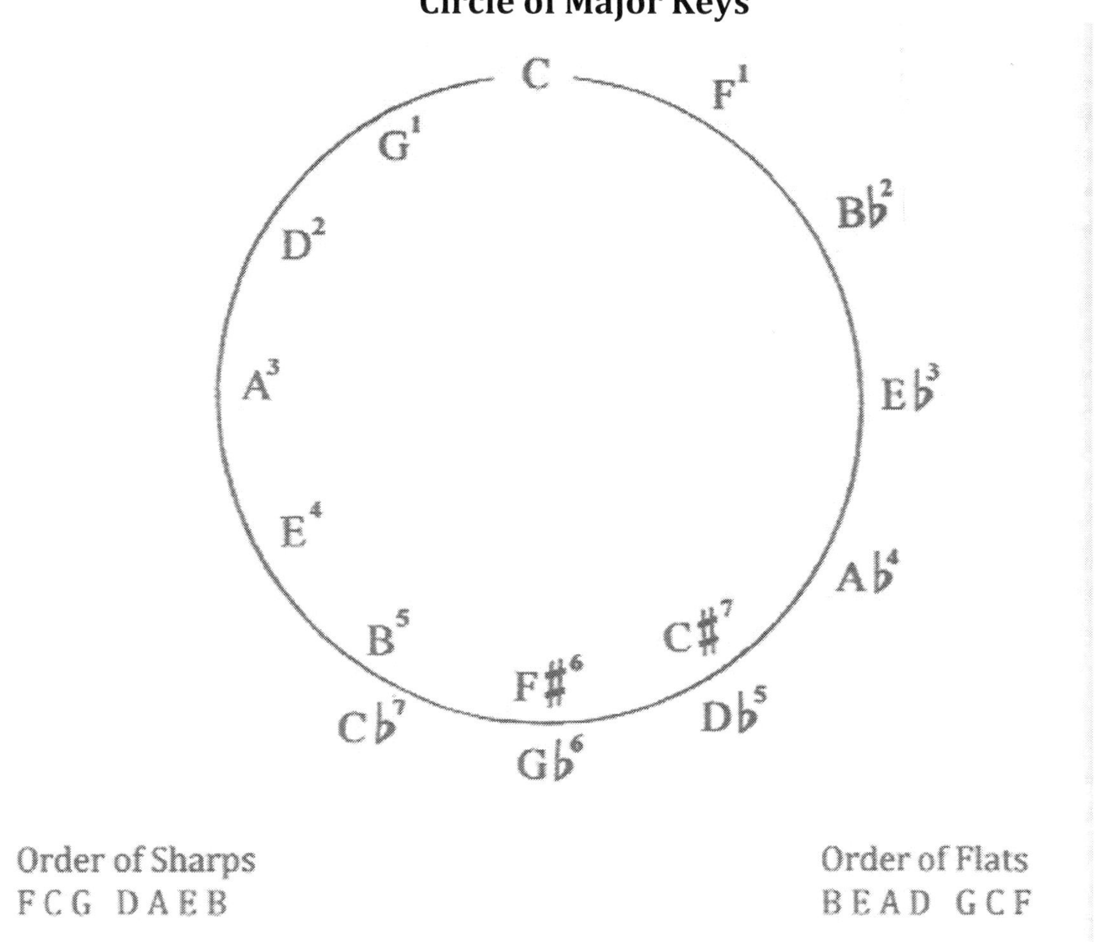

The major keys on the inside/left of the circle all have sharps in the KS and those on the outside/right have flats. If you are already familiar with the circle of keys it is likely you have seen it in the reverse order, with the sharps on the right side and the flats on the left. The reason for the order here will be discussed later.

Orders of Sharps and Flats

The numbers beside the keynotes in the circle indicate the number of sharps or flats in the KS. The sharps or flats are always placed in the key signatures in the orders given below the circle. *E. g.,* the KS of E-flat major is 3 flats: B-flat, E-flat, and A-flat. Those flats will appear in the KS from left to right in that order. See Example 6-C below.

Example 6-C

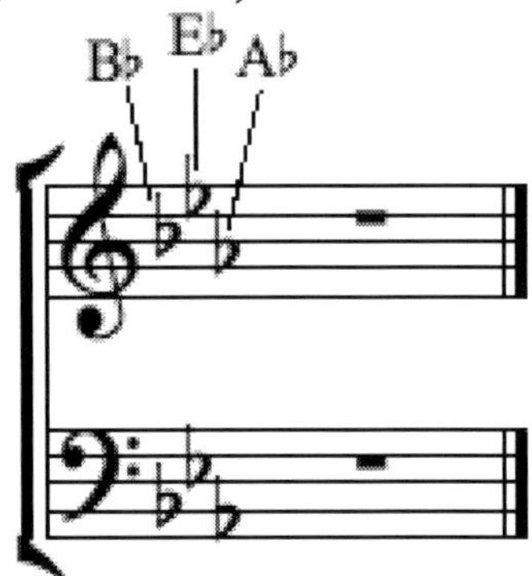

The word "bead" is a big help in remembering KSs and the orders of sharps and flats. It is spelled twice moving clockwise around the circle and also in the order of flats. Since the order of sharps is the reverse of the order of flats, "bead" appears backward in the order of sharps. The keys of G, C, and F major are at the top of the circle and G-flat, F-sharp, C-sharp and C flat major at the bottom. The rest of it is "bead." There are some good mnemonics there if you can just remember them. BTW, middle D is also in the middle of the order of sharps and the order of flats.

The 6 major keys at the bottom of the circle – 3 with sharps, and opposite them, 3 with flats – are enharmonic. That means that all the pitches of one major key are the same pitches and played on the same keys as the pitches in the major key on the opposite side of the circle, but the notes are different. *E. g.,* the keynote of G♭ major is the same *pitch* played on the same *key* as the keynote of F♯ major, but they are two different *notes* on a music staff. And so it is with all the other PNKs of the G♭ and F♯ major scales.

Computer exercise 6.1

KS Patterns on the Keyboard

There are some helpful patterns of KSs on the music keyboard. The first flat – B♭ – is at the top of the large group of 3 black keys. The second flat – E♭ – is at the top of the small group of 2 black keys. From there you work your way down alternating between the two black key groups ending with the two white key flats. For the sharps you reverse that by starting at the bottom of the large group of 3 black keys for the first sharp – F♯. The 2nd sharp – C♯- is at the bottom of the small group of 2 black keys. You then proceed up through both groups ending with the 2 white key sharps. Playing these patterns on your keyboard will help you remember the orders.

Example 6 D – Order of flats.

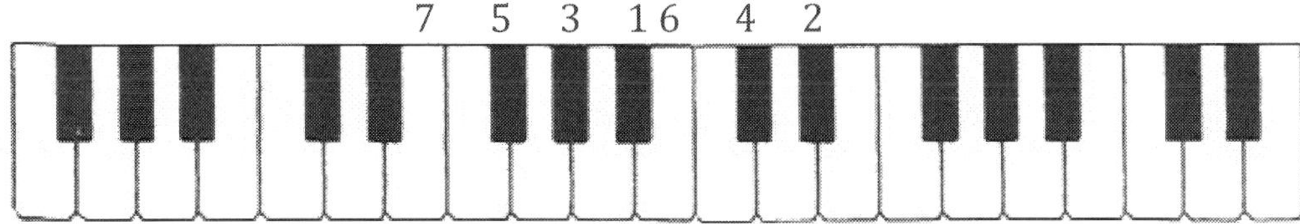

Example 6 E – Order of sharps.

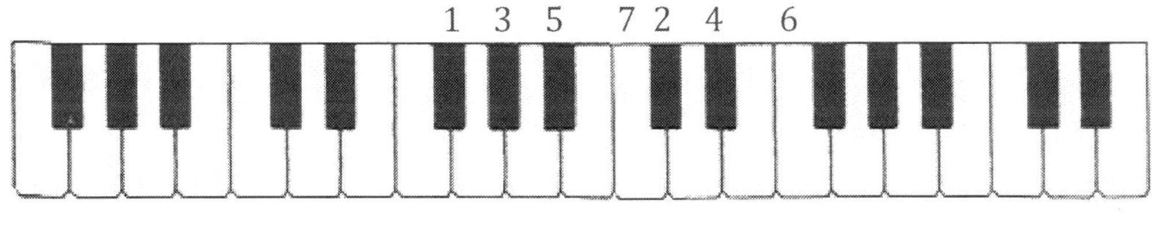

Computer exercises 6.2, 6.3, & 6.4

Exercise

Practice playing all the major scales now from their KS. Start with C major – no sharps or flats – and proceed clockwise around the circle with F major - 1♭, B♭ major - 2♭s, etc.

Accidentals

When one of the chromatic signs – a sharp ♯, flat ♭, or natural ♮, - is placed beside a note head (as opposed to being a part of the KS) it is called an **accidental**. That is an unfortunate misnomer because the composer most likely didn't place it there by accident. Be that as it may, that's what musicians call them.

An accidental affects all the following notes on the same line or space *to the end of the measure.*

A bar line cancels the accidental.

An accidental does <u>not</u> affect other octaves of the note.

See Example 6-F below.

Example 6-F

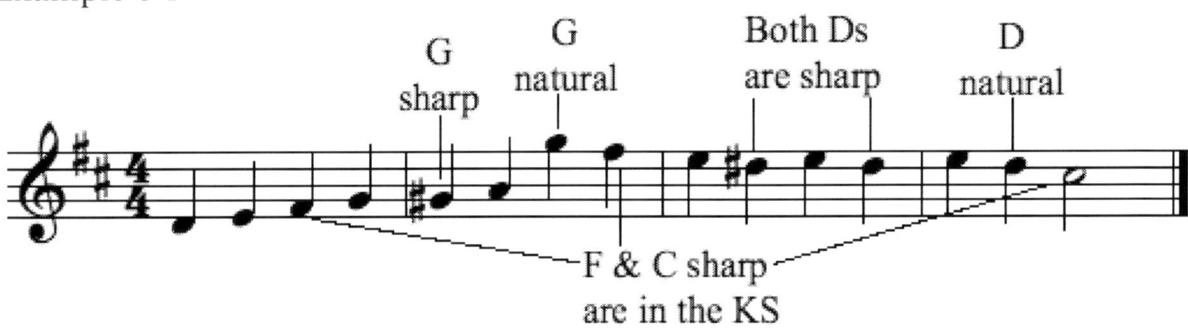

Add "accidental" with its definition (a sharp, flat, or natural which is <u>not</u> in the KS) to your mental music dictionary. FYI there are some publications and teachers whose definition of accidentals includes sharps or flats in the KS. I don't.

Computer exercise 6.5

Exercises

For each of the notes in Example 6-G below, write the correct letter name and chromatic sign below each note. The first three are done for you.

Example 6-G

Draw/write the circle of keys and the order of sharps and flats by memory. With practice you should be able to complete both in less than 45 seconds.

Practice writing the KS of 7 sharps and 7 flats on a grand staff, as given below, on the G and F clefs until you are confident of the proper placement of the symbols on the staves. The flats in both staves are consistently up-down-up-down-up-down. The sharps are down, up, down, down, up, down, with two downs after the 3rd sharp. Note that the symbols use only the available lines and spaces of the staff with no leger lines, *ergo*, the two downs in the sharps. Always say out loud the letter names and chromatic signs while you're drawing them.

Example 6-H

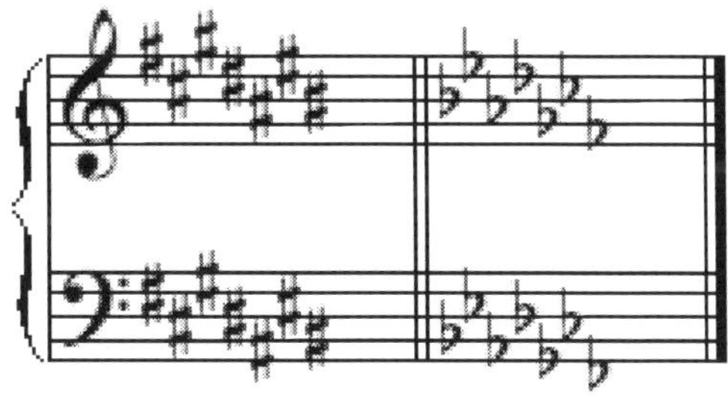

You have learned the music alphabet circle forward and backward. In Chapter 10 with the study of chords you will learn it by every other letter. Once you know the order of sharps and flats you will have also learned the music alphabet circle by every third letter (order of flats) and every fourth letter (order of sharps). These are not ends in themselves. They are tools that you must know thoroughly so you can concentrate on the building (the music) and not the tools.

Chapter 7
Keyboard Scale Fingering
The 4th Finger
The Modes
Relative Keys

Keyboard Scale Fingering

The scale fingering that I was taught as a budding young pianist has been around for many decades (centuries?) and may still be the most common. When I started getting serious about the piano at Arizona State University I spent a lot of practice time warming up with technique exercises including scales. The metronome was always employed to push the speed envelope.

While working on scales it became apparent that the defining limit to speed – the "weakest link in the chain" - was when the thumb and 4th finger crossed. This action is easier if the 4th finger is on a black key. (You can check this out by putting the thumb on a white key, crossing the 4th finger to the adjacent black key, and trilling the two keys. Then try it with both the thumb and 4th finger on white keys.) I then worked out a scale fingering system that puts the 4th finger on a black key in all the major scales (except C major). Compared to the old system it only required changing fingering for 4 different major scales, all in the left hand.

In addition to strengthening the "weakest link," it turned out that there were other important benefits from these changes. Many are especially helpful to students just beginning to learn the scales.

1. There are consistent patterns to the fingering that apply to all the major scales.

2. There is a close relationship between the fingering and the key signature (KS).

3. Nearly all the mistakes made by students involve the 4th finger. By concentrating on the placement of the 4th finger these mistakes are avoided.

4. The fingering applies to all the modes. (The modes are 6 scales/keys with half step and whole step patterns different from major or minor. They are discussed later in this chapter. The two minor scales are discussed in Chapter 12.) Initially the study of modes may not seem important, but Mozart and Beethoven used way more modal scales in their piano sonatas than major or minor scales. (For a prime example check out Mozart Sonata No. 16 in C major, measures 5 through 8, measures 50 through 53, etc.). The same is true of other composers' works as well. An analysis of these scale passages reveals that, although they occur in a context of major or minor tonality, a *big majority* of them don't begin and/or end on a major or minor keynote. As far as keyboard technique is concerned that is the same as playing a modal scale, and it is technique that concerns us here. The new fingering system works the same for modal scales as for major scales because it is based on the *key signature* (actually the *key context* discussed in Chapter 21) and not on the *keynote.*

5. The topography of the keyboard becomes more comfortable with this fingering. The arrangement of the black and white keys begins to "feel right." This is related to the 4th finger being on a black key, and if there are 2 or more black keys in the scale the 3rd finger gets to cross onto a black key also.

The 4th Finger

Here's how it works: On a music keyboard there are seven different keys in a major scale. The finger pattern will be 4 + 3 in each octave for those seven keys. That means you use the 4th finger just once in each octave. If you know which key the 4th finger plays the rest of the scale is 1,2,3 or 3,2,1 depending on the direction. You really only need to think about the key played by the 4th finger.

The placement of the 4th finger in a major scale is determined by the KS as follows:

For the scales with 1 to 5 sharps, the left 4 goes on the first sharp in the KS (F sharp) and the right 4 goes on the last sharp in the KS.

For the scales with 1 to 5 flats, the left 4 goes on the last flat in the KS and the right 4 goes on the first flat in the KS (B flat).

For the three enharmonic scales with 5, 6, and 7 sharps or flats the left four is always on F sharp/G flat and the right 4 is always on B flat/A sharp

As mentioned earlier, if there are 2 or more black keys in the scale the 3rd finger also gets to cross to a black key.

The 3 enharmonic major scales are the easiest to learn. You only have to remember which white keys to play with the thumb. They can be the best scales to start with for beginning students.

The two minor scales (discussed in Chapter 12) present fingering problems that don't fit any system. In the harmonic minor scale the awkward interval of 3 half steps between scale degree numbers 6 and 7 presents a challenge to the crossing of the 4th and 3rd fingers. The changes in the ascending *vs.* descending melodic minor scales sometimes require a change in fingering. Nevertheless, the easier crossing of the 4th and 3rd fingers to black keys is a good point of departure for finding your best fingering. It also applies to arpeggios or any situation where a finger and the thumb cross.

If you would like a more in depth explanation of the system and the details of the research on the Beethoven and Mozart sonatas, there is a small booklet published in 1970 by this author titled, "Keyboard Scale Fingering," All the major and minor scales are notated with the fingerings.

Computer exercise 7.1

The Modes

The major scale is a scale "mode" that can be described as a diatonic scale with a specific progression of whole steps and half steps as discussed in Chapter 5. However, when musicians talk about "the modes" they most often are referring to 6 diatonic scales with Greek names, which have a pattern of whole steps and half steps different from the major and minor scales. (The major scale also has a Greek name in this context – the Ionian mode.)

The history of the modes predates that of the tonal centered music of the Baroque period. Composers today like to use the modes for their subtle harmonies but still create tonal centered music with them. In such a case it would be proper to refer to a composition, for example, as "in the key of D Phrygian." That would be a tonal center on D with a KS of two flats.

All the modes can be played with any PNK as the keynote, the same as the major scales, as long as the correct whole and half step patterns are maintained. This is accomplished by utilizing the same KS as the major scales but starting with a different keynote. There is a neat system that makes this pretty easy to understand and play, especially with the fingering system based on KS given above. Let's learn the names of the modes first:

7-Locrian
6-Aeolian
5-Mixolydian
4-Lydian
3-Phrygian
2-Dorian
1-major (Ionian)

The number in front of each mode's name is the scale degree of a major scale. That PNK is the 1st scale degree (tonic) of the mode whose name follows the number and has the same KS as the major key.

You can almost make the acronym DIPLOMA out of the initials but not quite. Maybe you can figure out how to pronounce "dplmal."

To play a one-octave Mixolydian scale you start on PNK #5 of a major scale and play one octave with that major KS. The whole steps and half step pattern will be WS, WS, HS, WS, WS, HS, WS, which will give you the sound of the Mixolydian mode. Remember that your fingering is based on the KS so you will use the same fingers on the same keys as you did for the major scale. You just start on a different key. In the case of the Mixolydian mode that is the 5th key of the major scale. See Example 7-A below for the fingerings for the B♭ major scale and 6 modal scales with the same KS.

Example 7-A

B flat major (Ionian) scale
Right Hand Fingering
4 1 2 3 1 2 3 4
3 2 1 4 3 2 1 3
Left Hand Fingering

C Dorian scale
1 2 3 1 2 3 4 1
2 1 4 3 2 1 3 2

D Phrygian scale
2 3 1 2 3 4 1 2
1 4 3 2 1 3 2 1

E flat Lydian scale
3 1 2 3 4 1 2 3
4 3 2 1 3 2 1 4

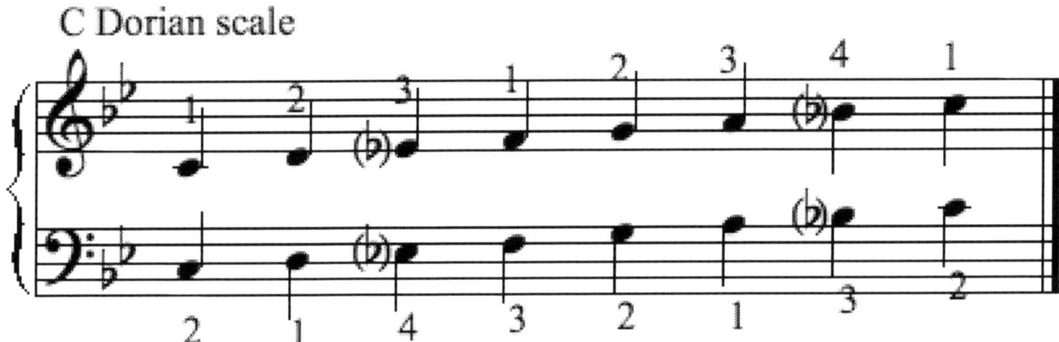

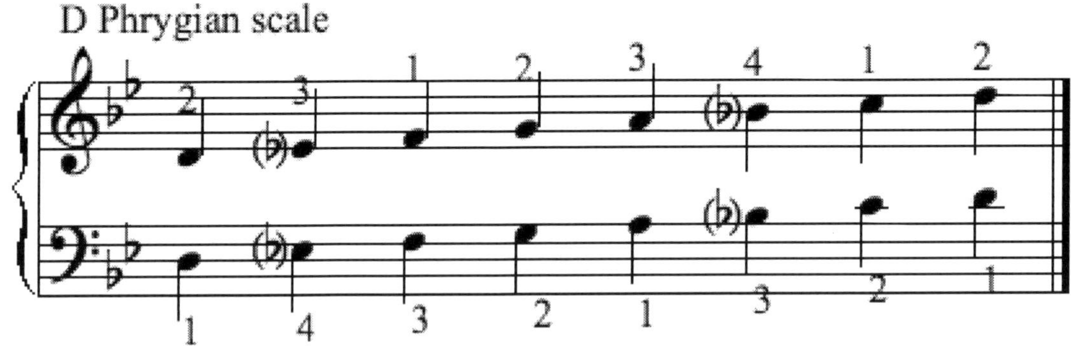

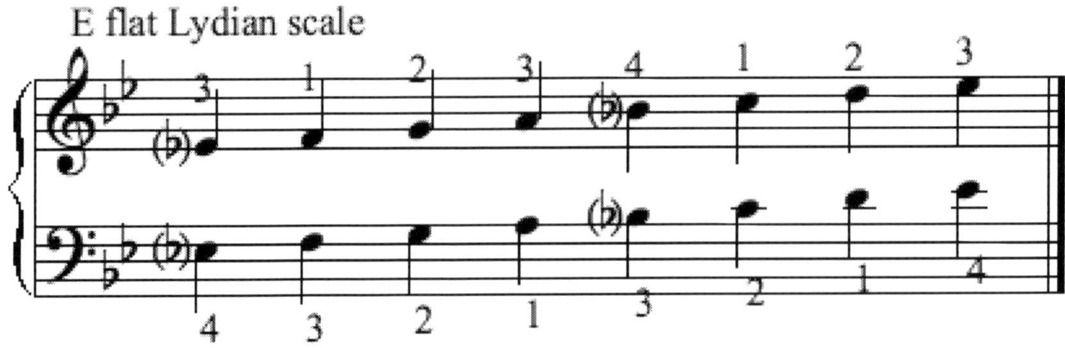

Relative Keys

This is a good place to introduce the term "relative key(s)." Two or more keys are said to be related when they have the same KS. All of the scales in Example 7-A above are related because they all have the same KS of 2 flats. B♭ major, C Dorian, D Phrygian, E♭ Lydian, F Mixolydian, G Aeolian & G Minor, and A Locrian are all related. Musicians often use the term for a major and minor key which share the same KS.

For the serious keyboard student the scales present an excellent device for technique development. Practice them hands separately first until you are entirely familiar with the fingering and KS. Always practice with a metronome to keep a steady beat and to plot your progress. Practice major scales and modes until you know them well enough that if someone asks for a keynote and a mode you can instantly play it with the correct fingering.

As mentioned earlier, fingering mistakes on the scales nearly always involve the 4th finger. It either crosses over the thumb to the key where the 3rd finger should cross or vice versa. The problem can be narrowed even further by noting that this mistake nearly always occurs when the left hand is ascending or the right hand is descending. When the hands are moving in the other direction the thumb crosses under the third or fourth finger and it does so instinctively when you've reached the end of the black key group. That's one of the consistent patterns that apply to all the scales in this system. What one learns from this is to pay close attention to the <u>4th finger of the left hand on ascending scales</u> and the <u>4th finger of the right hand on descending scales</u>. This is especially helpful when playing hands together.

Computer exercises 7.2 & 7.3

Exercises

With the metronome, practice playing the major scales ascending and descending for 3 octaves at 3 PNKs per beat, then 4 octaves at 4 PNKs per beat. Four PNKs per beat at 150 bpm is a good goal to go for. You will never be able to play the scales fast enough. Just keep pushing the envelope.

After you get pretty good with all the major scales, include all the modes in your practice. Play all the modes relative to each KS, then play each mode in every KS. If your principal instrument is not keyboard, you should practice all scales on your own instrument as well as on the keyboard.

Chapter 8
An Interval's Number
Perfect and Major Intervals
Double Sharps and Double Flats
Minor Intervals,
Diminished Intervals
Augmented Intervals
Inverted Intervals
Compound Intervals

An Interval's Number

An interval is the distance from one note to another. (The reason the notes of an interval are not called PNKs in this discussion is because the identification of intervals cannot be applied to the ambiguity of sounding pitches or keys on a keyboard, only to a notated interval. That disclaimer can be ignored at this time because you may not have a clue what it means yet.)

An interval has two identifying components: a number, which represents the number of alphabetical letters in the music alphabet circle from one note to another, and a qualifier. The number of an interval is the number of *diatonic* pitches from one of the notes to the other, *counting both notes.* From **D** to the next higher **B** is the interval of a 6th. From **D** to the next higher **B-flat** is also a 6th, because it still involves six letter names. From **D** to the next higher **A-sharp** is a 5th, because it only involves 5 letter names. The interval from **D** to **B-flat** is the same on the music keyboard as the interval from **D** to **A-flat,** but they don't look the same on the music staff, *i.e.,* they are the same *keys* and the same *pitches* but not the same *notes, i. e.,* they are **enharmonic** . See Example 8-A below.

Example 8-A

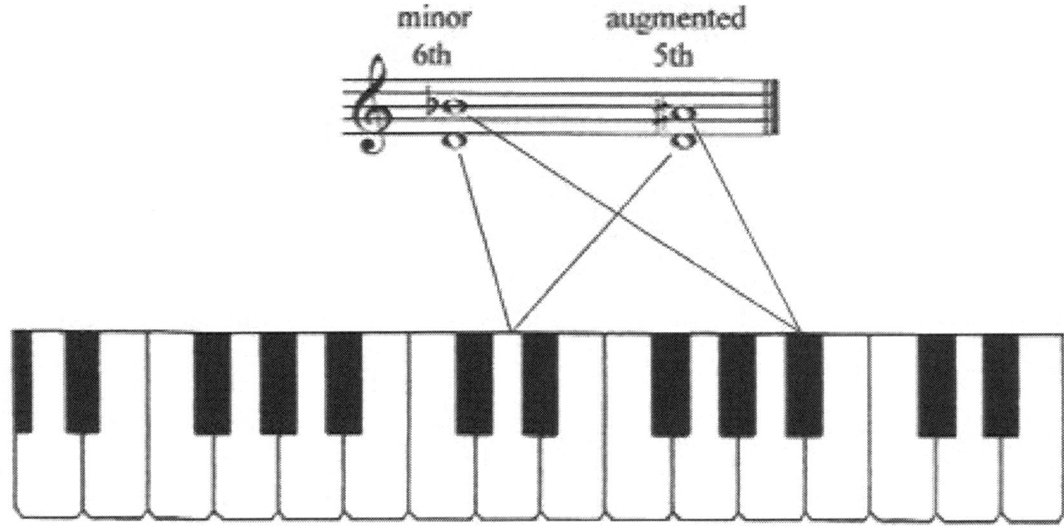

These two intervals don't sound the same either. (Gasp! How can this be?!) At this point a knowledgeable musician, *e. g.* your teacher, should play the following two phrases.

Example 8-B

Both phrases ended with a repeated interval played on the *same 2 keys on the keyboard.* But these two intervals *look different* (on the music staff) and they *sound different*. In the first phrase the last interval from D to B♭ is quite happy to stay where it is and end the piece. In the second phrase the last interval from D to A♯ is crying to expand to D and B♮. The context in which an interval is played will influence one's perception of the interval *and* the correct way to spell the notes. This is where we get to the qualifier part of the interval identification.

Perfect and Major Intervals

Your knowledge of the major scales becomes an important tool in understanding the identification of intervals. Example 8-C below gives the numbers and qualifiers of all the intervals from the keynote **D** to the other notes in a one-octave **D** major scale.

Example 8-C

Perfect and Major Intervals

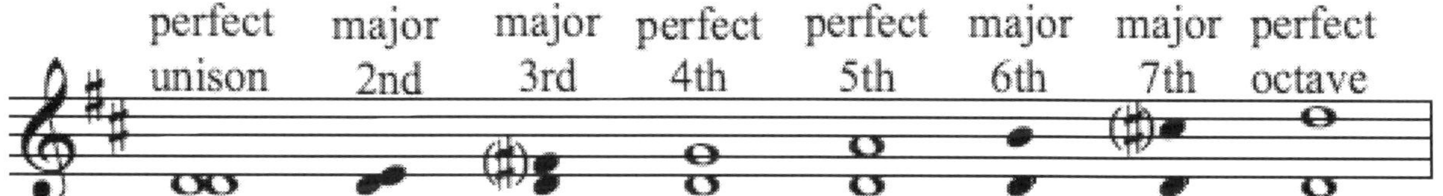

I realize that a unison is technically not an interval but we're studying music, not geometry. The math of intervals is also weird.

Perfect and **major** intervals have the upper note in the major key/scale of the lower note. The difference between major and perfect intervals is in the numbers. A **major** interval is a 2nd, 3rd, 6th, or 7th in which *the upper note is in the major key/scale of the lower note*. A **perfect** interval is a unison, 4th, 5th, or octave in which *the upper note is in the major key/scale of the lower note*. This is easier to remember when you consider that the perfect 4th and perfect 5th are halfway between the perfect unison and perfect octave with two major intervals on either side of them. You can see the pattern in Example 8-C above with the open *vs.* filled-in note heads.

Exercise

At this point you should start training your ear to identify intervals. Play and sing the pitches of any major scale. Sing the scale degree numbers. *E. g.*, for the F major scale, F = 1, G = 2, A = 3, B♭ = 4, C = 5, D = 6, E = 7, F = 1. (Always call the keynote 1, never 8.) When your ear is oriented to the F major scale, play and sing the keynote, then sing *without playing* one of the other tones of the scale above F, then check yourself by playing it. Sing the scale degree numbers or the functional names, not the letter names. Practice this in all the major keys/scales.

As you become more skillful, pick any pitch as a keynote, No. 1, and practice singing at random other scale degrees, always singing the scale degree numbers or functional names. Eventually you should be able to do this confidently without any prompting from the piano. *N. B.* We're not working for perfect pitch here. Don't sing letter names. When you're away from the piano we don't care what the notes are. It is pitch relationships we're concerned about.

The above exercise will give you one of the **essential** tools for being a musician – the ability to understand what you are hearing. As stated earlier, music is sound. In order to understand music you must understand the written *and* sounding relationships of PNKs. You should thoroughly learn this skill or change your major before drop/add expires.

Computer exercise 8.1

Double Sharps and Double Flats

Before we go further with the study of intervals you need to know about double sharps and double flats. A sharp is a half step higher than a natural. A double sharp is a whole step higher than a natural. F-sharp is the first key to the right of F, which is a black key. F-double sharp is the second key to the right of F, which is enharmonic with G.

Double flats work the same in the other direction: B-flat is the first key to the left of B - a black key – while B-double flat is the second key to the left of B which is enharmonic with A.

By extension we could discuss triple sharps, triple flats, quadruple sharps, quadruple flats, *etc., etc., ad nauseum,* but we won't.

The sign for a double sharp is 𝄪. The double flat is 𝄫. See Example 8-D below.

Example 8-D

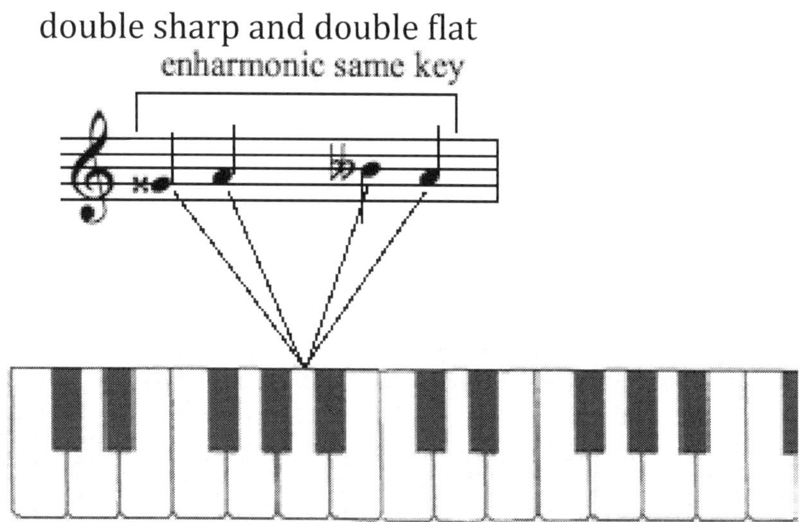

Now that you are totally confident in recognizing written and sounding major and perfect intervals, lets learn some more types of intervals and their qualifier names.

Minor Intervals

If we shorten a **major** interval by either raising the lower note a half step or lowering the upper note a half step, while retaining the same letter names, we have changed the major interval to a **minor** interval. All major 2nds, 3rds, 6ths, and 7ths can be changed to minor 2nds, 3rds, 6ths, or 7ths by shortening them one half step. There are no *minor* unisons, 4ths, 5ths, or octaves. *Only major intervals can be changed to minor intervals.* The definition of a minor interval is an interval one half step smaller than a major interval.

Example 8-E

Major and Minor Intervals

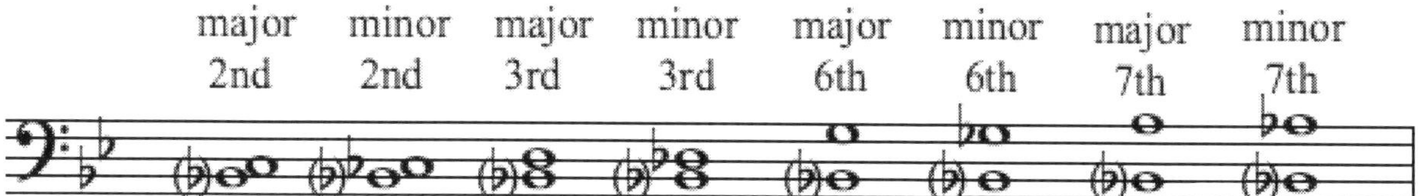

Diminished Intervals

A **diminished** interval is one half step smaller than a **minor** or a **perfect** interval. From A up to C♯ is a major 3rd. From A up to C♮ is a half step smaller so it is a minor 3rd. From A up to C♭ (enharmonic with B) is a half step smaller yet so it is a diminished third.

From A up to E is a perfect 5th. From A up to E♭ is a half step smaller so it is a diminished 5th. The major, perfect, minor, and diminished intervals above A are given in Example 8-F below.

Example 8-F

Major (maj), Minor (mi), Perfect (p), and Diminished (dim) Intervals

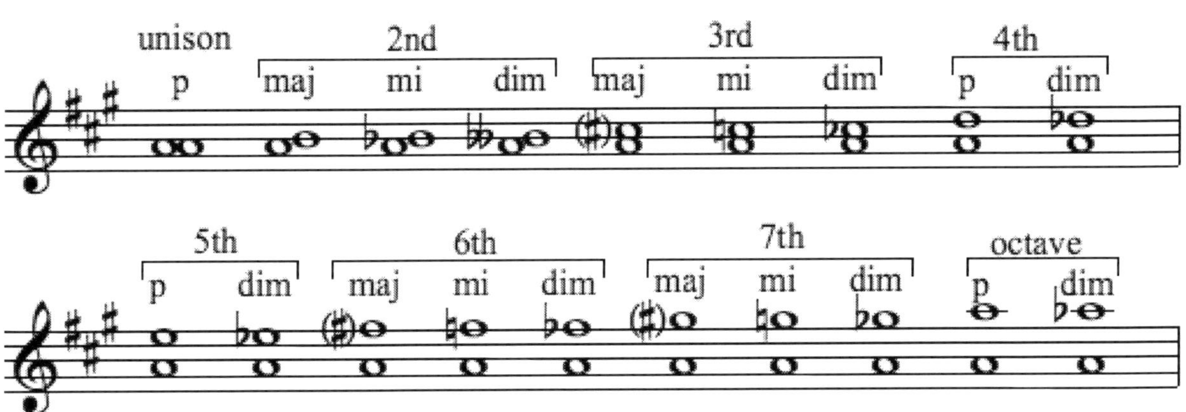

You'll notice that the unison is included in the example in its perfect form only. I tend to agree with the Oxford Dictionary of Music in that several of the intervals ". . . have little beyond a theoretical existence." In their article on intervals the unison is not even mentioned, which I think is a mistake. If two voices of a Bach fugue happen to converge on the same note it justifies the notation of a unison, but a diminished or augmented unison is stretching it a bit.

Augmented Intervals

We just have one more tweak for the intervals. If you expand a **major** or a **perfect** interval by a half step and keep the same letter names it becomes an **augmented** interval. If the upper note of <u>any</u> interval is a half step higher than in the major scale/key of the lower note, the interval is augmented. See the augmented intervals above A in example 8-G below. Since the key of A major has sharps on the 3rd note C♯, the 6th note F♯, and the 7th note G♯, the augmented 3rd, augmented 6th, and augmented 7th above A require double sharps in order to keep the same letter names of the notes and the same number of the interval.

Example 8-G

Perfect (p), Major (maj), and Augmented (aug) Intervals

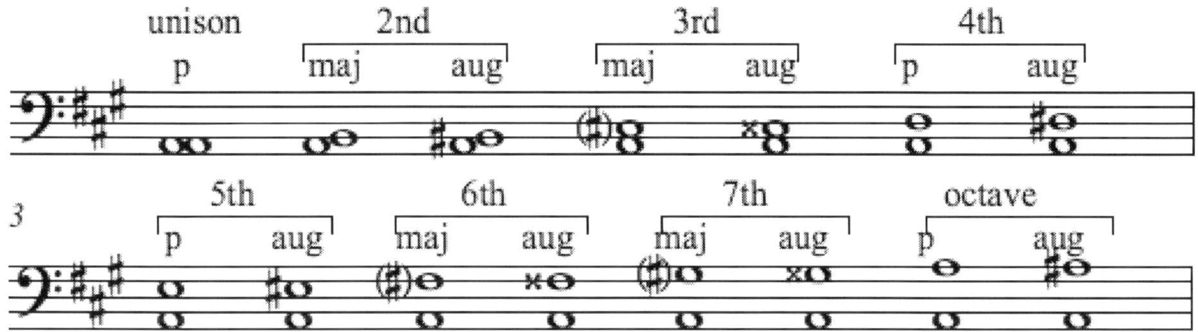

All intervals can be respelled enharmonically: dim 3rd/maj 2nd, mi 3rd/aug 2nd, dim 4th/ maj 3rd, dim 6th/p 5th, dim octave/maj 7th, etc. When you encounter the diminished and augmented intervals especially, either as a composer or a performer, be sure you are hearing them as such, and not as their enharmonic equivalents. The **diminished** intervals want to **contract** and the **augmented** intervals want to **expand.** If you feel an interval wants to move in the opposite direction or is stable without needing to be resolved, consider rewriting it. These ideas make for interesting discussions with other musicians. Always keep in mind that this is art. Different ears hear different things.

If you like you can double-tweak, triple-tweak, etc.-tweak the diminished and augmented intervals. *E. g.,* A quadruply augmented third above G flat would be B triple sharp. A doubly diminished 6th above F would be D triple flat. If you want to learn to hear those relationships then you are much more curious about your hearing capabilities than I am about mine.

Computer exercise 8.2

Inverted Intervals

To invert an interval you move the lower note an octave higher or the upper note an octave lower. When an interval is inverted, <u>both the number and the qualifier change</u>, *except for perfect intervals.*

A major 2nd inverts to a minor 7th, a minor 2nd inverts to major 7th, a major 3rd inverts to a minor 6th, a minor 3rd inverts to a major 6th.

Augmented intervals invert to diminished intervals and vice versa. An augmented 4th becomes a diminished 5th and a diminished 3rd inverts to an augmented 6th.

A perfect interval inverts to another perfect interval. A perfect 4th inverts to a perfect 5th.

Example 8-H

Intervals and their Inversions in F Major

Using the PNKs of a major scale/key with no accidentals you can construct 4 major intervals, 4 minor intervals, and 4 perfect intervals, but only one augmented interval and its inversion, the only diminished interval. This interval is the augmented 4th/diminished 5th formed by the 4th and 7th scale degrees. It is known as the "tritone" because the PNKs are 3 whole tones (whole steps) apart in both intervals.

The tritone splits the octave in half. (An octave is 12 half steps, the tritone is 6 half steps.) If you start from one PNK and go up 3 whole steps you will have the interval of an augmented 4th or its inversion the diminished 5th, depending on how you notate it. If you continue from the upper PNK for 3 more whole steps you will arrive at the octave above your original starting PNK. The tritone in the key of F major is notated in Example 8-I below.

Example 8-I

tritone in the key of F major

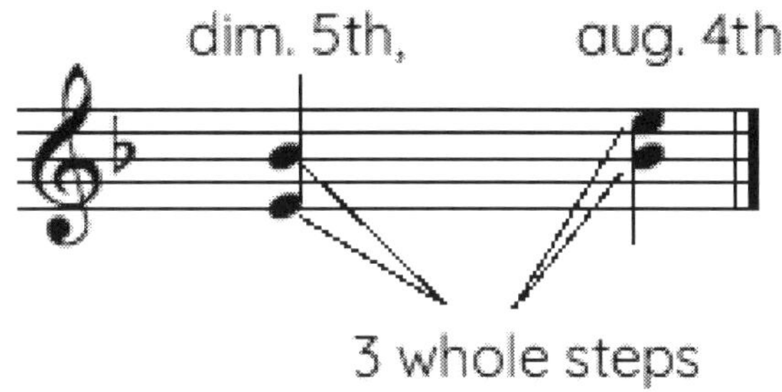

The tritone is a very important interval, loaded with information about the key, as you will learn in Chapter 21. Your knowledge of key signatures and the orders of sharps and flats will allow you to access that information.

Compound Intervals

An interval wider than an octave is called a compound interval. A compound interval will have the same qualifier as it would if reduced by one octave. A major 3rd expanded by an octave becomes a major 10th. (3 + 8 = 10, right?) See Example 8-J below.

Example 8-J

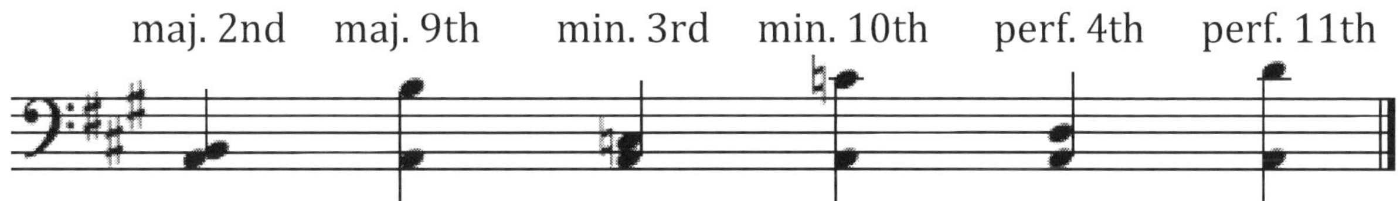

Musicians frequently refer to a compound interval as, *e.g.*, "... an "octave plus a 3rd ..." except when discussing PNKs added to chords. We'll get to that in Chapter 10.

Computer exercise 8.3 & 8.4

Exercises

Learn to quickly recognize in notation all the major, perfect, minor, augmented and diminished intervals. The Bach chorales, hymn books, piano music, etc. will provide a wealth of material. Compared to the other intervals there will not be many augmented and diminished intervals other than 4ths and 5ths. For practice you may want to "pretend" by imagining a major or perfect interval to be expanded into an augmented interval, and a minor or perfect interval contracted into a diminished interval.

Learn to identify intervals involving both clefs of the grand staff. Identify the compound intervals as though the two notes were within one octave, *i.e.*, not compound intervals. This will be an important skill in recognizing triad chords later.

Computer exercise 8.5

If you are thoroughly confident about singing the major and perfect intervals you should start singing the minor, diminished and augmented intervals. *Sing* a major or perfect interval, then change it to one of the other types and check it on the keyboard. Sing intervals both above and below the starting pitch. The goal is to hear any pitch and be able to sing any interval above or below that pitch. When you've accomplished that you'll be well on your way to becoming a musician.

Computer exercise 8.6

Chapter 9
Triads
Fake Music
Major and Minor Triads
Inverted Triads
Root Definitive Intervals (RDI)
The Circle of Chords
Chord Groups
Other Types of Triads

To fully understand this chapter you should know how to play on the keyboard all the major and modal scales and notate their key signatures (KS) on a grand staff (including A-double sharp major and D-triple flat Mixolydian) and likewise all the intervals from a given note (including the doubly diminished 2nd and the quadruply augmented 7th). You should be able to play from a score an unknown melody written on the grand staff while counting out loud.

Triads

A triad is a three-note chord with a **root, 3rd,** and **5th**. There will be two different methods of identifying triads in this text: **Fake music** in this chapter and **Roman numerals** in Chapter 11. In both cases the root, 3rd and 5th definition applies.

There are five different kinds of triads: major, minor, diminished, augmented, and suspension. The suspension chord is technically not a triad, since it has a root *fourth* and fifth, but for convenience sake we will include it in our study of triads.

Fake Music

"Fake music," is a term applied to popular and jazz music that is scored with a melody line with chord symbols written above the staff and lyrics often written below the staff as in Example 9-A below.

Example 9-A

The notes of the melody line are played or sung as written while the chords are played by an instrument or group of instruments capable of playing more than one pitch at a time – piano, guitar, band, orchestra, etc. The rhythm and octaves of the notes of the chords are not notated. They can therefore be improvised according to the whims and abilities of the musicians. The chord symbols also provide material for improvisation on single pitch instruments for the musicians who know how to read them. The potential for a great deal of creativity is available in fake music.

The chords used in fake music are the same as those used in classical music. The difference is that in classical music every note of the chord is notated so that the precise rhythm and octave of every pitch is prescribed, whereas in fake music the musician makes those up as she/he goes.

Major and Minor Triads

The first type of triad you should learn is the major triad. Once all the major triads are thoroughly learned the other types are more easily understood as variations of the majors.

The letter names of the root, 3rd and 5th of a triad will be in the order of three adjacent lines or three adjacent spaces on a music staff, or every other letter of the music alphabet: **a c e, b d f, c e g, d f a,** *etc.*

An F triad will be F A C. An E triad will be E, G B. However, when using only naturals (white keys on the piano) they are not the same type of triad. There are 4 half steps (hs) from the root to the third of the F triad and 3 hs from the third to the fifth. For the E triad those intervals are reversed. See Example 9-B below.

Example 9-B

F-4hs-**A**-3hs-**C**
E-3hs-**G**-4hs-**B**

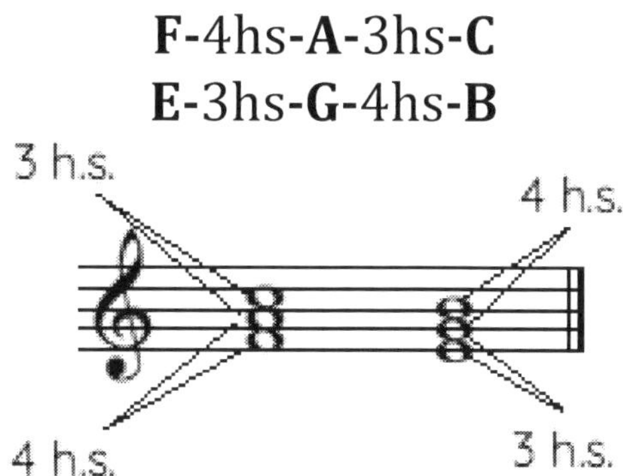

When played only with naturals on the white keys, the F triad is a major triad and the E triad is a minor triad. We can define the major and minor triads thus:

major triad = Root-4hs-**3rd**-3hs-**5th**
minor triad = Root-3hs-**3rd**-4hs-**5th**

The difference between a major and a minor triad is that in a minor triad the 3rd is a half step lower than in a major triad. We could change the F major triad to an F minor triad by lowering the **A** to **A♭.** Likewise, we could change the E minor triad to an E major triad by raising the **G** to **G♯.**

Example 9-C

F-3hs- **A♭**-4hs-**C = F minor triad**
E-4hs-**G♯**-3hs-**B = E major triad**

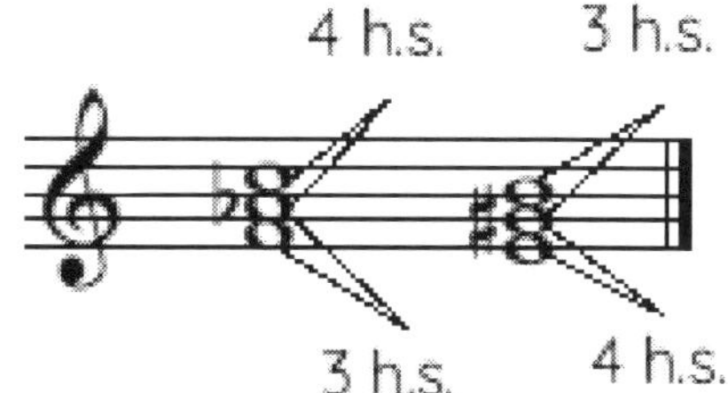

Notice we have *not* changed the letter names of the 3rds. The whole issue becomes very confused, especially later, if you misspell notes by interchanging sharps and flats. Our definition of a triad with a root, 3rd, and 5th would not include the chord **F G# C.** That would be a root, 2nd, and 5th. Your ear wouldn't know the difference between that and an F minor triad but your understanding of a whole bunch of stuff coming up would be totally defunct if we called that a triad.

Go to your music keyboard now and play a **major** triad on every key, *i. e.* use every black and white key as the root. Apply the above formula of half-steps as you play. Say the letter names as you play, being sure to identify them as every other letter in the music alphabet. You will find several different combinations of black and white keys functioning as the roots, thirds, and fifths of these triads. If you run into some double sharps, respell the root enharmonically as a flat. The F major and E major triads are notated and indicated on the keyboard below.

Example 9-D

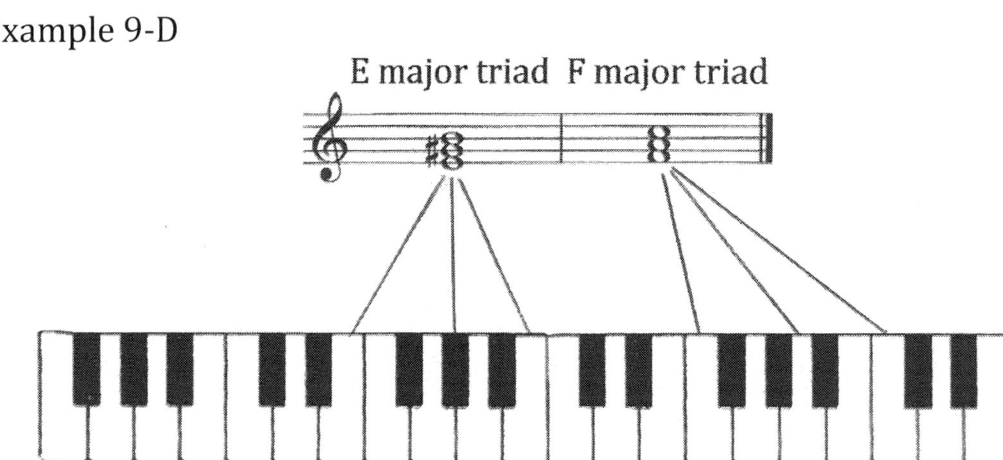

Inverted Triads

When the root of a triad is the lowest sounding PNK, the triad is in **root position.** A triad with the 3rd or 5th as the lowest PNK is **inverted.** If the 3rd is on the bottom the triad is in **1st inversion.** With the 5th on the bottom it is in **2nd inversion.** Triads can also be constructed with the tones spread over more than one octave (in **open position**) and/or with some of the tones doubled, tripled, etc. These various configurations do not change the names or functions of a chord or its PNKs. The root, 3rd, and 5th retain their I. D. regardless of their vertical positions. See the Example 9-E below.

Example 9-E

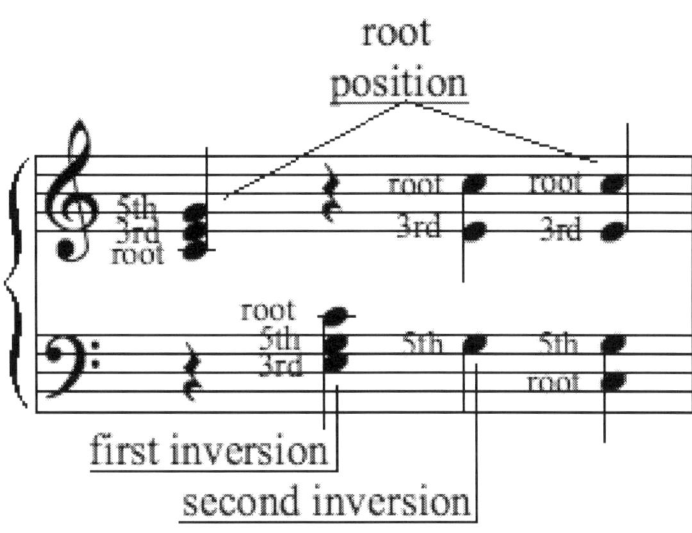

Root Definitive Intervals (RDI)

The perfect 5th in a major or minor triad in root position defines the *bottom* PNK of that interval as the root of the triad. The *top* PNK of a perfect 4th in an *inverted* major or minor triad is the root. (For more information on RDIs see Chapter 22.) The ability to recognize the perfect 5th and its inversion, the perfect 4th by *sound* is very helpful in determining whether the triad is in root position or inverted. See the various positions of the F major triad in Example 9-F below.

Example 9-F

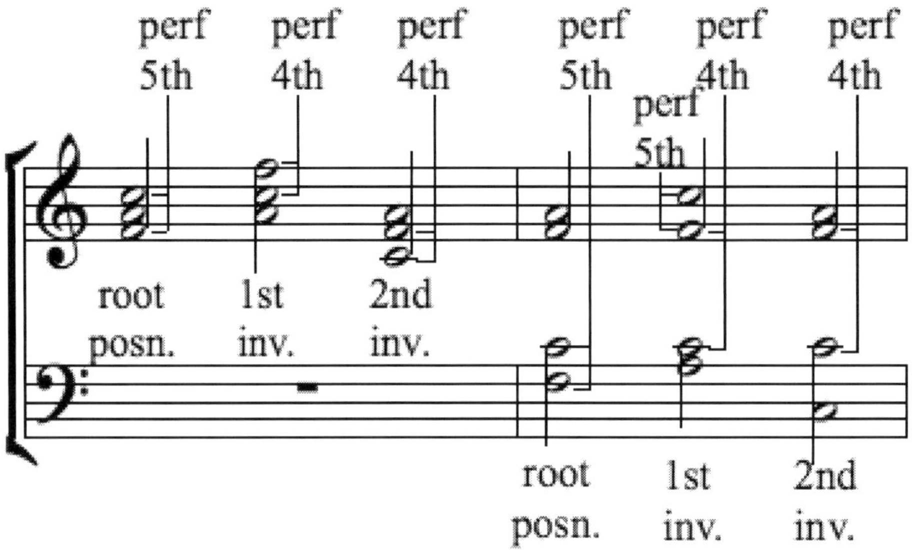

Exercise

Practice playing some perfect 5ths and perfect 4ths, one PNK at a time, while singing, "The end." See which combination really feels like "The end." If the bottom of the perfect 5th and the top of the perfect 4th don't sound finished at the word "end," then you need to find another way to identify RDIs.

Learn to recognize the 3 PNKs of a triad and which of the 3 is the lowest sounding pitch, *i. e.*, whether the triad is in root position or inverted. Practice singing a pitch, identify it as a root, 3rd, or 5th, then sing the other 2 pitches above it. Check your accuracy with a keyboard.

The Circle of Chords

You are about to receive the most valuable tool ever invented for the understanding of traditional harmony - the circle of chords. (Drum roll and blaring trumpets!!) A thorough understanding of the circle of chords in Example 9-G on the following page and the "Other Types of Chords" in the next chapter will equip you for gleaning much information from a music score and applying that information to the production of music. If you aspire to become a working musician you must have it all conveniently stored in your head.

Example 9-G

Circle of Chords

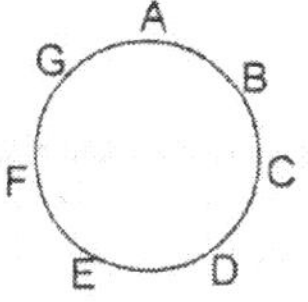

Triad – Root, 3rd, 5th

C

F

G

all ♮

B♭ ← B♭, D, F

D

MAJOR TRIADS

Root (4 h.s.) 3rd (3 h.s.) 5th

A

#3rd

E♭

E

♭ root and ♭ 5th

A♭

B

B, D#, F# →

F#

all #

D♭

G♭ all ♭

The circle of chords is a guide to playing all the major triads. They should be practiced in clockwise order around the circle. That will result in a dominant to tonic progression which is discussed in a later chapter.

In fake music the symbol for a major triad is the letter name of the root, sometimes with a sharp or flat added, just as they appear in the circle. All twelve black and white keys of the keyboard are represented in the circle. For the many other types of chords the fake symbols will have other symbols in addition to the letter name of the root to indicate a type of chord other than a major triad. Those are coming up in the next chapter.

Chord Groups

In the circle there are 12 major triads (if we count the F-sharp/G-flat triad as one) with three triads in each of the three groups. The three triads in each group have the same black and white key configuration and utilize the same hand position for playing them on the music keyboard.

The "all ♮ " at the bracket for the G, C, and F chords indicates that these three major triads are played using only white keys.

Example 9-H

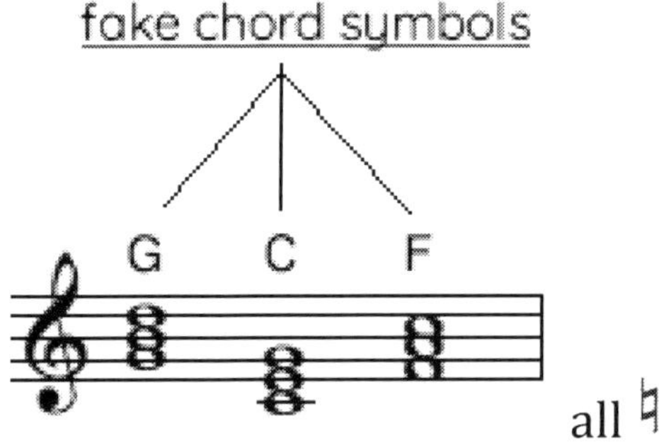

The "♭ root and ♭5th" for the E♭, A♭, and D♭ major triads tell you the root and 5th will be black key flats.

Example 9-I

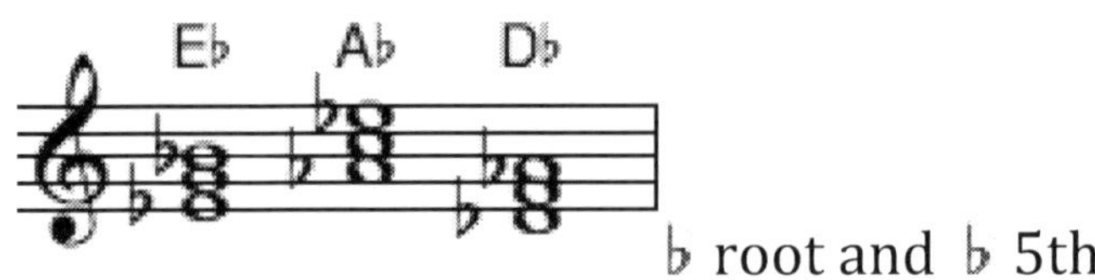

For the E, A, and D major triads the 3rds will be black key sharps.

Example 9-J

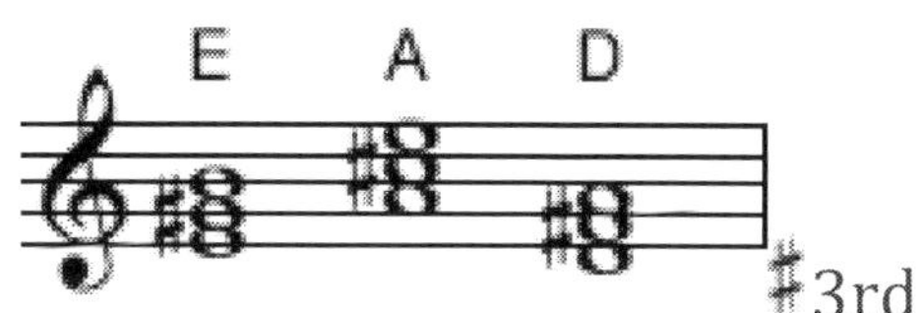

The F♯ and G♭ major triads utilize the same three black keys but with different names: F♯ A♯ C♯ *vs.* G♭ B♭ D♭ - the same keys spelled enharmonically. (See Example 9-K below.)

Students find the B♭ major and B major triads are the ones most often played incorrectly. That is because they are asymmetrical. All the other major triads have either a white key on both ends (root and 5th) or a black key on both ends. The students that misplay the B♭ and B major triads on the keyboard will either make the root and 5th both black or both white. You will probably want to put some extra practice on these chords. When practicing the triads in groups you can make a fourth group out of the B♭, F♯/G♭, and B major triads in that order.

Example 9-K

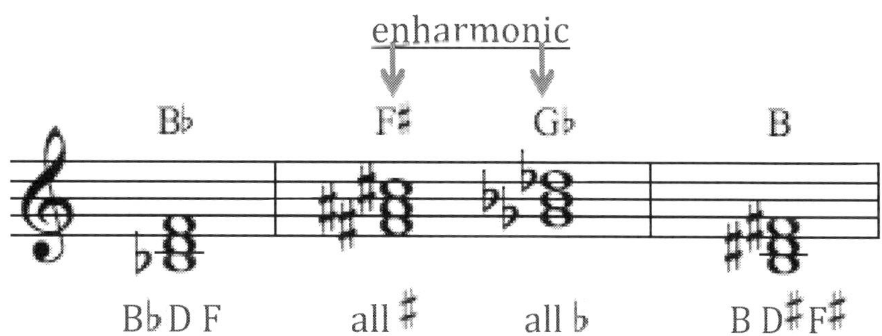

In the Circle of Chords, Example 9-G, the major triads on the right/outside of the circle (except for F at one o'clock) include flats. The major triads on the left/inside of the circle (except for G at 11 o'clock) include sharps. When you get to the F♯/G♭ major triads at six o-clock you cross over from flats to sharps.

Computer exercise 9.1

Exercises

Learn to draw the Circle of Chords from memory. You should be able to draw it in less then 45 seconds. (Just the circle with the roots properly placed and the groups bracketed.) If you know the Circle of Keys from Chapter 6 you shouldn't have any trouble with the Circle of Chords. The word "BEAD" is in there twice.

Practice each of the 3-chord groups until each group is easy. Then practice playing the triads around the circle until you know them thoroughly. If you make a mistake don't just practice the chord you missed but approach it from the preceding chord. That is a good habit for practicing anything in music. You need to know how to get **to** the PNK(s) you missed.

The more familiar you are with playing the circle of major triads the less difficult the following challenges will be. Use both hands, playing the same triad with each hand in two different octaves, as in Example 9-L below. You should be able to play them at 120 per minute (with your metronome).

Example 9-L

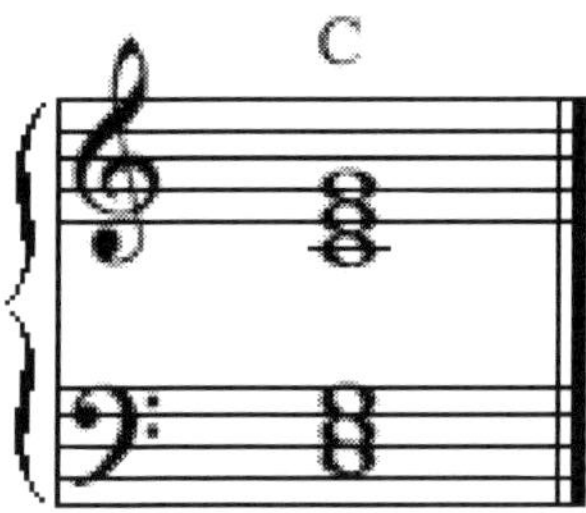

Other Types of Triads

There are 5 types of triads – major, minor, and 3 others:

The augmented triad is like the major triad with the 5th raised one half step.

The diminished triad is like the minor triad with the 5th lowered one half step.

The suspension is like the major triad with the 3rd raised one half step (which makes it a 4th which means it isn't really a triad but we'll pretend that it is).

Example 9-M

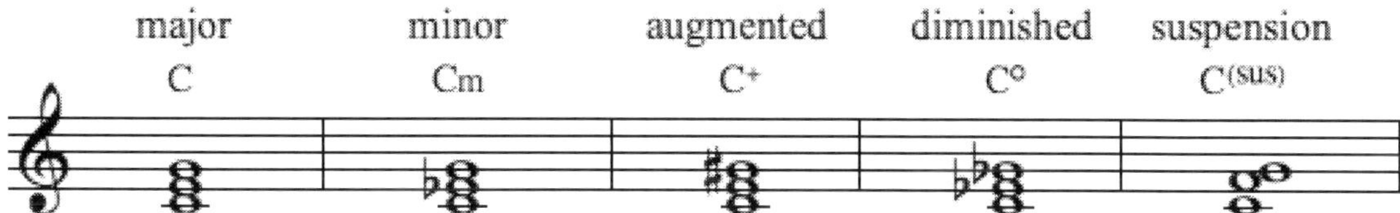

The augmented, diminished, and suspension triads are problematic when considering inversions. The augmented triad has the same spacing of PNKs (with enharmonic spelling) in every position. The diminished triad has no root definitive interval (RDI). The suspension has 2 RDIs that interchange with the different positions. The diminished triad is the only one of the three whose position can be determined by listening and that must be accomplished without the aid of a RDI. It would be easy to hear an inverted diminished triad as a diminished/diminished 7th chord (discussed in the following chapter).

Computer exercise 9.2

Exercises

Once you have mastered the major triads, practice the minor, augmented, diminished, and suspension triads. Play the 5 different types of triads on each root around the circle, then practice each type of triad around the circle.

Practice the triads in various positions – root position, 1st inversion and 2nd inversion. All 12 keys of a music keyboard – 7 white and 5 black - are included in the span of a major 7th (a half step short of an octave). This means you can play every major triad within a major 7th by inverting some of them. Between C and B - a major 7th above C - using inversions when necessary, play all the major triads around the circle. Then move your major 7th up a half step to D♭ - C and play all the major triad within those boundaries. Continue the process until you've fitted all the major triads within every major 7th interval. Then do the same with the other 4 types of triads.

Learn to sing and to recognize by sound the different types of triads in all positions – root position, 1st inversion, and 2nd inversion.

Computer exercises 9.3 & 9.4

If your principal instrument is trumpet, clarinet, oboe, or other single pitch instrument, in addition to learning the triads on a keyboard you should play them one pitch at a time on your own instrument.

You can have some fun while playing triads. With the left hand play the root of the triad down low in the bass on beat 1, then play the triad with the right hand above C4 on beat 2, then the next bass/root on beat 3, and the triad on beat 4. You can also do a waltz beat with root, chord, chord while counting "1, 2, 3." See Example 9-N below.

Example 9-N

You can be creative with different types of rhythms. You can play the PNKs of the triads one at a time as an arpeggio. See Example 9-0 below.

Example 9-O

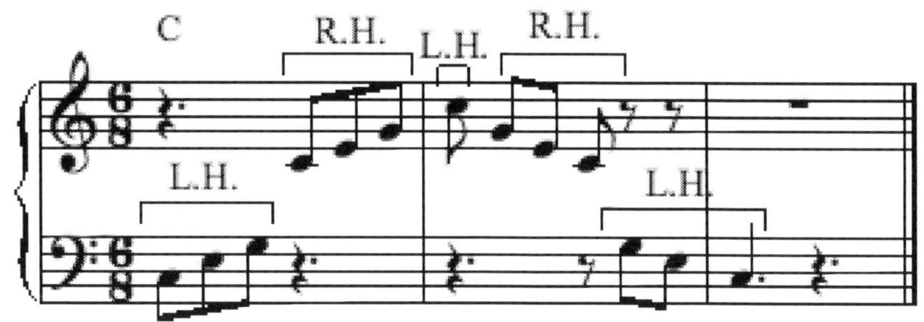

When playing close position triads, if the 3rd of the triad gets below C3 it starts to sound muddy. There is a scientific acoustical reason for this but it's more important to hear the *sound* than to understand the *why*. You should check it out by playing close position triads descending toward the lower areas of the keyboard. See if your ears confirm that from about C3 down, the lower you get the muddier they sound. (You may know a better adjective than muddy.)

To avoid this and still get the rich sounds of the lower piano strings, try playing the triads with the pattern in Example 9-P, below. This left hand pattern is used frequently, with various modifications, in both popular and classical compositions.

Example 9-P

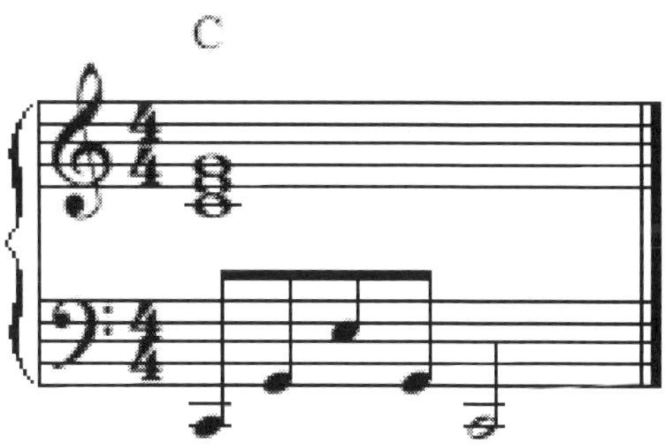

Play all the above exercises on each type of triad around the circle. Use your metronome and challenge yourself for speed and accuracy. If there is the slightest confusion about which PNK is root, 3rd or 5th, go back to square one and play in closed root position. Get together with other students/musicians and experiment. This is called improvisation.

Sooner or later you will find music with chords on roots *not included in the circle. E. g.,* it is not unusual to find C♯, C♭, G♯, D♯, chord symbols etc. in popular music. It's easy enough to figure out how to play them by applying the **root**-4hs-**3rd**-3hs-**5th** formula for a major triad. However, it will probably be easier and faster, once you know the circle well enough, to find the *enharmonic equivalent* on the circle. The C♯ major triad is played on the same keys as the D♭ major triad. When you really know this stuff you should be able to improvise on a G ♭♭♭ major triad with minimal thinking time. It is enharmonic with the E major triad, just as the A𝄪 major scale is enharmonic with the B major scale.

The Circle of Keys (Chapter 6) and the Circle of Chords can be extended in infinite spirals of enharmonic keys/roots. That's a rather significant and quite useful bit of information to contemplate. Be sure you understand it.

Chapter 10
Other Types of Chords
Triads with Added 6th
Other Added PNKs
Bass Non Chord Tones

Other Types of Chords

In the preceding chapter you learned about major and minor triads and you can now play all the major triads around the circle with ease. Example 10-A below gives you a bunch more chords which you will want to learn to play around the circle with ease.

Example 10-A

Other Types of Chords

chord type	fake symbol(s) & examples	description
minor	m Fm Gm	Like a major triad with the 3rd lowered one half step
augmented	+ *or* +5 B♭+ D+5	Like a major triad with the 5th raised one half step
suspension	sus *or* sus4 Asus E♭sus4	Like a major triad with the 3rd raised one half step (*i. e.*, a root, *4th* and 5th)
sixth	6 C6 G♭6	A major triad with a 6th added a whole step above the 5th
minor sixth	m6 Fm Dm6	A minor triad with a 6th added a whole step above the 5th
seventh	7 A♭7 E7	A major triad with a PNK added a minor 7th above the root (a whole step below the root)
minor seventh	m7 Bm7 D♭m7	A minor triad with a PNK added a minor 7th above the root (a whole step below the root)
major seventh	Δ *or* maj7 G♭Δ F♯maj7	A major triad with a PNK added a major 7th above the root (a half step below the root)
half diminished	ø *or* m7♭5 Cø Fm7♭5	Like a minor seventh with the 5th lowered one half step
diminished 7th	° *or* dim A° B♭dim	Four PNKs separated by three half steps *or* Like a seventh chord with the 3rd, 5th, and 7th lowered one half step *or* Like a seventh chord with the root raised one half step

The first column lists the common names of the chord types.

The second column gives the fake symbols that represent the chords with two examples for each. If there are two different symbols for the same chord type, musicians generally prefer the first of the two. The less ink on the page the better. However many publishers use the second of the two. You need to know both.

The third column tells how the chords are formed. As you can see, we are presuming that you know the major triads thoroughly as a starting point. For the 7th chords it's easier to measure the 7th in half steps *below* the root rather than a major or minor 7th *above* the root. Hence the remarks in ( ).

Example 10-B

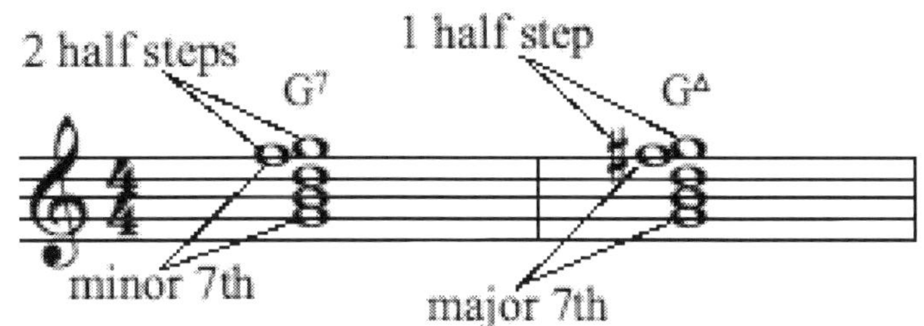

A fairly common way of identifying 7th chords is to state the type of triad followed by the interval of the 7th above the root. With this type of identification a C7 chord would be called a C major-minor chord, meaning a C major triad with a 7th added – B♭ - a minor 7th above the C root. *I. e.,* a C7 chord can also be called a C major-minor chord. See Example 10-C below for all the chords discussed so far with a C root.

Example 10-C

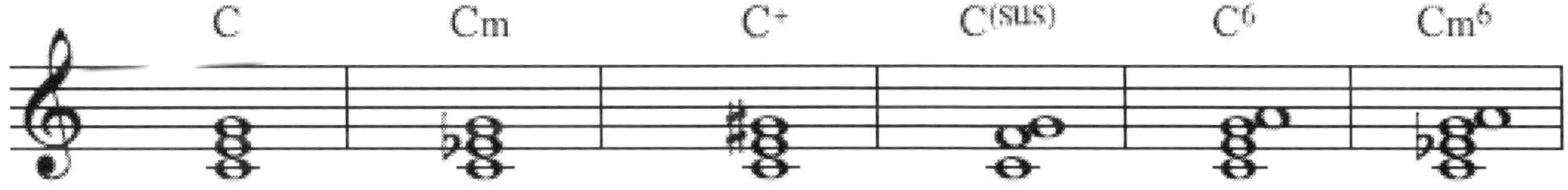

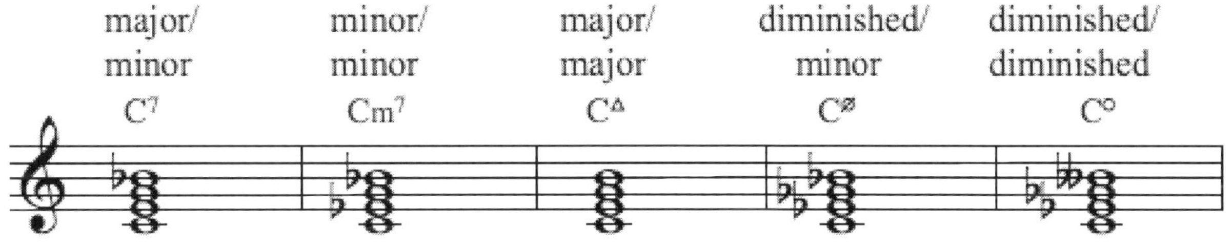

Computer exercises 10.1 & 10.2

Triads with Added 6th

The sixth and minor 6th chords – rows 4 and 5 in Example 10-A – are comprised of the same PNKs as inverted minor 7th and half-diminished 7th chords – rows 8 and 10 respectively. See Example 10-D below.

Example 10-D

The pitch that *sounds* like the root will probably be influenced by the lowest sounding pitch, *i. e.*, to be determined by the bass player. Different tonal and rhythmic environments and root definitive intervals (RDIs) (Chapters 9 & 22) are also determining factors.

Other Added PNKs

There can be other PNKs added beyond the 7th. Chords with 9ths, 11ths, and 13ths are not uncommon in jazz. (Why not 15ths?) Any time an odd number is added to the chord symbol, you assume all odd number intervals below the given one are also in the chord, *and* you are to assume that all PNKs are in the major scale/key of the root *except the 7th* unless otherwise indicated.

Example 10-E

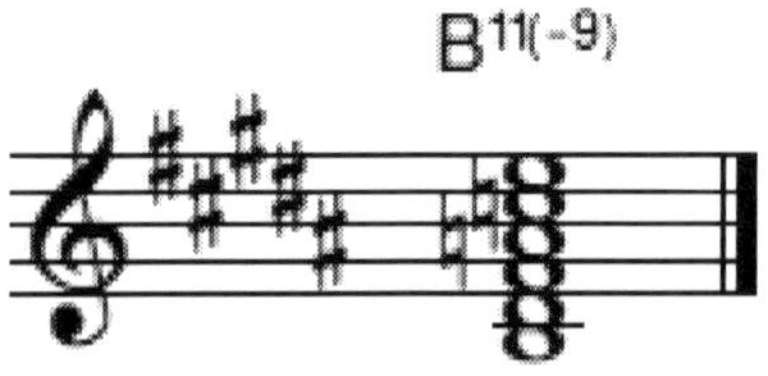

The 7th (A♮) and the 9th (C♮) are a half step below a major 7th and major 9th and are not in the major scale/key of the root.

Please note: Any fake symbol with a 6th, 7th, 9th, etc. added can always be substituted with just the triad. It won't sound as rich but it will work.

Inverted 7th Chords

In Chapter 9 we learned that triads can be inverted with PNKs other than the root on the bottom. The same is true of the other types of chords. Inversions are indicated in the fake chord symbols by a / followed by the letter name of the PNK in the bass. (If the band has a bass player you can ignore the /PNK.) (Unless you are the bass player.)

Example 10-F

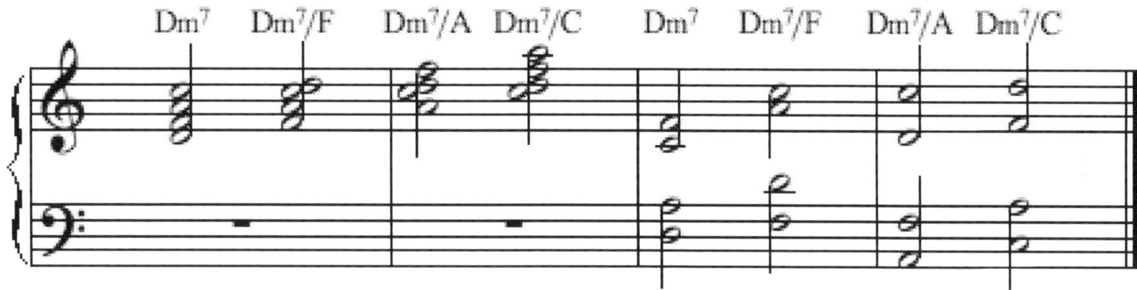

Bass Non Chord Tones (NCT)

Sometimes the /PNK is not in the chord. That can be a pretty powerful sound, possibly because the strong bass PNK is a dissonant NCT. In the progression in Example 10-G below the effect is like a rich jazz V^{11} with the 3rd and 5th omitted. It's in, *e.g.,* Carol King's "You've Got A Friend" and in the Beatles' "With A Little Help From My Friends."

Example 10-G

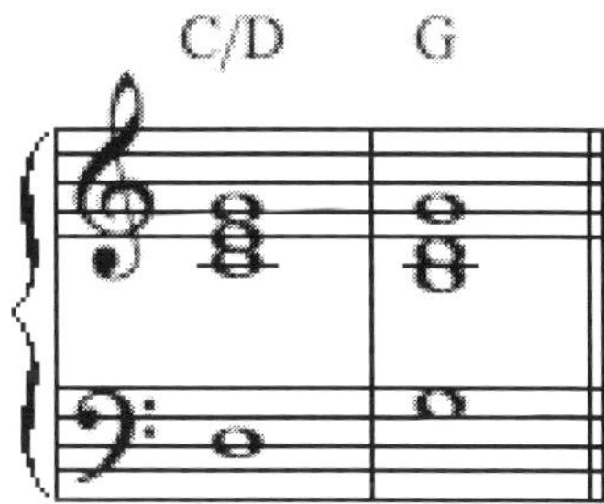

Exercise

It's time now to start the hours/days/weeks/months/years of practice necessary to learn all these new chords. Play them around the circle the same as with the exercises given for the major triads in Chapter 9. In one of the exercises you played all the major triads within the interval of a major 7th. Since the major 7th includes all 12 keys of the music keyboard you can also fit all the 7th chords (any conceivable chord for that matter) into a major 7th with the proper inversions.

Again, the best kind of practice as well as the most fun is playing a gig.

Chapter 11

Roman Numerals
Triads in Major Keys
Common Chords
Chord Inversions
7th Chords and Roman Numerals
Inversions of 7th Chords
Borrowed Dominants

Roman Numerals

Like fake symbols, Roman numerals represent chords. Roman numerals indicate the position of a chord root in the major or minor scale. *I. e.,* the Roman numeral is the scale degree number of the root of the chord. Roman numerals appear under the staff immediately below the notated chords. Many theory books and teachers use capital Roman numerals for major and augmented chords and small case Roman numerals for minor and diminished chords, so we'll do that here. Immediately preceding the first Roman Numeral in an analysis will be the name of the major or minor key.

In a composition in the key of E♭ major, Roman numeral I, placed below the staff, stands for the tonic E♭ major triad while it's fake symbol, placed above the staff, would be E♭. The supertonic triad is represented by the Roman numeral ii and the fake symbol Fm. Usually you don't find both but it helps to understand the systems if you can see them together. All the triads in the key of E♭ major are notated below in Example 11-A with their fake symbols written above the staff and their Roman numeral designations written below.

Example 11-A

Triads in Major Keys

There are three different types of triads in <u>all</u> major keys:

I, IV, and V are major triads.

ii, ii, and vi are minor triads.

vii is a diminished triad.

Since

1. all major scales are formed with the whole/half step formula given in Chapter 5 – W W H W W W H.

and since

2. all triads of a given type are formed with the same intervals from root to 3rd and from 3rd to 5th,

therefore

3. all major scales will have major triads on I, IV, and V, minor triads on ii, iii, and vi, and a diminished triad on vii. An augmented triad cannot be found in a major scale/key. It requires an accidental.

Common Chords

Considering this concept from the reverse perspective can provide material for smoother transpositions from one key to another. (That is not to say that smooth transpositions are always better.)

Since

1. all major keys contain 3 major triads and 3 minor triads,

therefore

2. any major triad can be found in 3 different major keys and any minor triad can be found in 3 different major keys.

The E♭ major triad can function as I in the key of E♭ major, IV in the key of B♭ major, or V in the key of A♭ major. See Example 11-B below.

Example 11-B

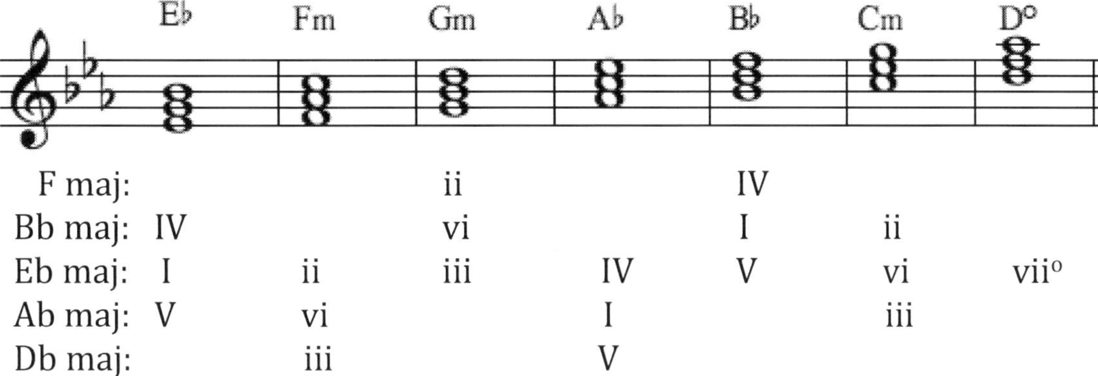

	E♭	Fm	Gm	A♭	B♭	Cm	D°
F maj:			ii		IV		
Bb maj:	IV		vi		I	ii	
Eb maj:	I	ii	iii	IV	V	vi	vii°
Ab maj:	V	vi		I		iii	
Db maj:		iii		V			

Notice that all the major triads can function as I, IV and V in 3 different major keys and all minor triads can function as ii, iii, and vi in 3 different major keys. Notice also that the D° triad is found only as vii° in the key of E♭ major and is in no other major key.

You can see that the key of Eb major has common chords with 4 other major keys, 2 on each side of E♭ in the circle of keys. The column of 5 keys on the left below the staff are in the order of the circle of keys – a descending perfect 5th apart. The number of <u>common</u> chords for each key represented by the Roman numerals are 2, 4, 6, 4, 2 in descending order. The closer the KS is to the original key the more chords the two keys will have in common.

Another device which will expand transposition possibilities is to change a major triad to a minor triad and vice versa. If the I, IV, and V chords in Eb major are changed to minor chords and ii, iii, and vi are changed to major chords it would provide common chords with 10 major keys, 5 on each side of E♭ in the circle of keys. See Example 11-C below.

Example 11-C

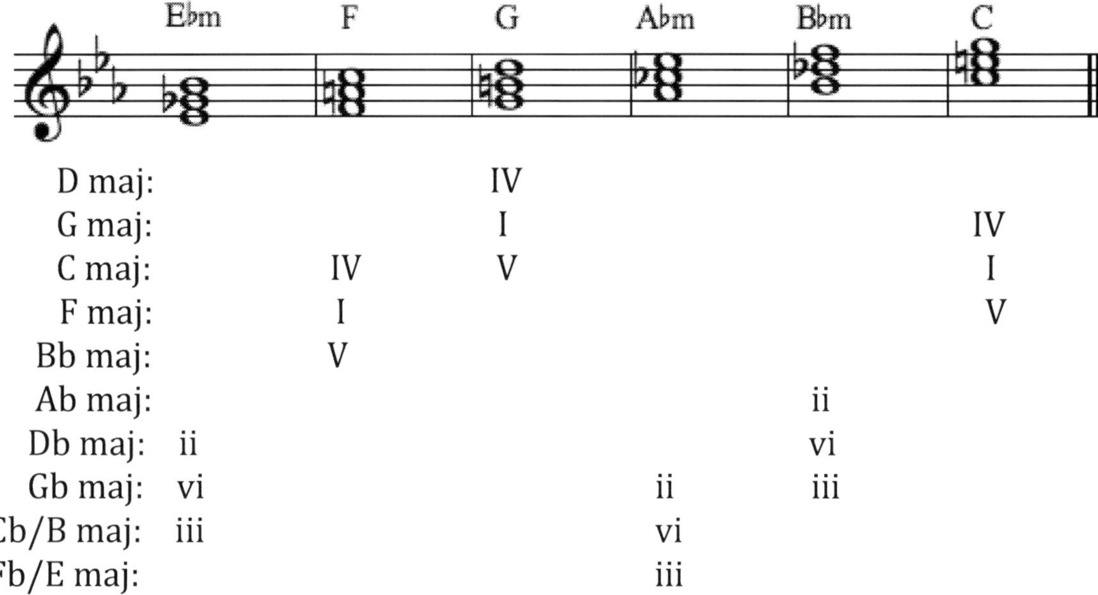

	E♭m	F	G	A♭m	B♭m	C
D maj:			IV			
G maj:			I			IV
C maj:		IV	V			I
F maj:		I				V
Bb maj:		V				
Ab maj:					ii	
Db maj:	ii				vi	
Gb maj:	vi			ii	iii	
Cb/B maj:	iii			vi		
Fb/E maj:				iii		

The same common chords would also be available with the relative modes of all these keys.

Chord Inversions

With fake chord symbols the inversions are indicated with a / followed by the name of the bass PNK. Gm/B♭ means a G minor triad with B♭ as the lowest sounding PNK.

With Roman numerals, inversions are indicated with added Arabic numbers. These Arabic numbers were used during the Baroque period for the keyboard accompanist in a system called figured bass. Instead of chord symbols, the bass notes (lowest sounding notes) of the accompaniment were notated in the F clef and the Arabic numbers indicated what intervals above the bass were to be played at the same time. The total effect produced what we now call a chord. See Example 11-D below.

Example 11-D Figured bass

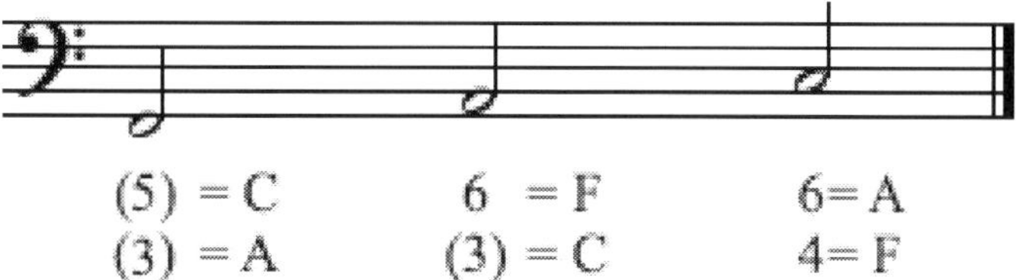

The numbers in ( ) would be implied and not written.

We now recognize Example 11-D as three F major triads in root position, 1st inversion, and 2nd inversion, thanks to a French musician named Jean-Phillipe Rameau (b. 1683, d. 1764). Rameau was contemporary with J. S. Bach (b. 1685, d. 1750). He codified the patterns of the figured bass into triad chords and 7th chords and their inversions, and identified the roots of the chords according to their position in the scale/key of the composition. The result was a combining of the Roman numerals for what we call the roots and the Arabic numbers from the figured bass for what we call 3rds, 5ths, and 7ths.

Note that it is not necessary to write *all* the interval numbers. The Roman numeral indicates the root. If no Arabic numerals are added it means a root position triad, a 6 means 1st inversion, and 6/4 means 2nd inversion.

Example 11-E

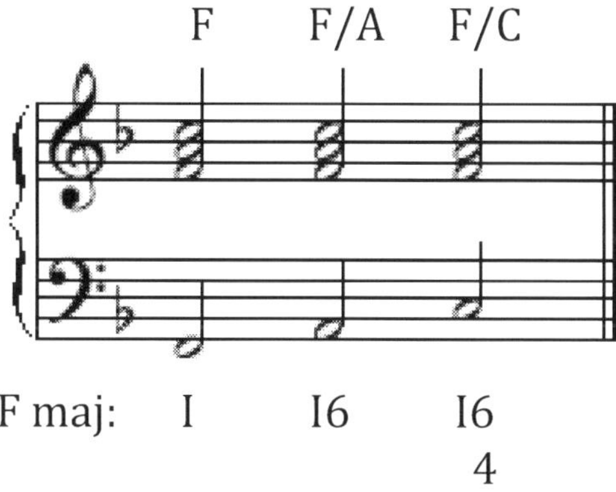

With figured bass the PNKs added above the written bass could be played in any octave, any rhythm, doubled, decorated with non-chord tones, or eliminated the same as we can with chord symbols. The Baroque musicians could improvise just like Dave Brubeck or Ramsey Lewis.

Exercise

Play all 7 triads of every major key around the Circle of Keys (Chapter 6) which you have memorized. Say out loud the scale degree number and the functional name, and the type of triad as you play each chord. *E. g.* "One tonic major, two supertonic minor, three mediant minor, . . . " See Example 11-F below for the triads in the key of C major.

Example 11-F

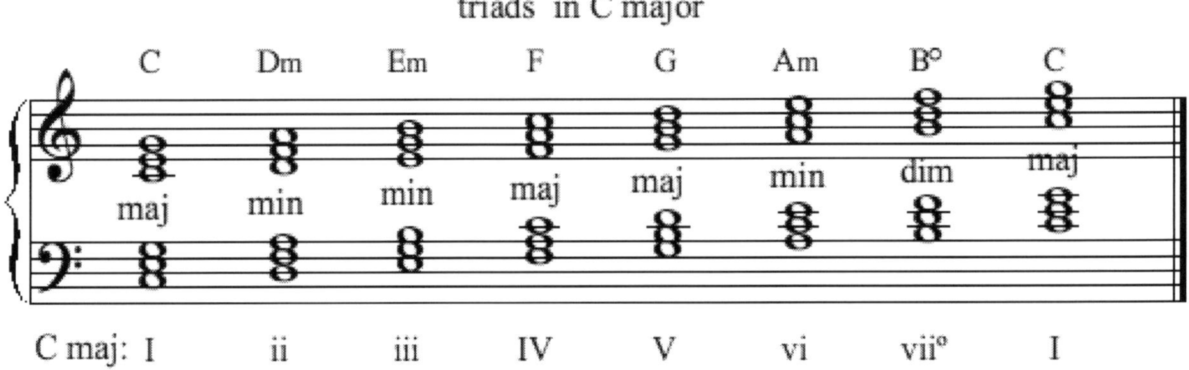

7th Chords and Roman Numerals

When a 7th is added to a triad in *root position* it is indicated with a 7 beside the Roman Numeral. See Example 11-G below.

Example 11-G

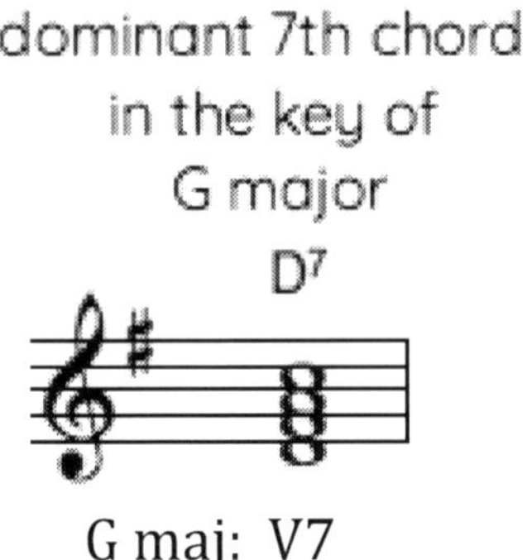

One important difference betweeen fake symbols and Roman numerals is that the fake symbols are independent of the KS of the composition. The D7 fake symbol in Example 11-G would represent the D major triad with a minor 7th above the root in any KS. With 2 flats in the KS the *notated* chord would need an accidental F♯ on the 3rd. The accidental would be indicated with a #3 in the Roman Numeral identification. The fake symbol would be the same in either KS.

Example 11-H

With Roman numerals you must indicate the alteration of any PNKs *not in the KS* to show the effect of the accidentals on the PNKs of the chord. If the alteration changes the chord from major to minor or minor to major, the large cas *vs.* small case Roman numerals will reflect the change. Instead of a chromatic sign, a < can be used to indicate an accidental to raise a note or a > can be used for a lowered one. If the symbol is placed *before* the Roman numeral it means the *root* of the chord is altered.

Please note that a diminished sign ° added to a *fake symbol* always indicates a diminished 7th chord. If the *Roman numeral* represents a diminished 7th chord, °7 must be added. ° alone just means a triad.

Computer exercise 11.1

Inversions of 7th Chords

Triads have 2 possible inversions. A 6 added to the Roman numeral means 1st inversion with the 3rd in the bass, 6/4 means 2nd inversion with the 5th in the bass. With a 7th chord there are 3 possible inversions. See Example 11-I below.

Example 11-I

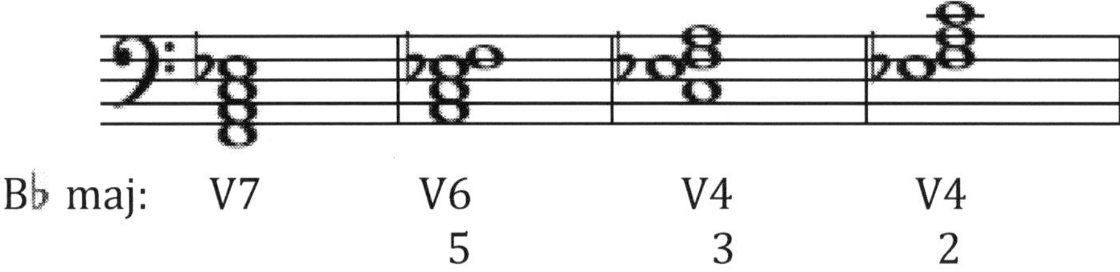

As in the triad inversions, the Arabic numbers added beside the Roman numerals indicate interval(s) above the root. One way to remember the numbers is to compare them to a phone number:

765-4342
7 65 43 42

The 7 is a root position 7th chord, 6/5 is first inversion, 4/3 is second inversion and 4/2 is third inversion. If you're going to be a musician it's worth remembering that phone number.

Example 11-J

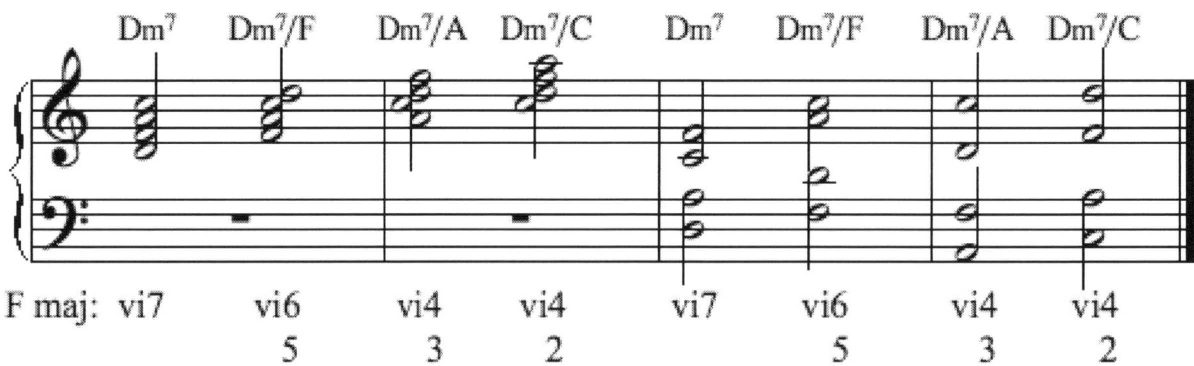

The advantage of fake symbols is their simplicity, which makes them faster to read in a live performance. The advantage of Roman numerals is they give you more information about the relationship of the chord to its musical environment and are therefore valuable for a detailed study of the music. Knowledgeable musicians are comfortable with both systems.

Computer exercise 11.2

Borrowed Dominants aka Secondary Dominants

This is a useful concept for explaining many accidentals and their effect on harmony. In the key of D major, a major triad on the supertonic – E – would require an accidental G♯. The E major chord could be considered as the dominant chord "borrowed" from the key of A major, as reflected in the Roman numeral analysis in Example 11-K below.

Example 11-K

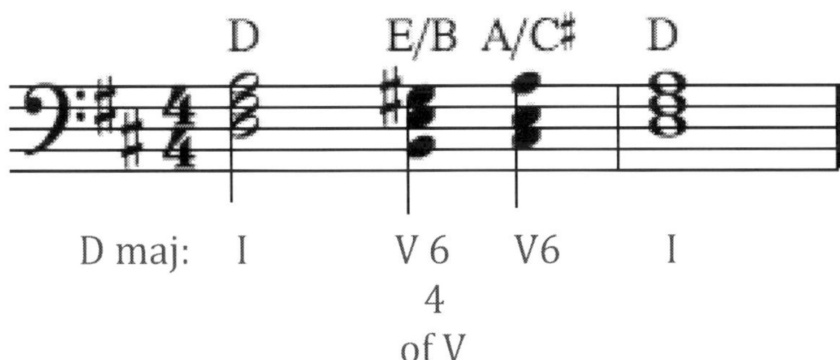

The accidental in the creation of a borrowed dominant need not be indicated in the Roman numeral analysis. The accidental is assumed as belonging to the new key from which the dominant chord is borrowed. Borrowed dominants are a more convenient way of justifying accidentals than identifying a brief departure from a KS as a transposition. See Example 11-L below.

Example 11-L

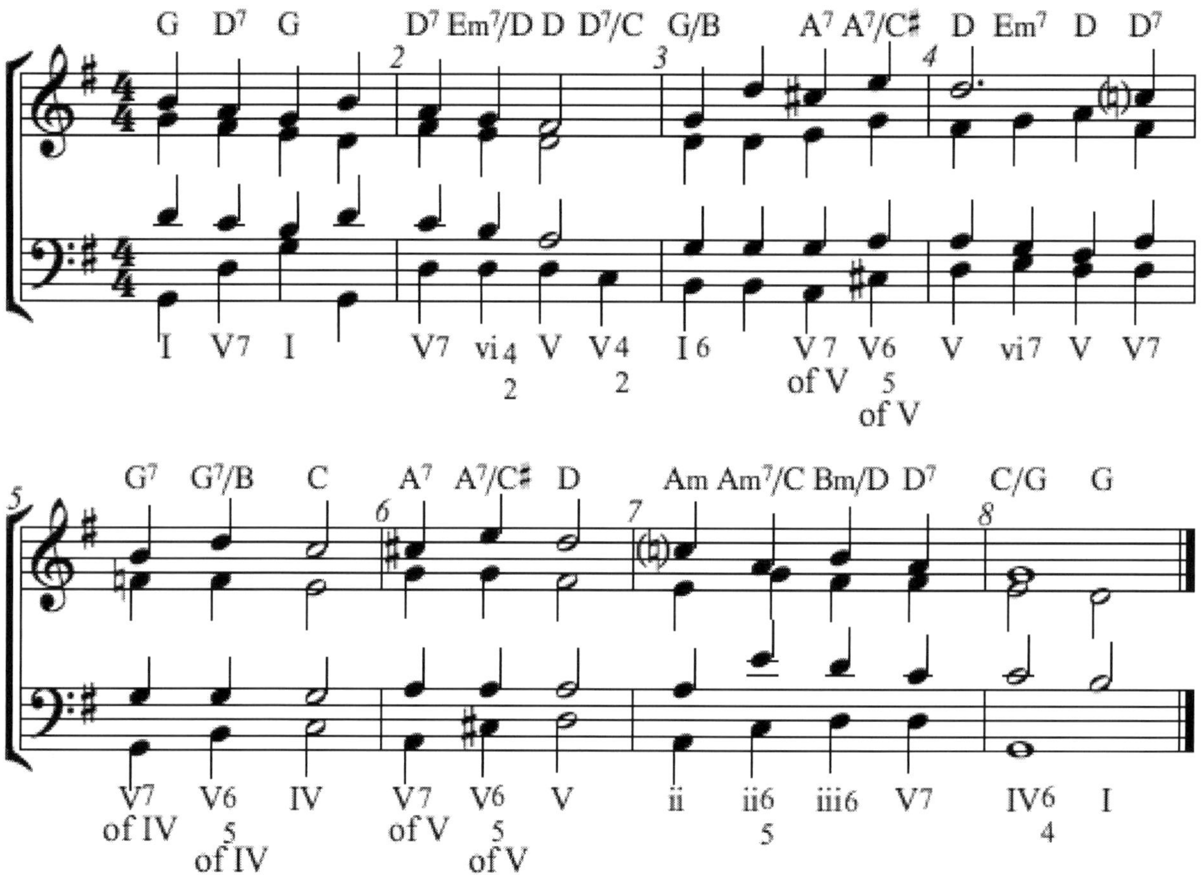

Bars 3, 5 and 6 have examples of borrowed dominants. Note the Roman numeral labels.

There is some disagreement among theorists about whether chords other than dominant chords can be borrowed. See Example 11-M below.

Example 11-M

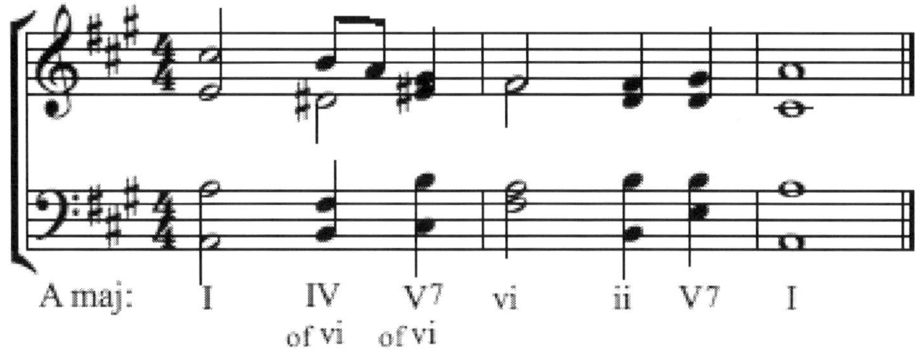

The analysis of the second chord as IV of vi seems more logical than labeling this brief episode as a modulation to the relative minor key. (The D♯ and E♯ are the accidentals in the key of F♯ minor. See Chapter 12.)

Exercises

Analyze some hymns and/or Bach chorales with figured bass and fake symbols. The first item is to identify the key. The root of the final chord will be the keynote. The KS plus the keynote will tell you whether it is a major or minor key. *N. B.* The key may change within the piece. The Roman numeral analysis must reflect the key environment of the chords. Notice in Example 11-N below that after a common pivot chord is analyzed in both keys the subsequent analysis continues in the *new key* until the next modulation occurs.

Use capital Roman numerals for major and augmented chords and small case for minor and diminished. Identify key changes. Indicate inversions and accidentals with appropriate Arabic numbers as in Example 11-N. Some non chord tones (discussed later in Chapter 16) are in parentheses and may be ignored for this analysis.

Example 11-N

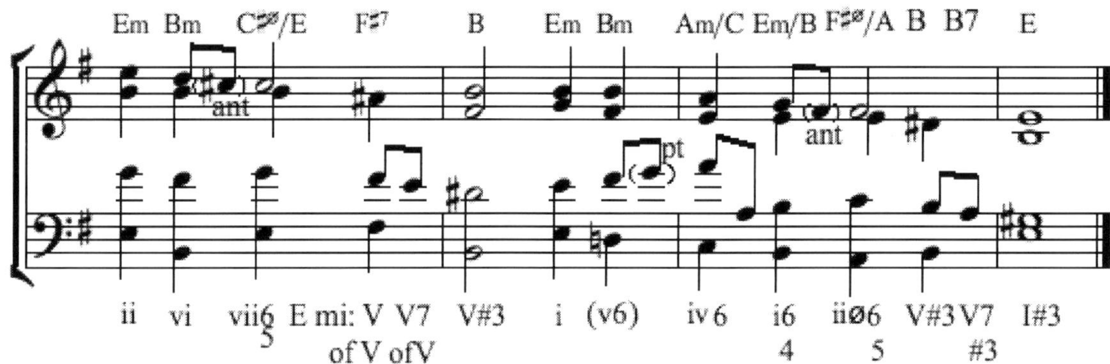

If you haven't already, you will learn a number of "rules" of four-part writing of this period, exceptions to most or all of which can be found in Bach's music somewhere. For example, an octave approached in similar motion, particularly in the outer voices (soprano and bass) is forbidden. But there it is in bar 2 beats 2 to 3 between bass and soprano. These rules are seldom or rarely broken so don't use one example as an excuse to ignore the rule. One professor told his class that when we had written as much music as Bach wrote we could break the rules as often as Bach did.

Chapter 12

The 2 Minor Scales
The Accidentals in Minor Keys
Chords in Minor Keys

The 2 Minor Scales

My teachers and the theory books I read all told me there are 3 forms of the minor scale: **natural minor**, **harmonic minor** and **melodic minor**. The so-called "natural minor" scale is exactly like the Aeolian mode which you learned in Chapter 7 with its key signatures (KSs) and its whole step/half step diatonic scale arrangement. In a composition, the use of the subtonic in the Aeolian mode as opposed to leading tone sets the sound of the Aeolian mode apart from the Baroque use of minor scales and harmonies. A composition in a minor key uses a leading tone raised with an accidental. A composition in the Aeolian mode does not. If a composer is writing in the Aeolian mode then that's what I would call it, not natural minor. However, for the sake of your grade average, remember what other books and other teachers mean by the term "natural minor scale". When you see the term "minor scale/key" in <u>this</u> text it refers only to the melodic or harmonic forms of minor.

The Accidentals in Minor Keys

Like the modes, the minor scales use the same KSs as the major scales. As you already know from Chapter 7, if you start playing a scale from the 6th degree of the major scale, you will be playing the Aeolian mode. The two minor scales – the harmonic minor and the melodic minor – also start from the 6th scale degree of the major scale but have accidentals added which raise the 7th and sometimes the 6th scale degrees a half step creating a leading tone. *N. B.,* these are accidentals and are <u>not</u> in the KS.

The sound of a seventh scale degree which is a whole step below tonic (aka subtonic) is one of the qualities you will learn to recognize as modal. Lydian is the only mode with a leading tone. A composition in the Lydian mode is sometimes mistaken for one in a major key for that reason.

The Baroque musicians used only the major and minor tonalities. The characteristic leading note with its strong tendency to resolve upward into tonic was important to establishing the keynote as the center of tonality, and tonal centered music was what it was all about. They also liked the sounds of the minor key. In order to have *both* a minor key *and* a leading note they raised the 7th degree a half step with an accidental. They still had the minor harmonies on tonic and sub-dominant, but you will find that the dominant triad in Baroque music is always major. (You may call me if you find an exception. I will probably weasel out by explaining that it's either an editor's mistake, not really a dominant chord, or not truly Baroque.)

Another accidental sometimes found in minor Baroque compositions is a raised 6th scale degree. Its purpose is melodic. In the ascending harmonic minor melodies the raised 7th created an awkward interval of 3 half steps between the 6th and 7th scale degrees. In Chapter 8 you learned the name of that interval - augmented 2nd.

The augmented 2nd caused intonation problems with singers, and the Baroque musicians didn't really care for its sound. So, when they wrote an ascending melody in a minor key they raised the 6th degree as well as the 7th. This gave them their leading tone and eliminated the awkward interval. They didn't really need a leading tone on a descending melody because it wasn't moving up to tonic, so in a descending minor melody the 7th and 6th degrees may be returned to their un-accidentalized states. *This is not a hard and fast rule.* You can find examples of descending minor scales with both the 6th and 7th degrees raised because of, *e. g.*, harmonic considerations. Later composers exploited the distinctive effect of the augmented 2nd in the harmonic minor.

The two minor scale forms that result from these accidentals are the harmonic minor with the raised 7th degree, (and its characteristic augmented 2nd) and the melodic minor with 6 and 7 raised ascending and returned to conform to the key signature descending. They are notated in the key of F minor in Example 12-A below.

Example 12-A

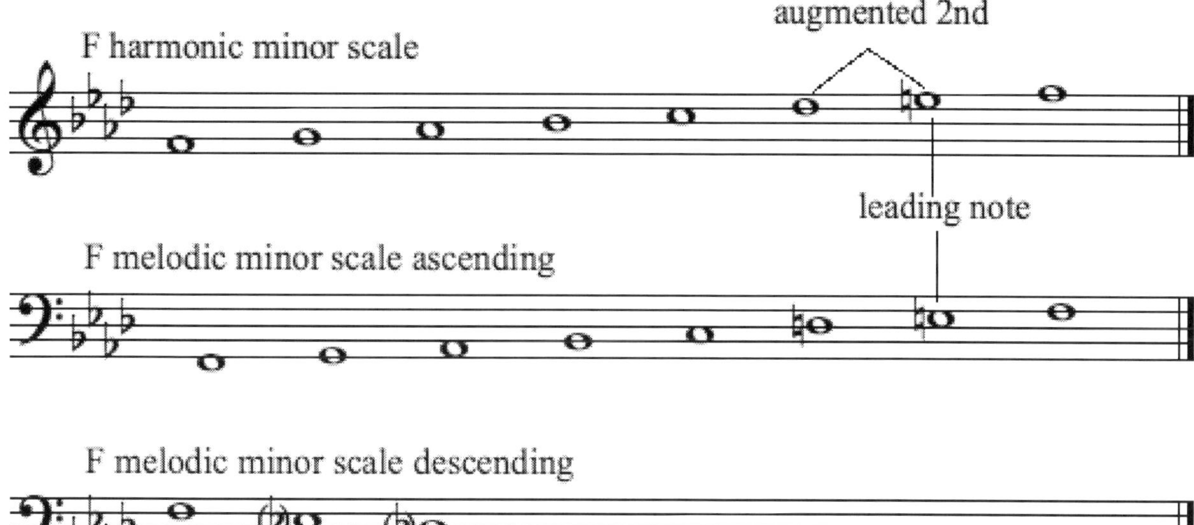

The above F minor scale is the <u>relative minor</u> of A♭ major because they share the same KS. Even though a composition in F minor has consistent accidentals, the KS is still 4 flats.

Computer exercise 12.1 & 12.2

Exercises

You now have two more scales in each KS to practice: the harmonic and melodic minor scales. There is no effective fingering *system* for these scales that works for all the minor scales. Because of the augmented 2nd in the Harmonic minor and the swapping around of black and white keys, depending on direction, in the melodic minor, the major scale fingering system based on KS won't always work.

Suggested fingerings for the minor scales are given in the above-mentioned "Keyboard Scale Fingering" book. However, different sizes and shapes of hands mean that each student should experiment to find his/her own best fingering. Crossing the 4th and 3rd fingers to a black key is a good point of departure, but it might not always be the least difficult for the minor scales.

Chords in Minor Keys

A minor key will include the same chords as its relative major plus the chords affected by the accidentals. An accidental changes not only a single melody note but also changes every triad and 7th chord that includes the accidental. The raised 7th in a minor key changes three triads and four 7th chords in that key. See Examples 12-B and 12-C below.

Example 12-B: Triads in A♭ major and F minor

Example 12-C: 7th chords in A♭ major and F minor

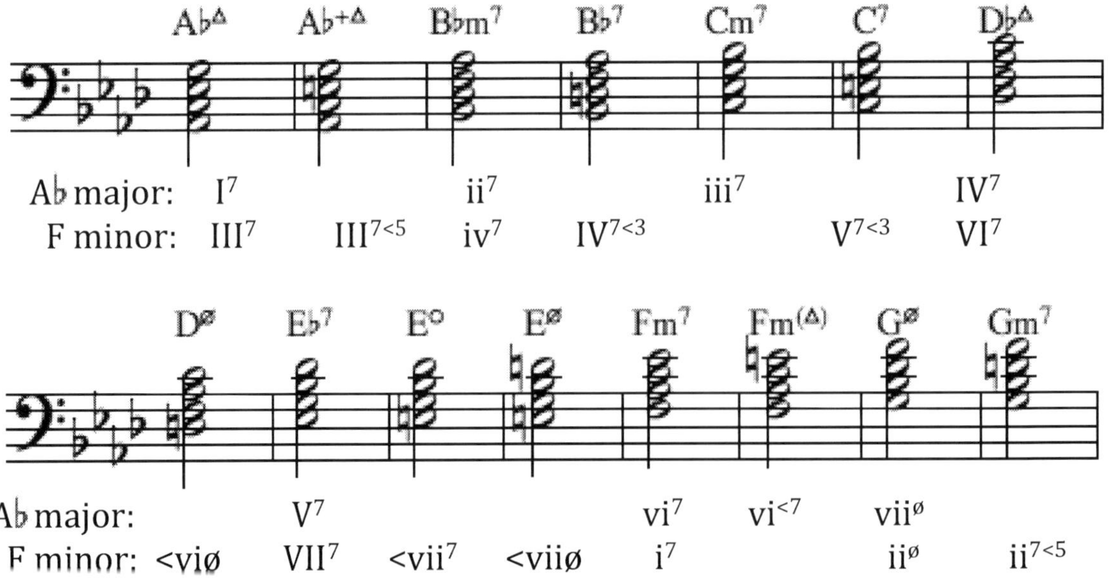

The raised 7th degree of the minor scales creates some chord roots off the charts of the circles. See Example 12-D below.

Example 12-D

To play these chords think their enharmonic equivalents. Remember, there are only 3 diminished 7th chords and their inversions.

In a minor key, the raised 7th creates an augmented triad on the mediant. It was not a favorite of the Baroque composers. In 61 of the chorales harmonized by Bach it is found only 6 times. It is clearly a mediant chord of a minor key in 5 of those 6 instances. Not so clear in the 6th. See Example 12-E below.

Example 12-E

excerpt from

Dein Glanz all Finsternis verzehrt

harmonized by J. S. Bach

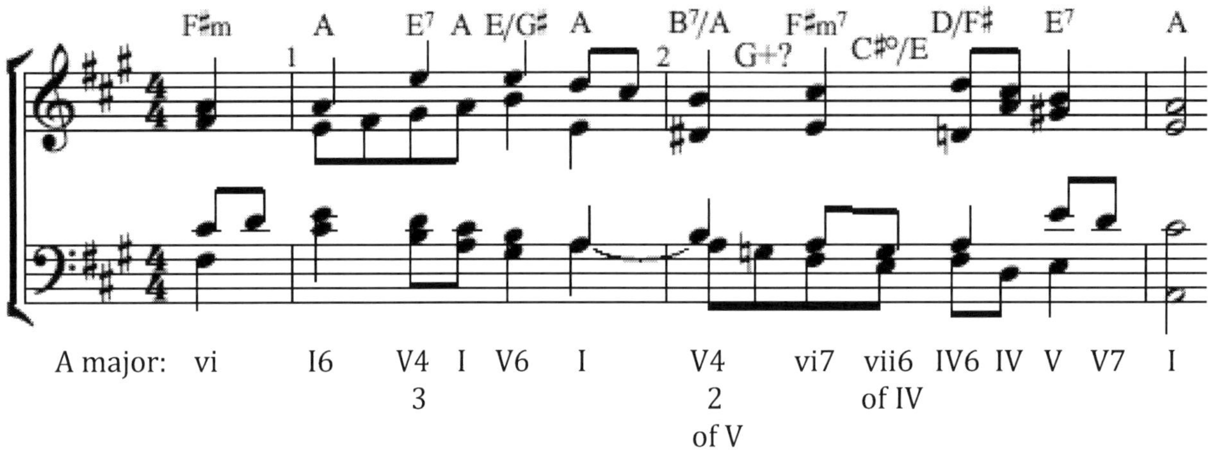

Bar 2 is an interesting chord progression. Beat 1 is a B7 chord, the V4/2 of V, but it's resolution into the V chord is delayed until beat 4. Why did Bach put a natural on the bass G in the 2nd half beat 1? It morphs the chord into a G+ chord, which is enharmonic with a B+ chord (which functions as V+ of V). B+ would have the G♮ spelled as F𝄪 which would resolve up to G♯ if it resolved into the V chord, but here the G♮ continues its descent to resolve to the F♯ root of the vi7 chord. I don't hear this as an augmented triad with a V+ of V function but instead as a non-chord tone. (See Chapter 16.) The second half of beat 2 is the vii° of IV (C♯°) resolving to IV (D) on beat 3. This is followed at last by the delayed resolution of the V of V earlier in the bar into the dominant chord (E7), bringing us back into 3♯.

Bach bounces us around between 2 and 4 sharps but the smooth voice leading makes it OK. This is a good example of why a performer – the singer – needs to know the implications of the accidentals in order to effect good intonation and to choose a direction in Bach's music.

Chapter 13
Early Church Music
Tonal Centered Music
Root Progressions
Circle Progressions
3-Chord Pieces
Other Tonal Center Influences

Early Church Music

Most of the written examples of the music of the medieval period (*ca.* 500 – *ca.* 1400) came from the Catholic Church. The Psalms and hours of the mass were sung as unaccompanied, single voice (monophonic) melodies or chants. Pope Gregory, whose papacy extended from 590 – 604, is popularly credited with collecting and codifying these chants and they are now referred to as Gregorian chant.

These melodies were based on the modal scales discussed in Chapter 7 and not on the major or minor scales. With no harmony and therefore no harmonic progression, and seldom a leading tone, they lacked a strong feeling of having a tonal center in what we call the keynote of a major or minor scale.

During the Renaissance period (*ca.* 1400 – *ca.*1600) polyphony (more than one melody sung at the same time) and accompanied melodies became more common. With the added harmony and the growing practice of raising the 7th scale degree a half step to create a leading tone, by the time of the Baroque period (*ca,* 1600 – *ca.* 1750) tonal centered music was firmly established.

Tonal Centered Music

An understanding of what we mean by "tonal centered" can be demonstrated by comparing the degrees of a major or minor scale to coming home from a trip to Europe. We will be using the functional names of scale degrees from Chapter 5 as given in Example 13-A below.

Example 13-A

scale degree #	functional name
7	leading tone (LT)
6	sub mediant
5	dominant
4	sub dominant
3	mediant
2	super tonic
1	tonic

The leading tone (LT) and dominant PNKs both want to resolve to tonic. After an extended trip away from home, returning to your hometown feels comfortable but not to the extent of being inside your house. Like the LT and the dominant in tonal-centered music, getting to your hometown makes the desire to walk into your home (tonic) that much stronger.

Exercise

Play a major or minor scale to establish a tonal center in your ear. Then play the dominant PNK followed by the tonic PNK, then the LT PNK followed by the tonic PNK and listen for the sense of direction in these pitch relationships. Try following other scale degrees with the tonic and compare that with dominant-to-tonic and LT-to-tonic. Then choose another scale/key and try it there. Do this until you can hear what other musicians hear when they talk about the sense of direction toward tonic that are inherent in the dominant and LT.

The dominant triad contains both the dominant PNK and the LT. See Example 13- B below.

Example 13-B

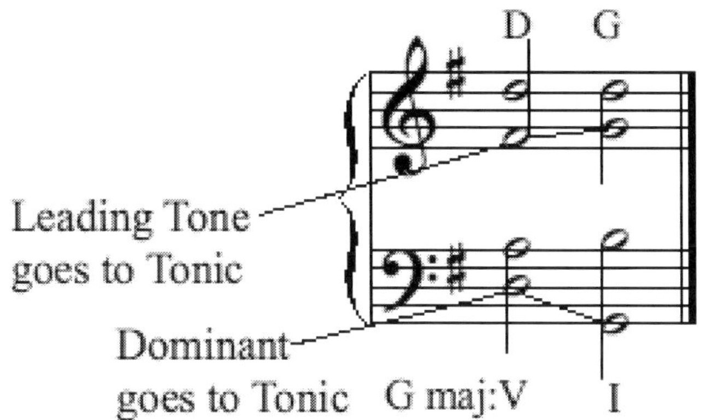

The dominant chord has a strong tendency to resolve to the tonic chord. This is not a "rule" chiseled in stone. A composer can choose any PNK to follow any other PNK and any chord to follow any other chord. Some of the most poignant moments in music are when your expectations are redirected, *e. g.*, when a V chord is followed by vi. However, too many surprises result in confusion, so we need a balance. If a long series of chords follows a strong progression pattern, then a surprise progression becomes more of a surprise and thereby more effective.

After a trip to a foreign country your return home would involve several levels of "going home": When you touch down on American soil, when you cross your home state line, when you drive into your home town, and when you finally reach your home. Each level can give you a closer feeling of going home.

In tonal centered music there is a tonal progression that relates well to that experience. The following chord progression could be from a song about returning from a European trip to home on Hollyhock Lane in Burlington WV.

Example 13-C

function/location -	leads to - function/location
mediant/Europe	submediant/USA (home country)
submediant/USA	supertonic/West Virginia (home state)
supertonic/West Virginia	dominant, LT /Burlington (hometown)
dominant, LT/Burlington WV	tonic /1465 Hollyhock Lane (home)

Play a major scale to establish a tonal center. Then play the order of scale degrees as in Example 13-C above: 3, 6, 2, 5 or 7, 1. Listen for the sense of direction in the progression.

Root Progressions

Musicians talk about root progressions. That has to do with the interval by which the root of one chord moves to the root of the following chord. A strong root progression is up a 4th or down a 5th. Both intervals progress to the same scale degree but in different octaves. This is commonly referred to as a root progression by perfect 5ths. (We'll see later how this is linked to the circle of keys and the circle of chords.) These are the same intervals by which the scale degree functions in the left column of Example 13-E above progress to the scale degree functions in the right column with the exception of the LT. See Example 13-D below.

Example 13-D

root progression up a 4th, down a 5th

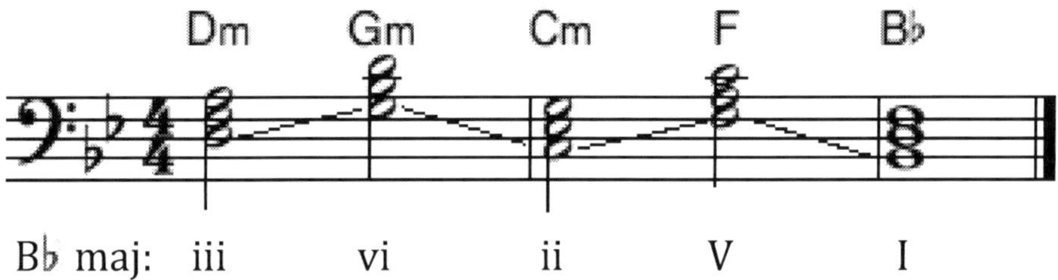

That progression will sound smoother with some inversions. The root progression is the same.

Example 13-E

root progression up a 4th, down a 5th.

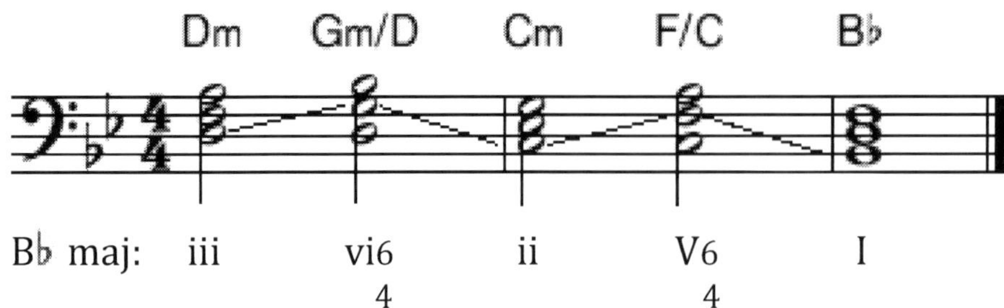

The root progression in Examples 13-D & E has been used, all or in part, in hundreds if not thousands of compositions of all genres, from J. S. Bach to Richard Rogers. See Example 13-F below.

Example 13-F

In the piano duet version played by the masses the 7ths are omitted. Also, the ii7 chord is often replaced by the IV6 chord, which is a lesson in chord substitutions. The ii7 chord and the IV6 consist of the same PNKs. It's the same chord in different inversions. However, the bass PNK is going to define the root. *I. e.,* even though a chord was analyzed as a ii6/5, with the subdominant PNK in the bass it would sound like a subdominant chord with an added 6th. The results are that you will *hear* a different root from the one indicated with the ii6/5 symbol. (This is how bass players can play with your mind.)

Example 13-G below is one of several instances of a root progression by 5ths in a piece by J. S. Bach.

Example 13-G

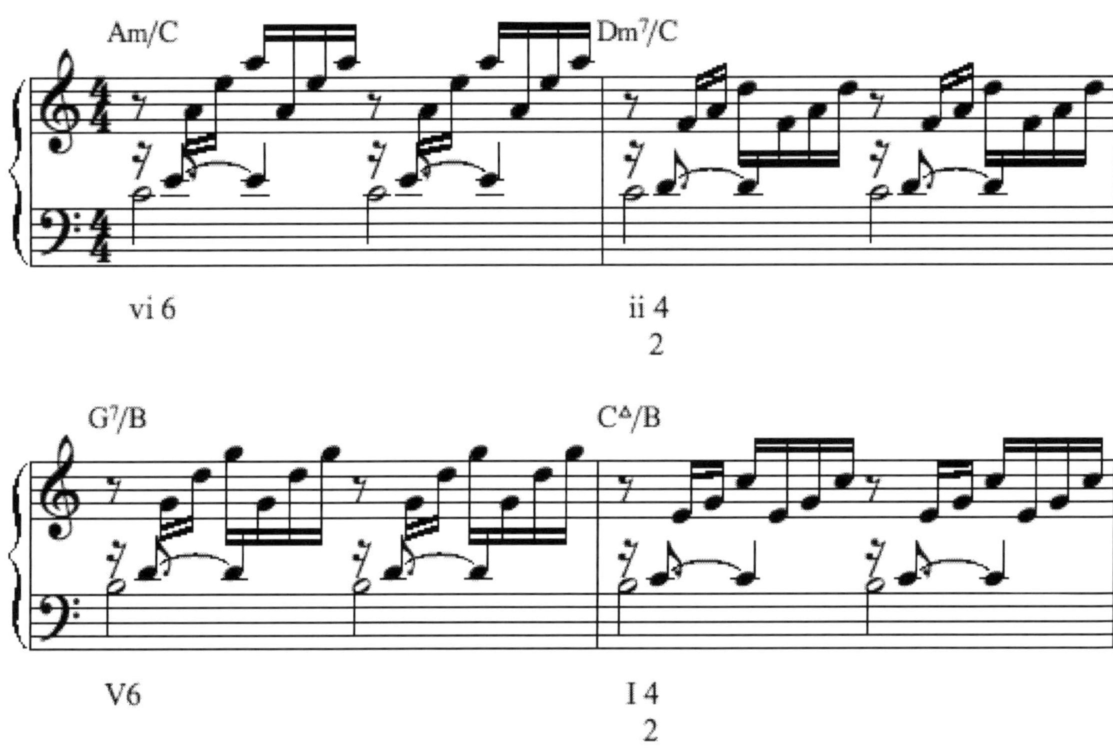

Let's see how the Circle of Keys from Chapter 6 relates to chord/root progressions. The circle is given below so you don't have to hunt for it.

Example 13-H

Circle of Major Keys

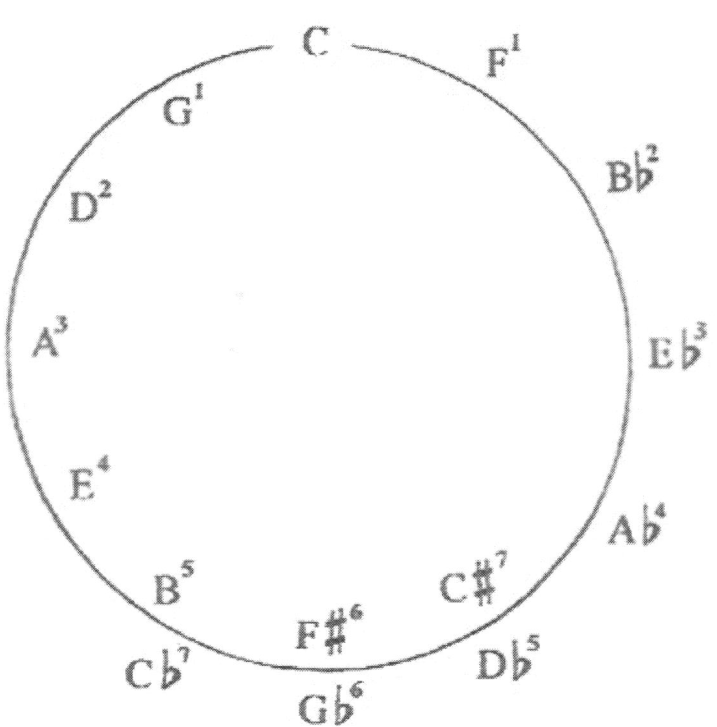

Circle Progressions

For the root progression vi, ii, V, I, (as in Hoagy Carmichael's "Heart And Soul" and Bach's "Prelude in C Major") pick any PNK on the circle as vi, and ii, V, I will follow it clockwise. If I'm playing in the key of G major, vi = Em, ii = Am, V = D, I = G. This would be called a circle progression because the roots are in the same order as clockwise around the circle. Any root progression in the same order as clockwise around the circle can be called a circle progression and may involve any number of chords. They would be in the same order as a Dominant to Tonic progression. A circle progression was referred to earlier as a progression by perfect 5ths. (Remember that the rest of the world runs their circle *counter-clockwise* from ours.)

3-Chord Pieces

There are hundreds of songs that can be harmonized with the I, IV, and V chords, *e.g.* "Me And Bobbie McGee", "Silent Night", "Amazing Grace". (If you add ii minor and/or II major you will find hundreds more.) These are often referred to as 3-chord pieces.

On the Circle, if you locate the key of a piece, which will be the root of the I chord, the root of the IV chord will be the next PNK clockwise and the root of the V chord will be the next PNK counterclockwise. *E.g.,* in the key of E major the I chord is E, IV is A and V is B. If you pick any PNK on the Circle as I, the IV and V will be on each side of it. To add the ii chord go one more step *counter*clockwise from V. If you want to sing or play one of these songs in the key of G major you can accompany it with the G, Am or A, D, and C chords.

Root progressions and chord progressions have a lot in common but they are not the same. See Example 13-I below.

Example 13-I

The <u>root</u> progression for III7, VI7, II7, V7, I is the same as for
♯3 ♯3 ♯3
iii, vi, ii, V, I, but the chords are different, *ergo*, the chord progressions

are different. BTW the altered chords in the above example could all be identified as borrowed dominants in the Roman numeral analysis.

Other Tonal Center Influences

There are several properties of music that can influence the center of tonality. We've discussed root progressions by perfect 5ths and the melodic tendency of the leading tone as two influences that indicate a tonal center. Perhaps one of the strongest influences today is that hundreds of years of music built around tonal centers makes us choose a tonal center by habit. We just want music to have a tonal center so we create one in our mind. Listen to the following example.

Example 13-J

There can be little question that the tonal center of this little piece is the last PNK, D, even though there is no harmony, no tritone, and no leading tone. Without close scrutiny it sounds like it's in D minor, but the subtonic C makes it modal. It could exist in 3 different key signatures (all♮, 1♭, 2♭) and 3 different modes (D-Aeolian, D-Dorian, D-Phrygian). It is created from a pentatonic scale – a scale with only 5 PNKs. Listen to the <u>same 5 PNKs</u> in another piece.

Example 13-K

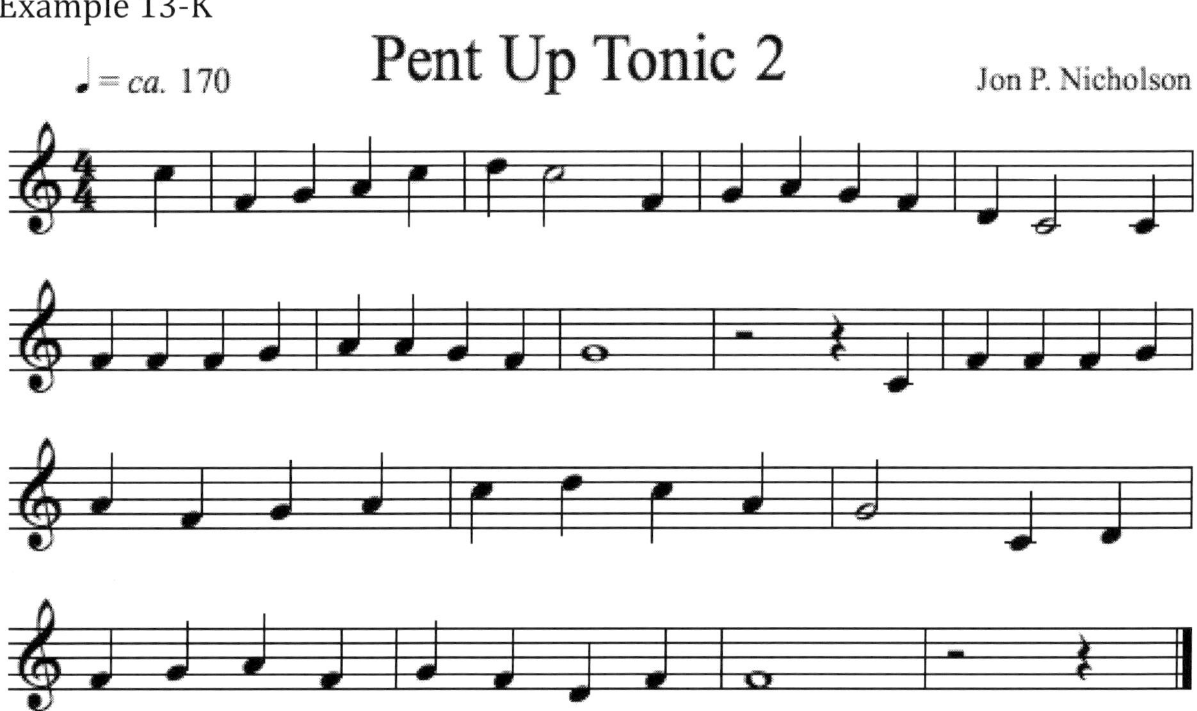

The tonal center here is obviously F. It consists entirely of the same 5 PNKs as Example 13-J but it sounds major. Since there is no subdominant or LT PNK we can't be sure of the key signature. As in the previous example there is no harmony, no tritone, and no leading tone. It could be in 3 different key signatures (all♮, 1♭, 2♭) and 3 different modes (F-Lydian, F-Major, F-Mixolydian). The experience of hearing tonal centered music for a lifetime may be the most important tonal center indicator of all.

Exercises

Play iii, vi, ii, V, I in every key around the circle *without looking at the circle*. Then add 7ths to the chords - iii7, vi7, ii7, V7, I△. The tonic 7th will be a major 7th chord. You may prefer a I6 instead if I△.

Play III7, VI7, II7, V7, I△ (or I6) in every key around the circle *without looking at the circle*. Same root progression as above but the first 2 chords are major/minor 7ths instead of minor/minor 7ths.

Since there are no IV chords in the above progressions you may want to add an "Amen" to the exercises with a IV, I (or IV6, I△) on the end. You may also substitute the viiø for V7 sometimes. I think it's a nice sound. If you add a dominant PNK to the viiø for the bass you will have a V9 chord.

Play by ear (no music) Heart and Soul in every major key around the circle. (Yes, both parts. That's why piano players have two hands.) The first four melody PNKs are tonic. The first melody PNK of bars 1, 3, and 5 are the root, 3th, and 5th of the tonic triad. The melody is all stepwise except for one skip down of a perfect 5th and a skip back up of a major 6th in bars 5 and 6.

Play by ear "Five Foot Two" in every major key around the circle. The first three melody PNKs are the 3rd and 5th of the tonic triad, the next three are the root and 3rd of the III7 chord, the next eight are the 5th and root of the VI7 chord, the next four are the 7th and 5th of the II7 chord. The first 5 measures are all chord tones. There are only two non-chord tones in the melody, the two submediants in bars 6 & 8.

If you apply these techniques to other melodies you have in your head you will be on your way to "Hum a few bars and I'll play it for you." "Happy Birthday", "Silent Night," "Jingle Bells" (with a V7 of V chord) and "Amazing Grace" should be cream puffs.

BTW you should always be prepared to play "Happy Birthday" by memory in F major. You are almost certain to be asked for it many times <u>without notice</u>. You will lose considerable credibility as a musician if you don't know it. (Speaking from experience here.) If you sing it loud enough you won't need to play the melody, just the chords. The first melody note is the dominant.

Computer exercise 13.1

Chapter 14
Consonance and Dissonance
Overtones and Partials
Harmonic Index
Parallel 5ths and Octaves

Consonance and Dissonance

Some combinations of tones are said to be consonant and others are said to be dissonant. This is a quality judgment and different people can have different opinions about what they consider to be consonant or dissonant.

Some intervals above C-4 in Example 14-A below are arranged from the most consonant to the most dissonant. (You don't have to agree with this particular order, even though millions of other musicians, teachers, authors, and composers do.) Listen to random pairs of these intervals in order to get a "feel" for what the terms consonant and dissonant mean. Also compare the same intervals sounding above other PNKs.

Example 14-A

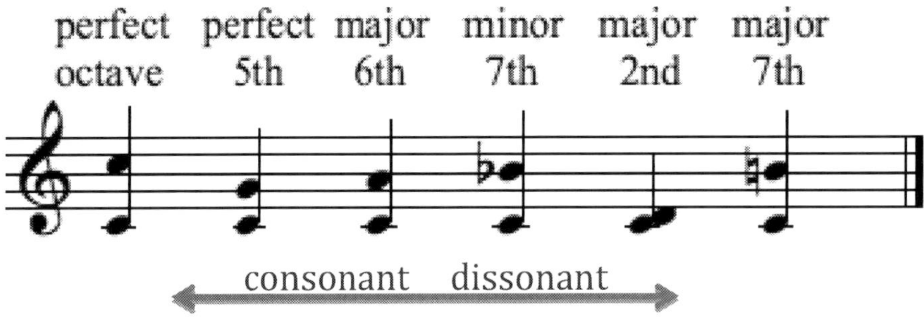

Historically there has been a progression of "acceptable" combinations of pitches sounding together. Originally there were just single line melodies but later the melodies were paralleled with octaves. Next came the addition of perfect fourths and fifths in parallel with the melody lines. This occurred about the 10th century. At that time nearly all of the music which was preserved in writing was unaccompanied vocal music for the church.

Later, two or more different melodies, sometimes with different lyrics, were sung simultaneously. This became known as counterpoint. The convergence of these melodies produced harmony, not yet important for its own sake but more of an unavoidable happenstance with several melodies going at the same time. Some of the intervals produced by counterpoint were considered pleasing and others were avoided.

Over time more intervals came into acceptance as pleasing and many which had been considered dissonant became okay as long as the dissonance was properly resolved. By the time of the Baroque period, with J. S. Bach and his contemporaries, dissonance was a very important part of their music and a long list of rules and regulations for their identification and proper use evolved.

Later in this chapter we will provide a method for determining relative consonance and dissonance and how it is reflected in acoustic phenomena. In Chapter 16 we will learn the rules and regulations for the use of dissonances in the Baroque style and learn to recognize them in the music of that period.

It is a mistake to define dissonance as a bad sound. Dissonance has a similar function in music as salt has to food. Most people don't enjoy eating salt by itself, but with the proper amount of salt food tastes better. So it is with dissonance in music. For the modern listener, music with no dissonance would become dull and boring very quickly.

The "correct" amount of dissonance, like the "correct" amount of salt, is a matter of personal preference. The more experience one has with contemporary dissonant music the more acceptable the dissonance will become. Over the centuries listeners have generally tolerated/preferred more and more dissonance in their music. As you study the stylistic changes in music history this becomes quite apparent. The way a composer employs dissonance in his/her music is an important factor in determining that composer's style and the historical period in which the music was created.

If dissonance is not to be defined as a bad sound, we need some other adjective to describe it. "Stress" and "tension" are terms often applied to dissonance. Today's musicians generally agree that the intervals of major and minor thirds and sixths, and the perfect intervals are consonant, while the 2nds, 7ths, augmented and diminished intervals are dissonant. (The perfect 4th is treated as a dissonance in some contexts.)

Another characteristic of some dissonances is the need to be resolved. I've heard that used as a definition of dissonance, but to me, some dissonances have an urge to be resolved while other dissonances do not. The minor 7th and the tritone, both tend to be restless and need to go someplace, while the minor 2nd and its inversion, the major 7th do not. My ear is quite satisfied to end a composition with a major 7th chord, but the tritone needs to be resolved. With all of these intervals, however, I think the terms "tension" and "stress" apply. Listen to the 2 sets of chords below. Both of them end with a dissonant chord. Decide whether one of them could end a piece while the other seems to indicate more to come.

Example 14-B

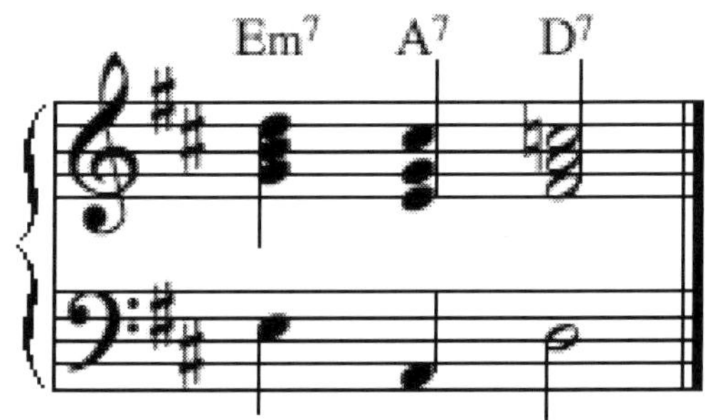

Overtones and Partials

In order to understand the theories of consonance and dissonance which follow, we need to understand what overtones and partials are and how they influence musical pitches. Every musical pitch, defined as a regular vibration rate between *ca.* 20 and 20,000 cycles per second (cps), is accompanied by overtones. The cps of these overtones can be calculated by multiplying the cps of the generated tone (aka the "fundamental") by every whole integer starting with 2.

The pitch A4 vibrates at 440cps. The first overtone above this fundamental would be 440cps X 2 = 880cps. This first overtone would be A5, one octave above the fundamental. The second overtone would be 3 X 440 = 1320cps which would be E6. Overtones # 3, 4, 5, etc. can be similarly calculated and the resultant pitches identified by their cps. The overtones diminish in volume the further they are from the fundamental to the extent that overtones above *ca.* number 15 are very difficult to hear.

Another name for an overtone is a partial, but the numbers are different. The first partial is the fundamental (the generated tone). Therefore the first overtone is the second partial and the first partial is not an overtone. The concept of overtones is useful to distinguish between overtones and the fundamental. However, our mathematical calculations are made with partial numbers.

The characteristic sound or timbre of a musical instrument is due to a great extent to the relative strengths of the partials. For example, a double reed instrument like the oboe produces stronger odd-numbered partials compared to a French horn which produces stronger even-numbered partials. These and other important elements of a sound generator (musical instrument) contribute to our ability to recognize what musical instrument is generating the sound.

Electronic sound generators can produce pure tones with no overtones, but any medium through which the tone passes, including air, will add overtones. Even the hearing mechanism in your head adds overtones. It would be safe to say that you have never heard a musical pitch without accompanying overtones.

When we hear a musical pitch we usually are not consciously listening to identify the overtones, but the overtones are there and they are an important part of what we are hearing. We have already mentioned the influence that overtones have on the timbre of an instrument. Piano tuners, guitar players, string players, etc. use overtones for accuracy in tuning.

There is strong evidence that overtones are significant in determining the relative consonance/dissonance of tonal combinations. One theory for the relative consonance of intervals was proposed by H. L. F Helmholtz.[1] According to Helmholtz, two musical pitches sounding together are more consonant the more their overtones coincide. Check out the perfect 5th in Example 14-C below.

---

[1] H. L. F. Helmholtz, On The Sensations Of Tone As A Physiological Basis For The Theory Of Music, trans. Alexander J. Ellis (4th edition; London: Longmans, Green & Co., 1912): Longmans, Green & Co., 1912.

Example 14-C

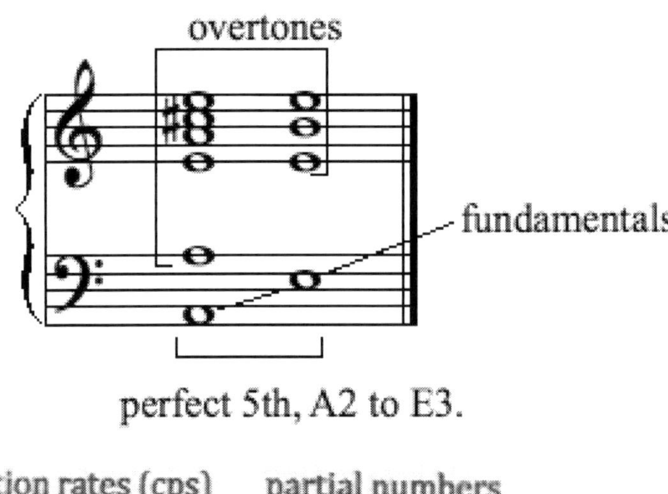

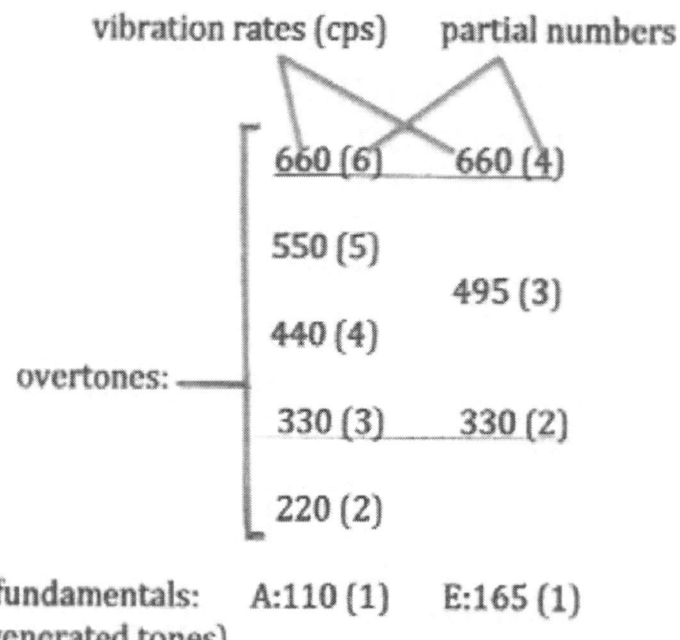

Example 14-C shows in notation and cps rates a projection of the overtones above the perfect 5th of A2 and E3 to the first coincidence of overtones at E4, and up to the second coincidence at E5. There is much more information here than we need to compare the coincidences of partials for the two tones of an interval. However, if you are unfamiliar with the overtone series Example 14-B will help you to understand what we're dealing with.

Overtones occur in a well-defined pattern above the fundamental. Notice that in the notes of the overtones above A3 in Example 14-B, the first six partials are all members of the A major triad. Every time you hear a musical pitch you are hearing a major triad, with that musical pitch as the root and the overtones supplying the 3rd and 5th. Could that be why the intervals of a perfect octave, perfect 5th, major third, and minor third were the first intervals to be historically accepted (in that order) as consonant?

In Example 14-B there are a total of five partials up to and including the first coincidence. Five more partials later there is another coincidence, and so it will be with an infinite projection of the partials of a perfect 5th: One coincidence for every five partials. We can express this rate of coincidences as 20%. All perfect 5ths have a ratio of 2:3 (110/165 = 2/3) for their fundamentals.[2] Therefore all perfect 5ths will have partials that coincide at the rate of 20%.

We don't need all the cps rates or the notation to figure this out. All we need are the fundamentals expressed as a ratio in lowest whole numbers so we can do some math calculations.

1. Reduce the cps of the fundamentals to the smallest whole number terms. 110:165 = 2:3

2. Add these terms together to get the total number of partials to the first coincidence. 2+3=5

3. Divide the number of coincidences (1) by the number of partials (5) to find the percentage of coincidences. 1/5=20%.

The formula for this operation would be:

$$1/(f1+f2)=n\%$$

where f1 and f2 are the vibration rates of the fundaments expressed as a ratio reduced to the smallest whole numbers, and n is the rate of coincidences of the partials.

---

[2] All calculations are based on just intonation. There is a wealth of publications available for students who want to know more about tuning systems and temperament. Just Intonation does not alter the order of relative consonance of tonal combinations when compared to equal temperament. In equal temperament the overtones have the same degree of "out-of-tune-ness" as the fundamentals.

A bit later when we consider the relative consonance of more than two tones, the calculations are a little more complex. Not much but a little.

Harmonic Index

From here on the "n" element in the above formula will be expressed as the "harmonic index" of the tonal combination, with a decimal figure to 6 places (with the remainder dropped). The harmonic index of the perfect 5th is .200000.

If we apply this formula to all the intervals available in a one-octave major scale, the order of relative consonance among those intervals would be as shown as in Example 14-D below.

Example 14-D

interval	ratio	harmonic index
p8	1:2	.333333
p5	2:3	.200000
p4	3:4	.142857
maj6	3:5	.125000
maj3	4:5	.111111
mi3	5:6	.090909
mi6	5:8	.076923
mi7	5:9	.071428
maj2	8:9	.058823
maj7	8:15	.043478
mi2	15:16	.032258
tritone	32:45	.012987

The order of intervals in Example 14-D above, as determined by the diminishing harmonic indices, duplicates the results of many tests whereby the test subjects were asked to rank intervals by *sound* according to relative consonance/dissonance. Probably the most remarkable of those tests in terms of its results exactly replicating the coincidence of overtones was one conducted by Akio Kameoka and Mamoru Kuriyagawa in Japan.[3] In their experiments these two scientists generated musical pitches electronically with various overtones suppressed. They could offer no reason why the orders of consonance/dissonance changed when certain overtones were not included in the generated pitches, but Helmholtz' theory of the coincidence of overtones matches their test results precisely.

The harmonic index as an expression of the coincidence of overtones can indicate the relative consonance/dissonance of tonal combinations of more than two pitches. As mentioned earlier, the math is a bit more involved. The formula as applied to the A4 major triad in root position follows:

1. Express the three fundamentals as a ratio in smallest whole numbers: The cps of the root, 3rd, and 5th of the major triad at A4 is 440, 550, and 660. This reduces to the ratio of 4:5:6. (This is the ratio for every major triad.)

2. Determine the first coincidence of all the overtones, which will be at the lowest common multiple (LCM) of these 3 numbers. (To find the LCM, multiply together the highest power of the prime factors of the ratio numbers.): $2^2X5X3=60$

3. Determine the total number of overtones to this first coincidence of all the overtones by dividing each fundamental into the LCM and adding together the results: 60/4=15, 60/5=12, 60/6=10. 15+12+10=37 overtones.

4. Find the total number of coincidences among all the overtones up to and including the first coincidence of all 3 sets of overtones:

   a - Determine the LCM of each fundamental to each of the other fundamentals: The LCM of 4 & 5 is 20. The LCM of 5 & 6 is 30. The LCM of 4 & 6 is 12.

   b – Divide each of these LCMs into the LCM from step 2 above: 60/20=3, 60/30=2, 60/12=5.

[3] Akio Kameoka and Mamoru Kuriyagawa, "Consonance of Complex Tones," The Journal of the Acoustical Society of America, 45;1460-1469, June, 1969.

c – Add the results: 3+2+5=10.
There are 10 coincidences of the overtones up to and including the first coincidence of all 3 sets of overtones of a major triad.

5. Determine the harmonic index by dividing the total number of coincidences in 4. above by the total number of overtones from 2. above: 10/37=.270270

The major triad has a harmonic index of .270270.

Example 14-E below is a list of the three triads in a major key in root position in the order of their relative consonance according to their harmonic indices.

Example 14-E

Harmonic Indices of Triads in a Major Key

type of triad	ratio of fundamentals	harmonic index
major	4:5:6	.270270
minor	10:12:15	.266666
diminished	25:30:36	.083333

We can measure heat, light, and loudness, but we can't measure cold, darkness, or silence. Cold, darkness, and silence don't exist. They are the *absence* of heat, light, and sound. Consonance and dissonance are not so easily defined and contrasted. Are they at opposite ends of the same spectrum or are they two different qualities that can coexist in the same tonal combination? If consonance is measured by the overtones that coincide and dissonance by the overtones that don't, then we can say yes, they can coexist. Consonance and dissonance are not mutually exclusive elements of a combination of tones.

Computer exercise 14.1

Exercises

Play all 12 intervals within an octave and write a list of them in the order of *your* feeling of their relative consonance/dissonance. Compare your list to Example 14-D above. Example 14-D is not the "correct" answer. Your opinion is "correct" for you and no one else. This can be an ongoing study. Your opinions can change over time.

According to Example 14-D the major 7th is less dissonant than the tritone. To me the major 7th is more harsh than the tritone but the tritone is less "stable," more needful of a resolution than the major 7th. That's my story and I'm sticking to it.

Parallel 5ths and Octaves

During the Baroque period there was an increasing trend toward the importance of harmony *vs.* melody in music. However, in four-part writing and in instrumental counterpoint, the melodic integrity of each of the voices was considered essential. The confluence of the voices created chords whose interrelationships produced their own sense of movement, direction, and form to a composition. But each individual voice was also crafted with independence and voice leading qualities that would allow them the musical significance to exist outside the harmonic environment.

When 2 voices move in parallel motion (by the same interval) the effect on the voices' independence from each other is determined greatly by the relative consonance of that interval. Listen to the 3 examples below.

Example 14-F

To the Baroque composers, in the first 2 phrases above, the intervals of an octave and a perfect 5th between the 2 voices made them sound too much like a single voice. The harmonic index of these 2 intervals indicates the highest coincidence of overtones compared to the other intervals. The major 3rds in the 3rd example, with much fewer overtone coincidences, sounds more like a duet, with each voice a melody independent but in consonant harmony with the other. In order to preserve the independence of voices in contrapuntal music the consecutive intervals of perfect octaves or perfect 5ths were avoided in Baroque compositions.

Example 14-G below shows examples of parallel 5ths and octaves that should be avoided when writing in the Baroque style.

Example 14-G

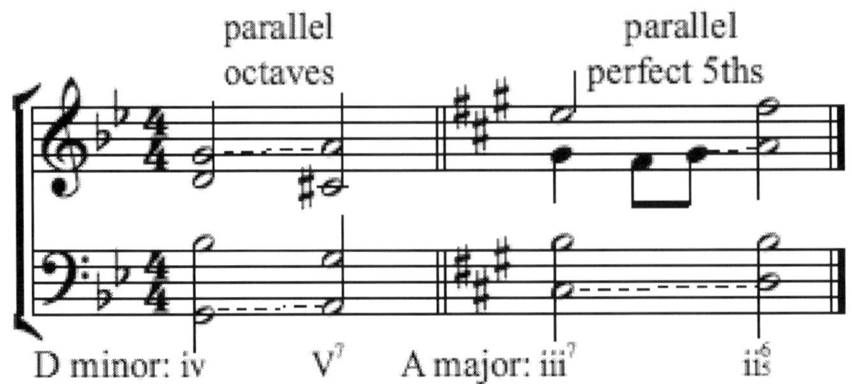

If one or more of the parallel 5ths is *not a perfect 5th*, the voice independence is maintained. The harmonic index of the diminished 5th is quite small.

Example 14-H

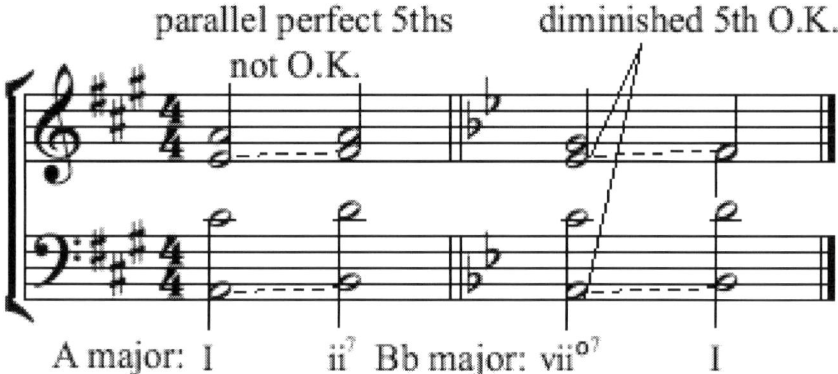

Check the Bach chorales and a hymn book for parallel perfect 5ths and octaves. Or just take my word for it that they are rare and save yourself a lot of frustration. If you are composing in the Baroque style you must learn to recognize parallel 5ths and octaves and learn how to use chord inversions to avoid them.

Computer exercise 14.2

Chapter 15 - Rhythm II

More Metric Signs
Hierarchy of Beat Divisions
4 Kinds of Meters
Hearing Meters
Syncopation

More Metric Signs

Before we get into the heavy stuff there are two time signatures you need to know about.

Example 15-A

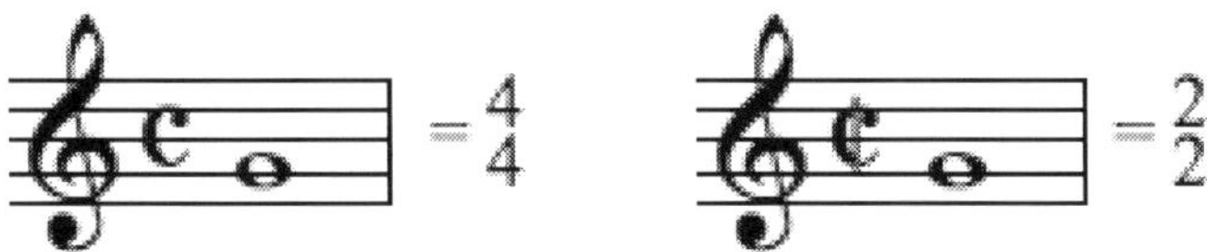

Both these symbols originated in the music from the early church hundreds of years ago. The number 3 (as in the Trinity) and a circle both represented perfection for the church. *Ergo*, a triple rhythm like 3/4 is perfect music, *ergo* a circle for a time signature stood for triple rhythm. The broken circle (in the staff on the left in Example 15-A) was for imperfect duple rhythm. Today it means the same as 4/4 meter.

The slash through the broken circle (in the staff on the right) is often called "cut time." It's like 4/4 that goes too fast for the conductor, so instead of waving the baton 4 times per measure he/she only beats the strong beats – 2 to a bar – the same as 2/2 meter.

You can't tell by listening to music whether it is 4/4 or 2/2 meter. They are both duple meters and both feel the same. You <u>can</u> tell whether a meter is triple or duple. We will learn about other types of meter a little later. The distinctions among the different types of meters is in the *top* number. The bottom number is always a power of 2.

Hierarchy of Beat Divisions

The first beat in a bar is the strongest beat. If the top number of the meter is 4 or larger there will be more than one accented beat, but none of them as strong as the first.

When the beat is divided with PNKs smaller than 1 beat there is a hierarchy of strength relationships among the beat divisions. The beginning of the beat is stronger than any PNK following in that beat.

Example 15-B

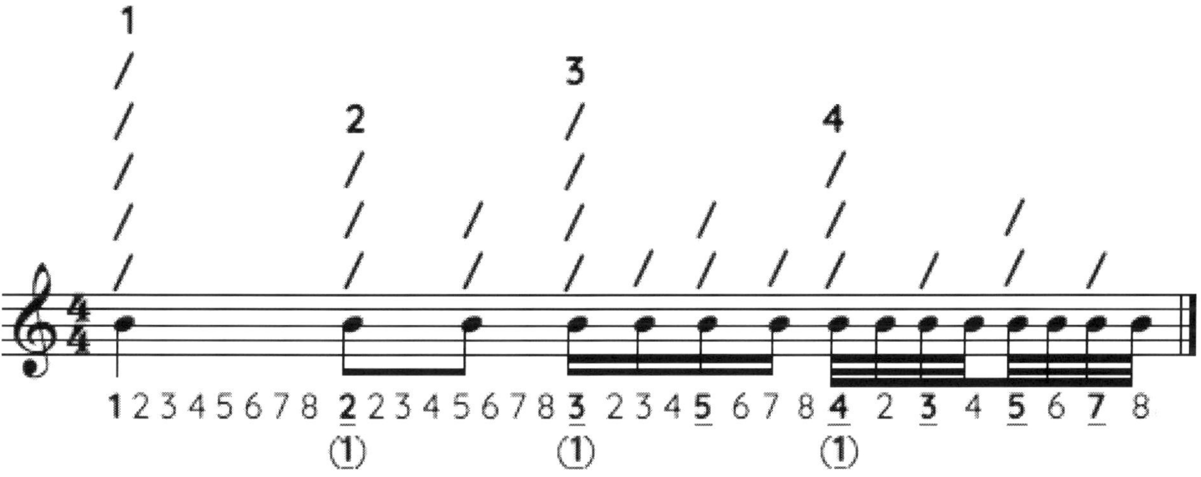

The / is <u>not an official music sign for an accent</u>. They are used here to show the relative strengths of beat divisions. The more /s you see stacked over a note the stronger is that beat or beat division.

As stated in Chapter 1, when counting beats you need to count the smallest beat division throughout the composition in order to assure that the longer PNKs are held long enough.

Each time a smaller note value is introduced in a composition it creates a new level of strong *vs.* weak. Notice that the / are only over the odd numbers. The (1) is a reminder that that is the 1st 8th of the beat and is therefore to be treated as an odd number.

Here's how the hierarchy works:

The beginning of beat 1 is the strongest beat in the bar. Any accented beats which follow in the bar will be less strong than beat 1.

The beginning of each beat is stronger than any beat divisions which follow in that beat.

An odd numbered beat or beat division is always stronger than an even numbered beat or beat division.

How is this applied to performing a composition? Must all the accented PNKs be played louder than the unaccented PNKs? No. The music could sound corny of you do. Notice that the terms "loud" and "soft" have not been used in the above explanation. The relative strengths of the beat divisions are an integral part of music even without dynamic emphasis. The "oom pah pah" of a polka band makes it obvious to the dancers that the "oom," played by the tuba is beat 1 and the "pah pah"s, played by the clarinet are beats 2 and 3, even without dynamic stress on the "oom." Strong *vs.* weak beats are felt even in unaccompanied melodies.

Understanding relative strengths of beats and beat divisions is valuable for the composer who wants to create points of emphasis in a composition. Also, understanding syncopation (later in this chapter) and dealing with dissonance and non chord tones (in a later chapter) will require a knowledge of metric stress.

The drummer and I did a bad thing one night at the club. It was "Olde Tyme Dance" night and we were bored out of our minds by all the 3/4 waltz beats we were playing. On a prearranged signal we switched our accompaniment pattern from 4 bars of 3/4 (= 12 beats) to 3 bars of 4/4 (= 12 beats) and then back to 3/4 on the next bar. The chords and melody were unchanged and the transitions were quite smooth. See example 15-C below.

Example 15-C

excerpt from

The Lovliest Night of the Year

Our poor front line trumpet player got totally lost, wondering how he could wreck such a simple piece. The dancers couldn't find their feet but I don't think anyone fell down. We didn't do that again.

Rhythm is such an essential part of living that we don't need obvious dynamic accents in music to relate to it. Equal divisions of a beat are as natural as breathing, chewing, walking, and heartbeats. You can probably think of at least one more.

Beats grouped in threes are understandably quite unnatural for us. I don't remember any exceptions to the students I've had who added a 4th beat to every measure of their first 3/4 piece. They count out loud, "one, two, three, (intake of breath), one, two, three, (intake of breath)" etc.

Besides even divisions of beats, the instinct for even numbers in music is further expressed by putting 4 bars in a phrase, with the first of every pair of bars being the accented bar. With a waltz the result is like an even number of beats with each beat divided into triplets. (One triplet = one bar of 3/4.) Check out some waltz music and see how the phrases consist of 4 bars. See if you can find one with an odd number of bars in a phrase. (Pickup bars don't count. The final bar of a phrase often includes the pickup into the next.) Many hundreds of popular songs from the 20th Century had 32 bars (not counting the introduction.) A notable exception was the 12-bar blues form - still divisible by 4 but not a power of 2.

Exercise

Add bar lines and meters to the following two examples. There is more than one meter that will work for each, but one is duple and the other is triple. You probably can work it out just by looking at the note values, but play it so you can *hear* the meter. In the second example the patterns in the F-clef are pretty revealing.

Any time you listen to music, think about whether it is in duple or triple meter.

The Preludes and Fugues and Two- and Three-Part Inventions of Bach are a good source of examples for beat divisions. Any music with small beat divisions will serve as well. Follow any voice and determine the relative strength of each note by its position in the measure and in the beat. See Example 15-D below.

Example 15-D

The beats and partial beats in order of relative strengths are:

The beginning of beat 1
The beginning of beat 3
The beginning of beats 2 and 4
The beginning of the 2nd half of every beat
The beginning of the 2nd and 4th fourths of every beat

In the example above the PNKs in the F clef will have the same relative strengths as the PNKs directly above them in the G clef.

The weakest PNK in the example is the 4th eighth of beat 3 with no / over it. If there was a PNK of lesser value (a 16th of a beat instead of an 8th of a beat} then this PNK would be an odd-numbered beat division. It would be the 7th 16th of beat 3 and would have a PNK weaker than it. In Chapter 16 you will learn that this non-chord tone is a passing tone because it is unaccented. If it had been rhythmically stronger than the following chord tone it would be labeled an appoggiatura.

Find some music with small beat divisions and analyze it as in Examples 15-B & E. It may help you to write out the counts as in Example 15-B.

4 Kinds of Meters

There are 4 kinds of meters:

1. Duple meter is one with the top number as a *power* of 2.

Example 15-E: Duple Meters

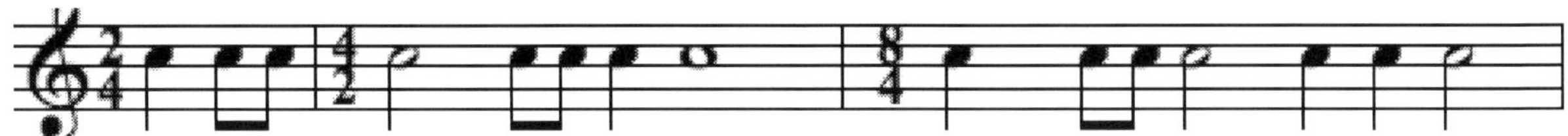

2. Triple meter is one with the top number 3.

Example 15-F: Triple Meters

3. Compound meter is one with the top number a *multiple* of 3.

Example 15-G: Compound Meter

4. Complex meter is one wherein the top number is a prime factor *bigger* than 3, or more than 1 top number.

Example 15-H: Complex Meters

Hearing Meters

How can you recognize a meter by listening? Do you listen for *louder* accented beats? It is not necessary for a performer to add dynamic accents in order for the listeners to hear meters. The rhythmic *patterns* in the music define the meters. The accompaniment patterns in piano, band, orchestra, or accompanied solos make the meters recognizable. As stated previously, even the meter of an unaccompanied melody is usually clear.

Notice how, in bar 3 of Example 15-H above, the eighth notes are beamed together to indicate the rhythmic pattern of the meter to the performer. Look for patterns of beams in your repertoire. You may wonder, as I do, why many publishers *don't* beam in metric patterns for vocal music. (Many hymns are published without metric beam patterns.) Look for it on referendum ballots so we can make it illegal.

There is no way to tell the *bottom* number of a meter by listening. The bottom number is always a power of 2. 4/2, 4/4, and 4/8 all sound the same, as do 3/2, 3/4 and 3/8 if the metronome is ticking once per beat for each meter.

Remember that tempo is <u>not</u> determined by the meter. 3/2 with each beat played at 100bpm will sound the same as a duple meter with beats divided into triplets if each triplet PNK is played at 100bpm. A slow 4/4 with triplets can sound the same as a fast 3/4 or 6/8 . I was surprised to discover that the original manuscript of "Silent Night" was written in 6/8 because 6/8 is usually reserved for faster tempos, but tempo does not determine meter. (Did I already say that?) Modern publications of "Silent Night" are more often notated in 3/4. The song "Memory," from the Broadway show "Cats," and "The Impossible Dream," from "Don Quixote," are two more examples of slow compound meters.

There are limited details of the <u>top</u> number that *can* be identified by listening. You can *categorize* the top number as being **triple, duple, compound,** or **complex**. You should practice identifying them in music you hear until it becomes easy for you. Of the 4 categories above in Examples 15-E, F, G, and H, you cannot distinguish by listening between triple (15-F) and compound meters (15-G) nor with duple meters with beats divided into triplets. Triple, compound, and meters with beats divided into triplets can all sound the same, but they can be distinguished from duple and complex meters.

Computer exercise 15.1

Exercise

Renotate each of the following examples twice, with 2 different sets of notes and 2 different meters that will <u>sound</u> the same as the given example. The first one is done for you. When writing notes with flags or beams be sure they are grouped to reflect the metric rhythm. You may add bar lines if needed as in the first example.

The <u>meter</u> in the third exercise above could indicate 3-2/8 or 2-3/8. However the <u>beams</u> show the composer's intention is 3-2/8.

Syncopation

Syncopation occurs in music when an unaccented beat or beat division is stressed more than an accented beat or beat division. One way to effect syncopation is to put more dynamic stress on the unaccented beat or beat division – play or sing it louder.

The symbol for a dynamic accent is >. In Example 15-I below, the metrically weak 2nd beat of the first bar and the metrically weaker 2nd half of the 2nd beat in the second bar are to be played louder than the metrically strong beats. The result is syncopation.

Example 15-I

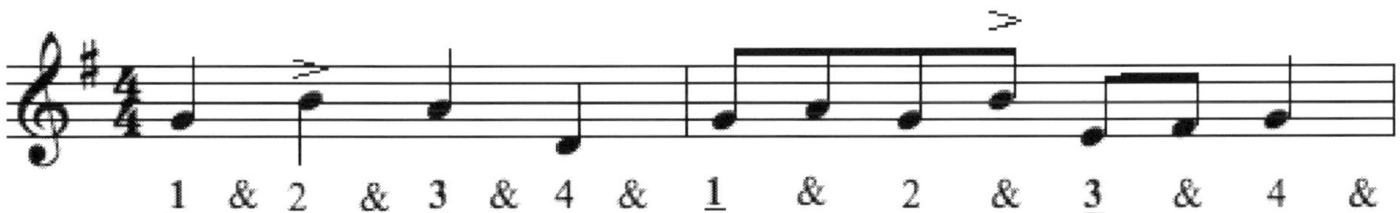

Tap and count out loud Example 15-I. Tap loudest on the accented notes and feel the syncopation.

A stronger feeling of syncopation is created when a metrically strong beat or strong beat division is not articulated – when no PNK is played or sung at the beginning of a strong beat or strong beat division.

Example 15-J

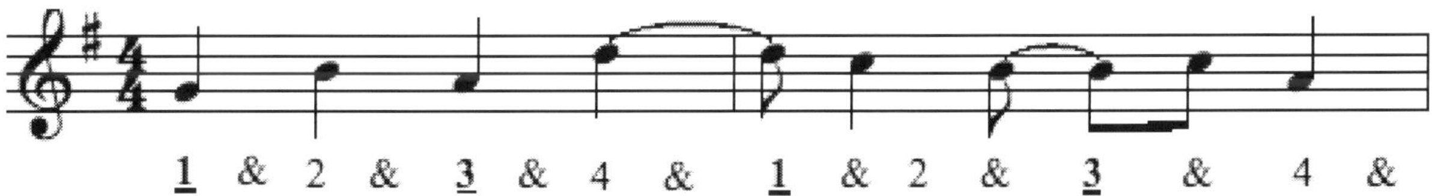

"Notable by it's absence." is appropriate here. If you're not familiar with that expression, it's like the loudmouth neighbor that shows up at all the neighborhood gatherings. After a while you get accustomed to hearing her rantings and ravings so that they are hardly noticed. Then one Saturday she doesn't show up. She is noticeably missed, like the strong beats and beat divisions in Example 15-J which are felt more strongly because they aren't articulated.

Tap and count Example 15-K below and feel the syncopation. You will probably find yourself accenting the syncopated notes - adding a dynamic accent - to emphasize the syncopation.

Example 15-K

excerpt from

If You Can Do Anything Else

Billy Livsey &
Don Schlitz

It is not difficult finding syncopation in published music. It is more difficult finding popular music that is not syncopated

Beethoven wrote one terrifically strong bit of syncopation in his Ninth symphony in the last movement when the chorus is singing “Alle Menschen.” It has been translated and included in many hymnals as “Ode To Joy.” It also appears in many beginning music method books for different instruments. (Unfortunately the rhythm is often rewritten to be unsyncopated.) See the excerpt below in Example 15-L.

Example 15-L

excerpt from

Alle Menschen

aka "Ode To Joy"

Ludwig van Beethovan

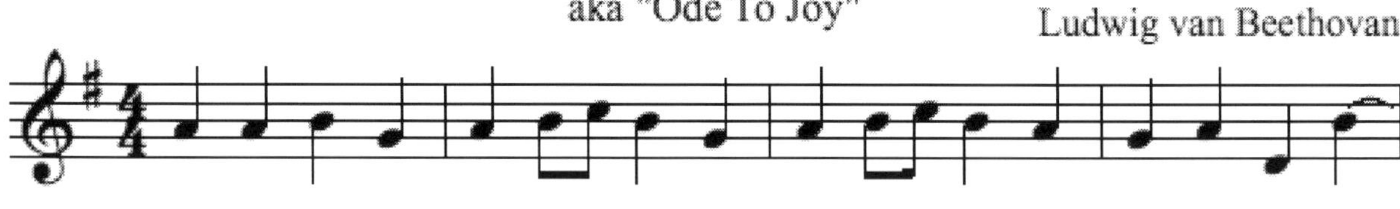

One reason the syncopation in bar 4 to 5 is so powerful is because the rest of the song has such uncomplicated rhythm. Then all of a sudden we are hit over the head with a syncopated mallet on the weakest metric beat - beat 4 - of a weak bar - bar 4 - followed by an unarticulated beat 1 on one of the strongest bars – bar 1 of a 4-bar phrase. Wow! The music may have lifted your spirit to the clouds before but at this point you are ready to leap to your feet and yell "Yay! Beethoven!"

Computer exercise 15.2

Exercise

An abundant source of examples of syncopation can be found in popular and especially rock music. Find some and count and tap the rhythms. Use your metronome. Practice until it's easy and the rhythm takes on a musical life of its own. Even with songs you know, counting and tapping while concentrating only on the rhythm can be a challenge. As a working musician you will be expected to *sight read* the syncopation with all the right PNKs and with the appropriate expression on your face. (A scowl of intense concentration is not an appropriate expression.)

Chapter 16

Non-Chord Tones (NCT)
NCTs and Rhythm
Passing Tone
Neighbor Tone
Appoggiatura
Suspension
Échapée
Cambiata
Changing Tone
Anticipation
Pedal Point

Non-Chord Tones (NCT)

Centuries before the Baroque period, music consisted primarily of single line melodies. By the time of J. S. Bach, harmonies to accompany the melodies became the norm and is still the norm today. Even with an unaccompanied melody, a harmony is usually implied.

The words "harmony" and "accompaniment" refer to PNKs, often sounding together as a chord, that go with a melody. As the terms suggest, these PNKs must "go with" the melody - be related to it. There are several ways a melody PNK can be related to a harmony. The most obvious would be if a melody PNK was included in the accompaniment chord. But even a melody PNK not included in the accompaniment chord must be related in some way. Such a PNK is called a non-chord tone (NCT).

NCTs will be dissonant with at least one PNK of the harmony. As discussed in the chapter on dissonance, the history of musical styles shows an increasing tolerance/desire for more and more dissonance. The frequency of NCTs in melodies reflects that trend. The question for the composer is, "How much dissonance is too much?" You can compare the tolerance/desire for dissonance to a rubber band. The further you stretch it the more tension you feel. Until it breaks. Then you feel no tension at all. At that point the NCT has lost its relationship to the harmony. The harmony/accompaniment is no longer harmonizing/accompanying the melody.

The breaking point is different for each listener. The more experience one has with dissonance the more dissonance will be tolerated/desired. If you are a composer, the more dissonance you use the more of the rest of the world of listeners will be left behind. A music critic at the first performance of one of Beethoven's symphonies reported the effect as ". . . a cacophony of sound." Beethoven had left him behind.

This chapter is about recognizing and identifying the relationships of melodic NCTs to the accompanying harmony. Play the melody in Example 16-A until you know it.

Example 16-A

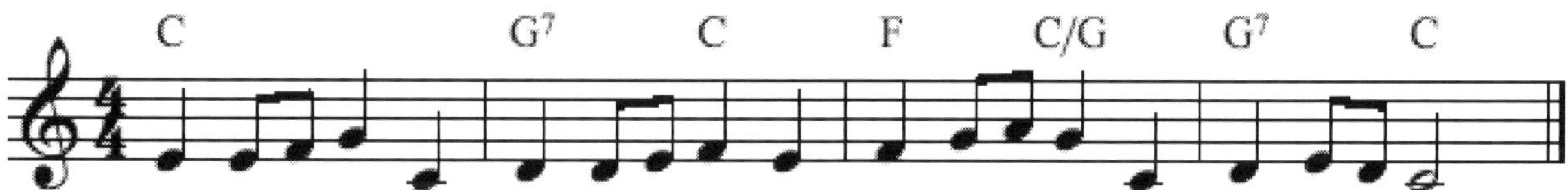

Now add the chords in the L. H. while you play the melody. Play a chord on the strong beats 1 and 3 of each bar.

Why do those chords work with the melody? If you analyze the music you will find that most of the melody notes are included in the chords, especially those on the strong beats struck at the same time as the chord. But not all of them.

Play the melody note and the chord on beat 3 of bar 2 – a C chord with the F melody note. The F is not part of the C chord and is dissonant with the E and the G. Played in isolation from the rest of the piece, the F sounds out of place, unrelated to the chord. It is a NCT. When the piece is moving and the F dissonance resolves into the E, it works fine. This is how dissonance gives motion and a sense of direction to a piece. When you hear the F melody note you expect it to resolve to a PNK in the next chord, which it does.

That same dissonant combination of the melody note F against the C chord occurs in the first bar on the second half of beat 2. It doesn't have nearly the punch that it has in the second bar because the dissonance occurs on the rhythmically weak part of a weak beat. The effect of dissonance is partly dependent on rhythm.

There are names assigned to the different ways that dissonant NCTs are related to chords. *E. g.* the dissonant F in bar 1 is called a passing tone. The dissonant F in bar 2 is called an appoggiatura, which is Italian for "leaning." Do those terms seem appropriate to you in these two cases?

Example 16-B below is a four-part piece in the key of G major. It could be a hymn, with Soprano and Alto voices in the G clef, and Tenor and Bass voices in the F clef. This configuration is called four-part writing and it is customary to refer to the four parts with these designations. In this setting a PNK in one of the voices, which is not a member of the chord formed by the other voices, is a NCT.

In Example 16-B, the fake symbols and Roman numerals are given for the first measure. Notice that in the first bar the 2nd half of beat 2 could be analyzed as F♯° with the G as a NCT. However the Soprano and Alto notes can both be treated as NCTs with the C chord. There are several NCTs in the example. Most are on the second half of the beat but a few occur on the beat.

Write the fake symbols and Roman numerals for the remainder of Example 16-B for the *first half of each beat*. Then place parentheses around, or circle, all the NCTs. The NCTs may make some of the chord identification confusing and some may be interpreted more than one way. It will become clearer later as you develop more understanding of how NCT's work. Check your analysis with Example 16-C which follows it.

Example 16-B

Example 16-C

Some of the NCTs have ? nearby. See if you can understand why these notes could have a double meaning. Stop reading and do that now.

In bar 2, in the soprano, the second half of beat 2, the note C does not belong to the V triad. However it could be considered as a chord change to vii°6.

In bar 5, in the alto, second half of beat 2, the note A does not belong to the IV chord. However all the sounding pitches at that point create a vi chord in 2nd inversion.

In bar 6, second half of beat 2, in the alto, the note D could be considered the 7th of the vi7 chord.

Different listeners may hear these examples in different ways. If you were in one of my theory classes and this was on a test, I would call any of these options a correct answer to the question. If you gave both options you would get extra credit. If you are in someone else's theory class you need to find out what that teacher wants.

If your goal is to become a working musician then probably all you need to know about NCTs is how to recognize them and their relationship to the tonal environment. If you want to get a degree in music from college or teach music theory or write a book like this one you will need know the names of the different NCTs, like passing tones and appoggiaturas.

NCTs and Rhythm

Unfortunately there are different variations of some of the names and descriptions of NCTs. Many of the discrepancies concern rhythm. Most of the NCTs occur on weak beats or weak parts of the beat. In the preceding Chapter 15 you learned how to distinguish between strong and weak beats and strong and weak divisions of the beat.

The beat divisions and subdivisions of the beats and the resultant hierarchy of rhythmic accents are very important in our perception of NCTs. A PNK that is articulated on an *un*even beat division is going to sound rhythmically accented, even though it is the beginning of the "weak" 2nd half of the "weak" 4th beat. If there are other PNKs sounding on the weaker 2nd and/or 4th fourths of that beat it will be rhythmically accented in relation to the rhythmically weaker PNKs. Consequently, if such a PNK is a NCT, then it is an accented NCT.

In your musical education so far and that which is yet to come you will probably encounter different specifications and a variety of names for the several different ways NCTs are prepared and resolved. Do not take any of them, including this one, as the final authority. The most useful of the lot will be those that sound right to you, and there is a good possibility that will change as you grow musically. That's OK too.

In the soprano, alto, tenor and bass format a NCT can occur in any of the four voices and more than one NCT may occur at the same time.

There are 3 parts to the identification of the various types of NCT dissonances: 1. The preparation - the PNK immediately preceding the NCT in the same voice. 2. The NCT itself. 3. Its resolution - the PNK immediately following the NCT in the same voice.

Some common names of eight types of NCTs are listed below.

Example 16-D

type of NCT dissonance	abbreviation
passing tone	pt
neighbor tone	nt
appoggiatura	app
suspension	sus
échappée	ech
cambiata	cam
changing tone	ct
anticipation	ant
pedal point	pp

Passing Tone (pt)

The passing tone is rhythmically unaccented, moves *by step* from a chord tone (the preparation) and continues *by step* to a chord tone *in the same direction* (the resolution). Moving by step means moving by the interval of a 2nd – either a half step or a whole step.

Example 16-E

There are two passing tones in Example 16-E, one ascending and one descending. They move by step from the E and G on beat one to become dissonant NCTs with the bass on the weak beat 2, then they each resolve by step to the chord tones on the strong beat 3.

There can be more than one passing tone in succession.

Example 16-F

Neighbor Tone (nt)

Aka auxiliary tone, embellishment. The neighbor tone is rhythmically weak. It is preceded by a chord tone, moves by step in either direction, then returns to the same chord tone. The chord of preparation may be different from the chord of resolution.

Example 16-G

Appoggiatura (app)

The appoggiatura occurs on a strong beat or strong part of the beat and moves stepwise to a rhythmically weaker resolution. Some theorists claim that the appoggiatura must be approached by leap rather than by step. I feel that the name "appoggiatura," which is Italian for "leaning," is appropriate to describe an appoggiatura regardless of its approach.

Example 16-H

appoggiatura (app)

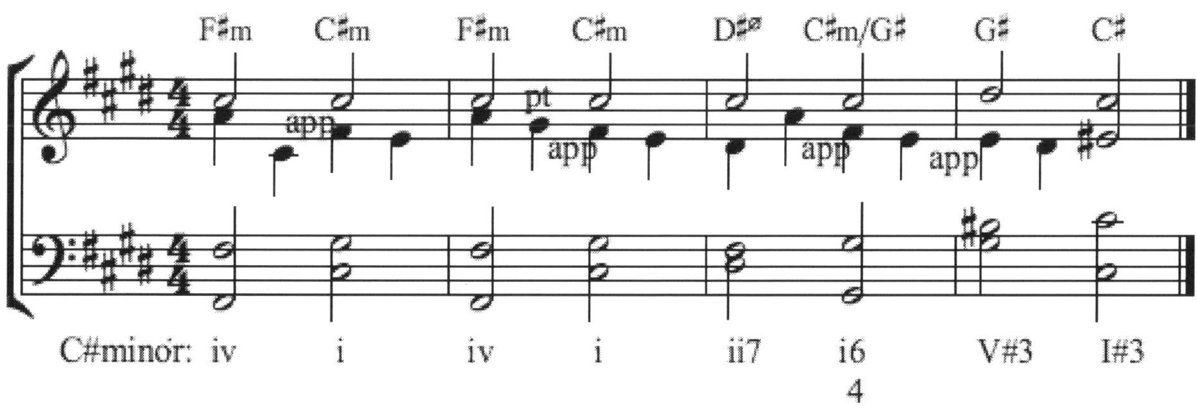

Different theory texts will have different opinions concerning appoggiaturas. One states that passing tones and neighbor tones can occur as accented NCTs, and, that an appoggiatura must be approached by leap and resolved by step in the opposite direction. Others state that an appoggiatura and a suspension (coming up next) are the only 2 NCTs that occur on an accented beat or accented part of a beat. According to the first definition, in Example 16-H above, bar 2, beat 3, the F♯ in the alto would be an accented passing tone. I think the term "appoggiatura" which means "leaning tone" in Italian is a more accurate description of the feeling of that F♯ than passing tone. You need to decide: 1. what the music says to you and 2. what your current teacher wants. Just know that in this text we are going with the second definition above – The only 2 accented NCTs are the appoggiatura and the suspension, and a so-called accented PT is really an appoggiatura.

A very expressive appoggiatura can be found in "Stormy Weather" in Example 16-I below. It occurs several times in the song.

Example 16-I

Suspension (sus)

The suspension, as its name implies, is a chord tone that is suspended over from one chord to become a dissonance with the following chord. It then resolves by step to become a chord tone with the new chord. The beat or partial beat at which it becomes a suspended NCT is rhythmically stronger than its resolution. Except for its preparation as a suspended chord tone it is like an appoggiatura, a rhythmically strong dissonance stepping to a rhythmically weaker resolution. See Example 16-J below.

Example 16-J

suspension (sus)

A NCT with the characteristics of a suspension – prepared as a chord tone, becomes dissonant with the following chord, resolves downward by step – but which is *articulated* with the new chord whereby it becomes dissonant, is labeled an appoggiatura by some theorists and a suspension by others. Both points of view are valid. In the following excerpt from Bach, the first PNK in bar 1 on beat 1 is repeated on beat 3. At the beginning of bar 2 it is articulated as a NCT with the C chord. It is finally resolved on beat 1 of bar 3. It could be labeled an appoggiatura or a suspension.

Bach gives us the opportunity with this "hold it and milk it" accented NCT to put some real feeling into the music. By adding just a bit of agogic and dynamic stress to Bach's masterful creation we can bring the audience with us on a great musical adventure. There are many similar opportunities with various dissonances in this little piece.

Example 16-K

excerpt from

Prelude In C Major

from The Well-Tempered Clavier

Johann Sebastien Bach

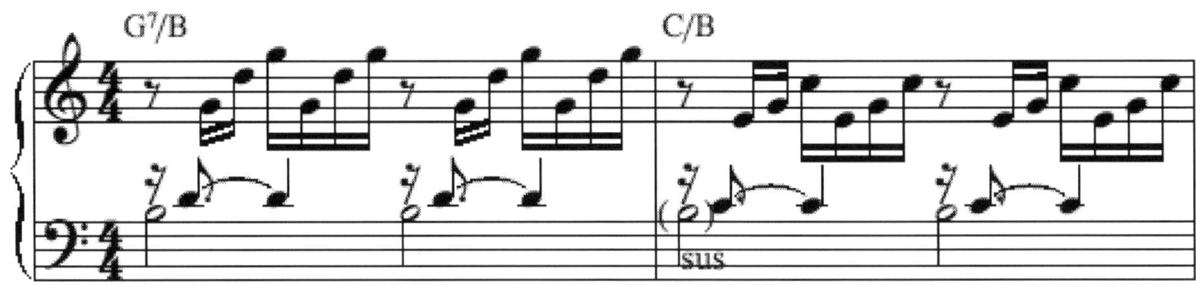

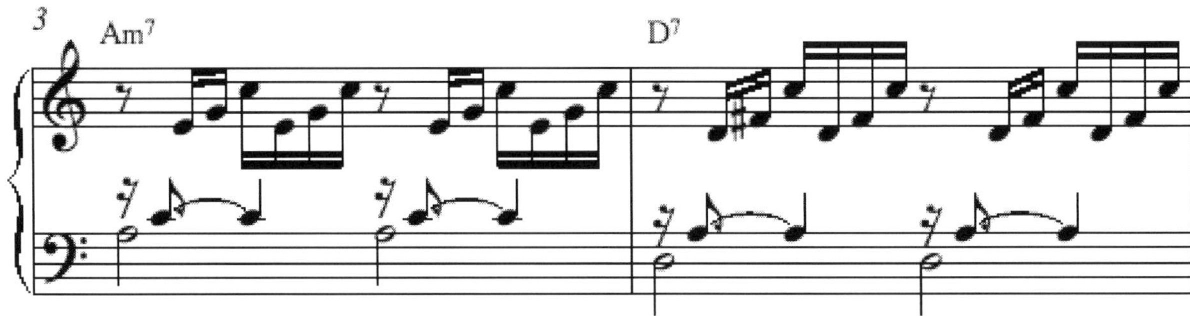

FYI, some authors say the suspension can only resolve downward and give a different name – "retardation" – for a suspension that resolves upward, as in Example 16-J, bar 2, beat 3 in the tenor. I don't see the point but it's something you may need to know.

Échapée (ech)

Échapée is French for "escape." The preparation is a rhythmically strong chord tone, the NCT is a step down or up in the "wrong" direction, the resolution is a skip of a 3rd in the opposite "correct" direction to a chord tone.

Example 16-L

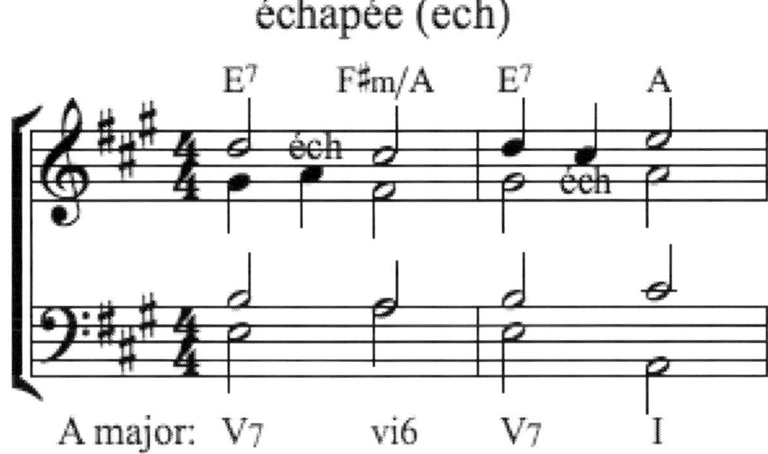

Cambiata (cam)

The cambiata is prepared as a rhythmically strong chord tone. It then leaps a step "too far" in the direction of its resolution. It resolves by step in the opposite direction to a chord tone.

Example 16-M

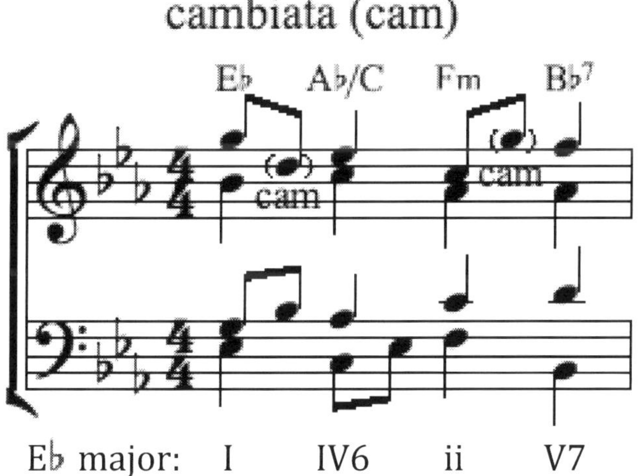

A comparison of the échapée with the cambiata can be helpful in remembering how they work. The échapée is approached by moving in the "wrong" direction from its resolution, after which it must skip in the opposite direction to resolve. The cambiata is approached by leaping "too far" toward its resolution, after which it must step back to resolve. Note that the approach of the échapée is always an interval of a 2nd and the resolution a 3rd. The cambiata can be approached by an interval of a 3rd or wider but resolves by a 2nd.

Changing Tone (ct)

A changing tone is prepared as a chord tone, moves up or down a 2nd to a NCT, moves in the opposite direction by a 3rd to another NCT, then resolves by a 2nd, returning to the chord tone which was the PNK of preparation. The description is more complicated than the notation. See Example 16-N below. Note that the chord of resolution may be the same as or different from the chord of preparation.

Example 16-N

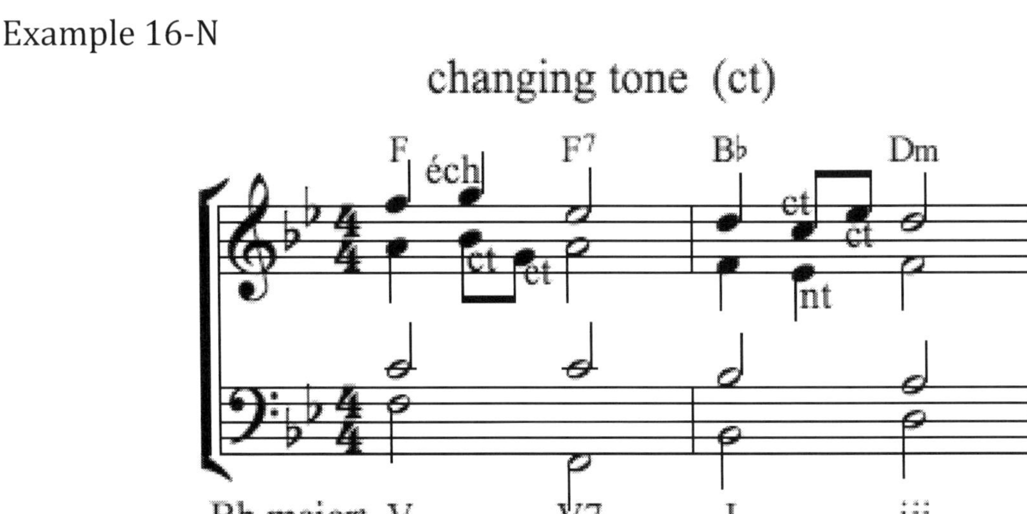

Anticipation (ant)

The anticipation is pretty well described by it's name. It can be approached by step or skip in either direction from a chord tone, and is usually shorter in duration than it's resolution, which is the same PNK.

Example 16-O

Pedal Point (pp)

The pedal point gets its name from the organ, when a bass pedal is sustained through several chord changes, some of which do not include the pedal PNK. The preparation is the initial chord which includes the pedal PNK. The resolution is the final chord which also includes the pedal PNK. The chord of resolution may be the same as the chord of preparation or it may be a different chord.

Example 16-P

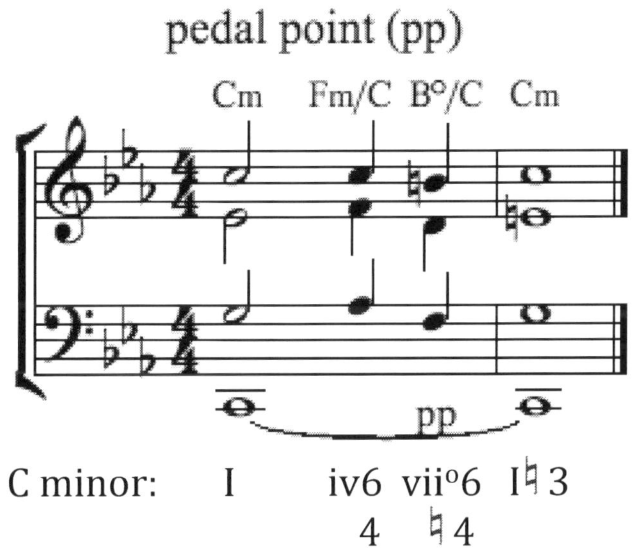

In the example above the bass C2 becomes a dissonant pedal point in bar 1 beat 4, where it is sustained through the B dim chord. It resolves on the last chord as the root.

The following example of a pedal point is from the theme song for the TV series The Golden Girls.

Example 16-Q

The bass player plays the G with the 1st chord and repeats it throughout the 7 bars. The G pedal point becomes a dissonant NCT with the D7 chord in bar 5, finally resolving in bar 7.

Not all NCTs fit neatly into the preceding descriptions. Music has evolved beyond the Baroque and Classical styles wherein these descriptions were appropriate. In both classical and popular contemporary music we hear unprepared and unresolved dissonances that are introduced into the music to effect dramatic increases in stress. There may be no attempt to justify them beyond that.

Computer exercises 16.1 & 16.2

Exercise

Play all the examples of NCTs in this chapter and learn to recognize them by sound. Do the same with NCTs you find in the Bach Chorales, hymn books, and/or your repertoire. Be especially cognizant of the different effects of the metrically accented *vs* unaccented NCTs. The accented NCTs demand more of our attention and help create high points in the music. If the performer is aware of them it becomes another tool for expression.

Chapter 17
Phrases
Harmonic Cadences
Picardy 3rd
Musical Form
Symbols of Repetition

Phrases

As discussed in Chapter 3, a musical phrase is similar to a sentence in language. Much of music could be compared to poetry, and when poetry is set to music, as in a hymn, the similarity is obvious. Each phrase is a thought or an idea, the thought or idea may be repeated, there is usually a space for breathing after each phrase, and there is usually punctuation after each phrase. In music the space for breathing is a longer held note and/or a rest, and the punctuation is called a cadence. (More about cadences later.)

Example 17-A

This apostrophe sign ❜ is a breath mark and is placed at phrase endings in music for singers to indicate where they can breathe. Note that they appear after long note values in the Example 17-A above and they coincide with punctuation in the lyrics.

Composers are not bound by a *rule* which dictates that a song must include longer notes and/or rests to allow singers to breathe. The following song is an example of what happens when a composer doesn't consider such things.

Example 17-B

In 1956 Johnny Marks wrote a new musical setting for this poem by Longfellow, but Marks used the exact same rhythm as the above example. Still no place to breathe. The words are quite worthy of a proper musical setting.

Exercise

That's your assignment for today - Compose a new setting for this song. You could use the same PNKs and chords and just change the rhythm, or start from scratch with a whole new melody, but please give the singer a chance to breathe after each phrase.

Harmonic Cadences

The chords used to end a musical phrase comprise a harmonic cadence. The drum patterns in a marching band are also called cadences, but they have no relation to our subject here. One of the strongest harmonic ends for a phrase is dominant to tonic. A dominant 7th chord has a particularly strong resolution to tonic and is used many thousands of times to end phrases in all styles from the Baroque period on.

The V or V7 to I progression is called an authentic cadence. If the two chords are in root position and the lowest and highest PNKs of the final chord are the tonic it is called a perfect authentic cadence. Check out any collection of any style of music from the Baroque period on and see how many pieces end with an authentic cadence.

Authentic cadences and cadences less strong than authentic cadences are found at the ends of phrases and sections of music. Three such cadences, in addition to the authentic, have been used so frequently as to have become codified and named. All 4 are listed below.

V or V7 to I is an authentic cadence.

IV to I is a plagal cadence. The "Amen" added at the end of a hymn is usually a plagal cadence.

Any cadence ending with V, V7, vii, or vii7, is a half cadence.

V or V7 to vi is a deceptive cadence. V or V7 to anything other than I may also be called a deceptive cadence.

See the examples of these cadences in the key of C major below. The identifications of these cadence types are the same whether in major or minor keys.

Example 17-C harmonic cadences

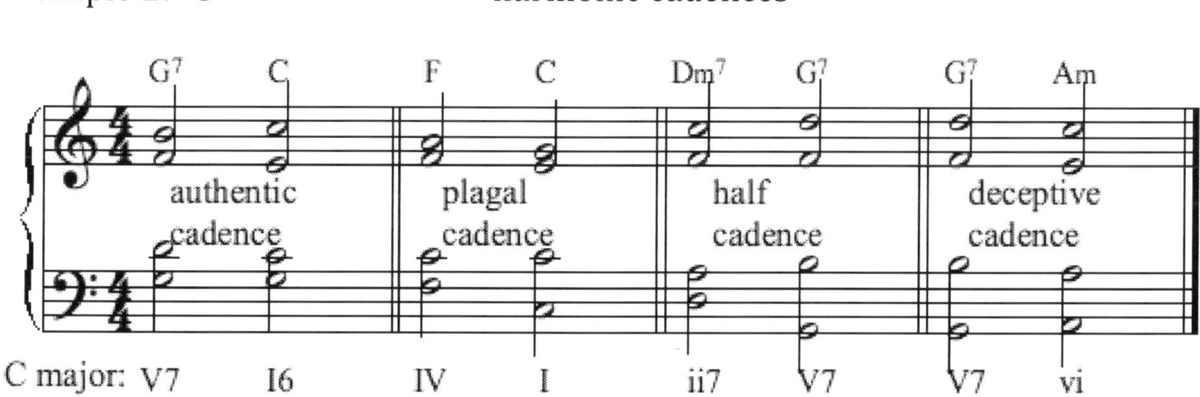

Following are some examples of cadences by various composers. The non-chord tones are in parentheses.

Example 17-D, authentic cadence

excerpt from

Carnival Of The Animals

Camille Saint-Saens

♩ = *ca.* C7 F C7 Dm Gm D Gm C7 F

F major: V7 I V7 vi ii V6 of ii ii V7 I

Example 17-E, half cadence

Example 17-F, plagal cadence

Example 17-G, deceptive cadence

Example 17-H, deceptive cadence

In both the deceptive cadences above the composers continued the compositions by repeating the same music leading up to the deceptive cadences but finally ending the pieces by following the dominant (7th) chord with the tonic chord for an authentic cadence. The final endings were even more convincing after we had been denied the resolution to the tonal center with the deceptive cadence. In these examples as in other occasions, the feeling produced by the deceptive cadence can be made more expressive when the performer is aware of the expressive potential in the music.

The most important indicator of a phrase end – a cadence – is not the harmony but the rhythm. There are V-I, I-V, IV-I, V-vi, etc. etc. chord progressions *within* phrases that are obviously not cadences, not the end of the phrase. All of the above-mentioned harmonic combinations found at the ends of phrases are quite common in music since the Baroque period, but are by no means exhaustive. Any chord(s) can be used to end a phrase. The real indication of a phrase end cadence is when the composer applies the brakes to the rhythm. There is another cadence not mentioned in any of the theory books I've read – the I-IV cadence. It figures prominently in "Happy Birthday" where the celebrant's name is sung. The IV-I cadence is called a plagal cadence. We could call I-IV a "lagalp" cadence.

The example below from one of Bach's chorales is another cadence that doesn't have a name.

Example 17-I

The 2-count chord in bar 4 obviously comprises a cadence at the end of a phrase. We don't have a name for a III-VI cadence. It could be argued that this is an authentic cadence in the key of F major, but the key of F major has a B♭ and just two beats before the F major chord is a B♮. Bach could easily have added a B♭ on beats 1 and 2 (creating a ii - V7 - I cadence in F) if he'd wanted it to sound like F major.

The point is, why do we need to label cadences with names? Why not just call an "authentic" cadence a V-I cadence? Probably because, since I had to learn all these names to get my music degree then you have to also. That's how it is folks. In real life you are going to have to jump through hoops. I would be remiss in my duty to prepare you for real life if I didn't require you to learn all these names. If you want to converse intelligently with other musicians you probably need to know them. But focus your attention on the ***sounds*** of music. What does a half cadence sound like? That's the real goal. Be aware of the many other "rules" of music theory that can become ends in themselves without having any significant revelations about what music sounds like. Learn to look (listen) beyond the rules.

Picardy 3rd

In a minor key the final tonic triad is often altered to a major triad with an accidental that raises the 3rd of the chord a half step. This altered 3rd is known as a Picardy 3rd. See the example below.

Example 17-J

It was unusual for a Baroque composition in a minor key to not end with a Picardy 3rd. No one seems to know who Mr. or Ms. Picardy was but he/she has been immortalized with major triads at the end of minor compositions.

Computer exercises 17.1 & 17.2

Exercise

Find examples of the 4 different above-named cadences in your repertoire. A hymn book is a good source. Frequently hymns will be arranged on the page with a phrase for each line of music and the musical phrases will exactly match with the poetic lines. If a hymn concludes with an "Amen," see how often it is harmonized with a IV - I plagal cadence.

Musical Form

Form in music has many similarities to form in writing. A phrase in music would be like a sentence. The "punctuation" at the end of a musical phrase could be a longer note value and/or a rest. A written paragraph, dealing with one particular idea would be like a section of music dealing with one particular musical idea. A chapter in a book would be a movement of a symphony or a sonata. An entire book would be like the whole symphony or sonata.

Symbols of Repetition

Repetition is usually involved in musical form. A section of music can be repeated for various reasons - more than one verse of lyrics, a different ending giving a question-and-answer effect, or just to extend the music to accommodate dancers, are three such possibilities. There are several symbols that are used to indicate repetition in music. See Example 17-K below.

Example 17-K: symbols of repetition

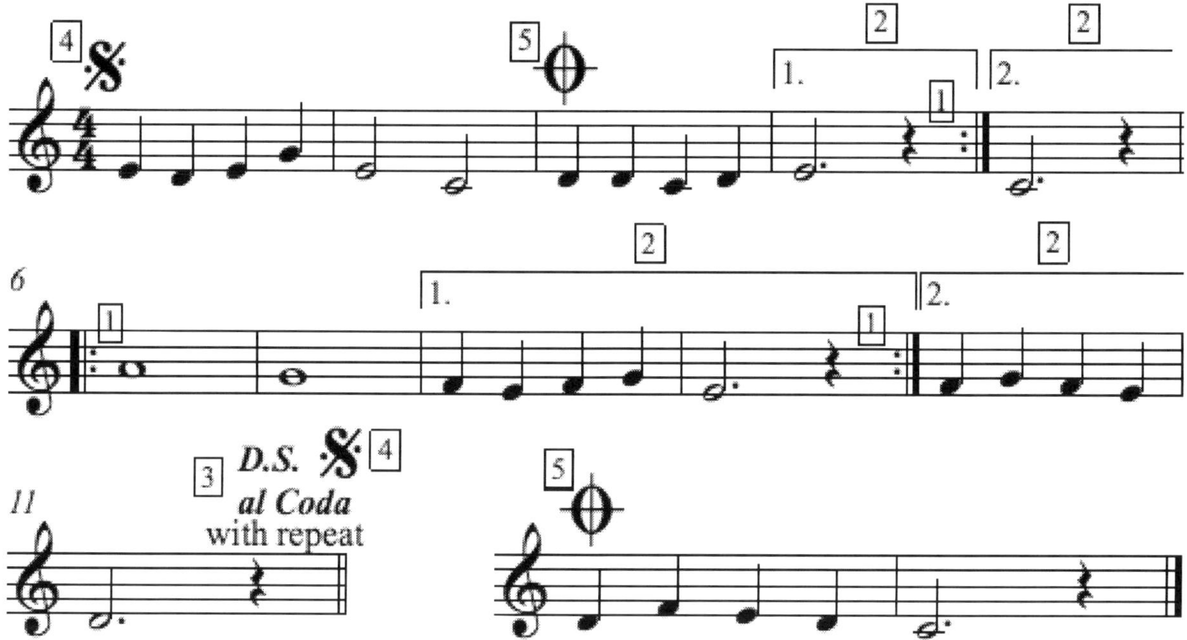

Each of the boxed numbers is a reference to the nearby symbol for the following discussion:

[1] There are 3 sets of repeat dots. In bar 4 the two dots placed on the staff to the left of the double bar tell you to play again from the beginning. When you get to bar 9, the repeat dots tell you to repeat from bar 6 where the two dots are on the right side of the double bar. Since there were no repeat dots on the right side of a double bar between the beginning and bar 4, the repeat dots at bar 4 tell you to repeat all the way from the beginning.

[2] There are 2 sets of first and second ending brackets. The first bracket, placed above the staff with the number 1. tells you to skip this/these bar(s) after you take a repeat indicated by repeat dots. This is called the first ending. The second bracket with the number 2. is the second ending. It indicates the bar you will skip to after the repeat, and proceed from there. The first ending bracket can include any number of bars. The second ending will include only the one bar from which you will continue with the piece.

[3] and [4] ***D. S. al coda*** with repeat. The Italian *"Dal Segno al coda"* translates to "From the sign to the coda." [4] is the *"Segno,"* the sign. When you first start playing the piece you will make a note of the *"Segno"* at the beginning of bar 1, knowing that you will be returning to it from later in the piece. "with repeat" means when you return to the *"Segno"* you will take the repeat before going to the coda. Without the "with repeat" you would not take the repeat but skip to the coda the first time after the "Segno."

There is another sign – *D. C.* – which is Italian for *"Da Capo"* which means "From the beginning." There would be no *"Segno."* You would just return to the beginning of the piece. It could have been used here instead of *"D. S."* but I wanted to show you the *Segno*.

[5] The coda sign. *"Coda"* is Italian for tail. After you have returned to the *Segno*, played to the repeat dots in bar 4, returned to the beginning, and repeated bars 1 & 2, you skip from the coda sign after bar 2 to the coda at the end of the piece and play the tail, the final two bars.

Without repeat signs music would take up a lot more pages. Turning pages is always a nuisance when you're trying to stay with a beat. Also, publishers save money using repeat signs rather than printing more pages. It also saves trees so everybody wins. Learning to read repeat signs is an essential skill for musicians.

Musical form is often expressed by assigning alphabetical letters to the various sections. Example 17-K above consists of 2 different 4-bar ideas or phrases. We will label them Phrase A and Phrase B. Phrase A comprises the first 4 bars. Phrase A is then repeated with a slight change – the last note is different. We'll still call it A.

The B phrase from bar 6 through bar 9 also has a different ending on the repeat, but notice that bar 10 is an inversion of bar 8. There is enough similarity in the repetition of B, even with the two different measures on the end, to justify labeling the repetition as B.

The coda is yet a third ending for the A phrase after the *Segno* repeat. We'll still call it A. The final form of this little piece then is AABBAA.

How much similarity is enough to justify using the same letter name? That is a judgment call. You need to learn to recognize differences and similarities in melodic contours, rhythmic patterns, chord progressions, etc. Similarities are often quite subtle. They are sometimes more obvious when heard than in the notation.

Exercise

Probably the best source for finding these symbols of repeats is in published popular music. Browse the music stores. In the popular music section study the music and identify the forms as in the AABBAA above. (Don't be intimidated into buying something because you want to look at some music. Just be careful not to crease the pages.) When listening to your favorite music or performing your repertoire be aware of repetition and form. Repeated sections should be performed with different expressive nuances in each repetition.

It is unusual to find music from the Baroque period to the present that has no repetition. We would call such a piece through-composed, meaning every idea is new. The form of such a piece would be ABCD etc. with a new alpha letter identifying each new phrase. See Example 17-L below.

Example 17-L

The only thing the 4 phrases have in common is their 4-bar length. The form of this piece is ABCD.

Chapter 18 – Rhythm III

Uneven Beat Divisions – Triplets
Swing Rhythm

Uneven Beat Divisions – Triplets

So far we have only discussed beat divisions and subdivisions by halves. It is possible to have any fractional beat division a composer might want. Any beat division different from a “regular” division by halves is called a **tuplet** or **uplet**. I will use “tuplet.” A common uneven beat division is the triplet. (In Chapter 20 we’ll look at some others.) Triplets divide a PNK into three parts instead of two. In the example below in 4/4 meter a quarter note is a one-beat note. One beat can be divided evenly into two 1/2-beat notes. It can also be divided into three 1/3-beat notes, called triplets, indicated by a 3 over or under the notes.

Example 18-A

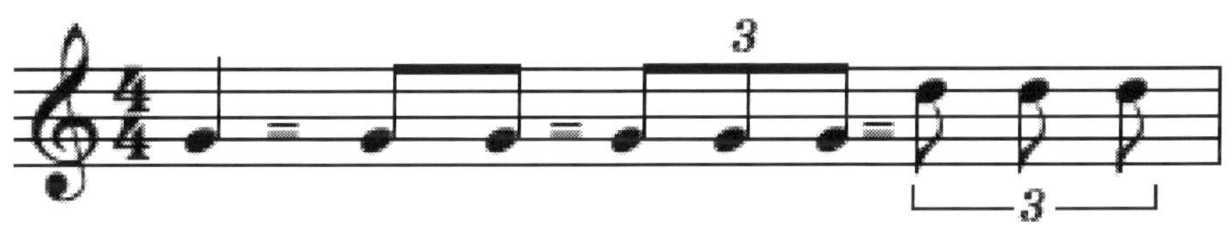

The triplets get 1/3 beat each. They are played slightly faster than the 1/2-beat notes in order to stay within the one beat allotted to them. (How much faster? No calculators allowed. Do it in your head.)

If you can play or sing in 3/4 time, counting triplet eighth notes 3 to a beat shouldn’t be a problem. Instead of “one-and, two-and” etc. for 1/2-beat notes you count “one-and-uh, two-and-uh” etc. for triplet 1/3-beat notes. In Chapter 15 it was mentioned that new students tend to add a 4th beat to each bar of 3/4 meter. With triplets the tendency is to subdivide a beat into 4ths instead of 3rds by adding a pause after the “uh.” Don’t do that.

Count out loud as you tap or play the notes in the example below. Set your metronome for one-beat notes and tap or play 3 even triplets for each click of the metronome, *ca.* 50 to 100 beats per minute (bpm).

Example 18-B

Example 18-B could be rewritten in 6/8 meter and eliminate the need for triplets. Count and tap and feel the same rhythm as before.

Example 18-C

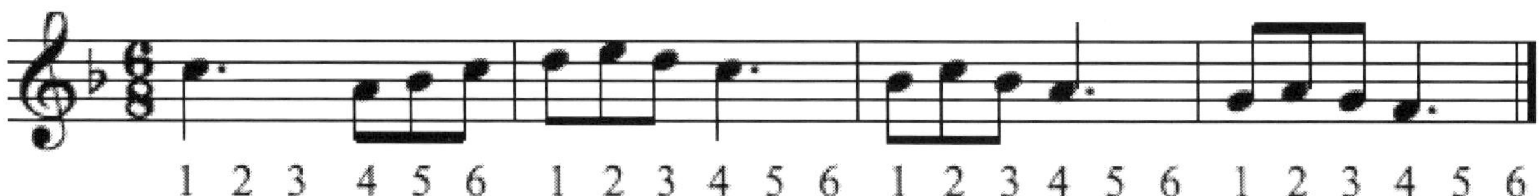

The rhythm of the melody in Examples 18-B & C is exactly the same. The 6/8 version would be easier to write because you wouldn't have to mess with all the triplet signs.

Swing Rhythm

In published music you will sometimes find the words "swing beat" above the first bar, the location for tempo and/or metronome information. The idea may be disguised in expressions such as "With a Gaelic lilt" or "In a lazy 4." Unfortunately if you haven't heard the song these expressions are not very instructive. The word "swing" always (or at least nearly always) means the beats are divided into triplets instead of duplets, even though they may not be written that way. (!?) In swing rhythm the first and third triplets of a beat are articulated, not the second.

Example 18-D swing rhythm

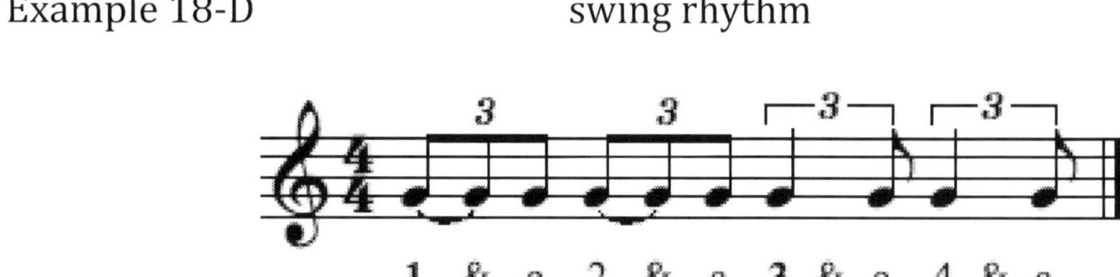

Count and tap the above example. Beats 1 and 2 have the first two triplets tied to demonstrate that the <u>second</u> third of the beat is *not* articulated. Beats 1 and 2 are played exactly the same as beats 3 and 4.

There are 2 ways that publishers commonly write swing rhythm, neither of which is the "correct" way to perform it. See the two versions of the excerpt below in Example 18-E.

Example 18-E

Ignore the "swing beat" instruction and play the first version <u>as written</u> while counting equal half counts. Then play the second version <u>as written</u> while counting even 1/4 beats, giving 1/4 beat to the sixteenth notes and 3/4 beats to the dotted eighths. If you are familiar with the song you will realize that neither way is how this song is supposed to sound. The first would be a syncopated rock version and the second would be too jerky.

The technically "correct" way to write the song in 4/4 meter is in Example 18-F below.

Example 18-F

It is simpler to read and simpler to write in the first and second versions in Example 18-E than in 18-F. The word "swing" tells the musician that it is to be played as in 18-F.

Go back and play the two versions in Example 18-E while counting triplet divisions of each beat – "one-and-a, two-and-a," etc. - and see if that sounds better.

The conflict between what is written and what it is supposed to sound like could be avoided by writing the song in 6/8 meter.

Example 18-G

Many popular songs have a combination of "correct" and "incorrect" versions of swing rhythm. A problem arises when all 3 thirds of a beat are articulated, so they must be written correctly with a triplet sign. See the published excerpt from "It's Beginning To Look A Lot Like Christmas" in Example 18-H below.

Example 18-H

excerpt from

It's Beginning To Look A Lot Like Christmas

There are very few bars in the song that don't include at least one set of triplets, some with the dotted eighths/sixteenths and some with the triplet sign. 6/8 meter would accommodate both versions.

Example 18-I

excerpt from

It's Beginning To Look A Lot Like Christmas

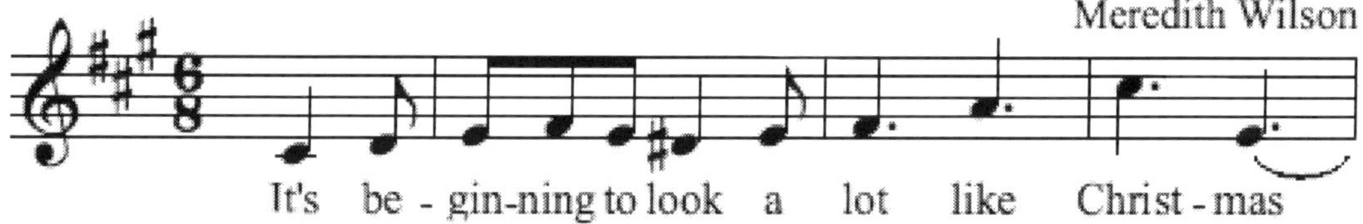

Finally, let's take a look at a song that was recorded with a combination of triplet quarter notes and triplet eighth notes.

Example 18-J

excerpt from

Blueberry Hill

Al Lewis
Larry stock
Vincent Rose
1940

recorded by Fats Domino, Louis Armstrong, etc.

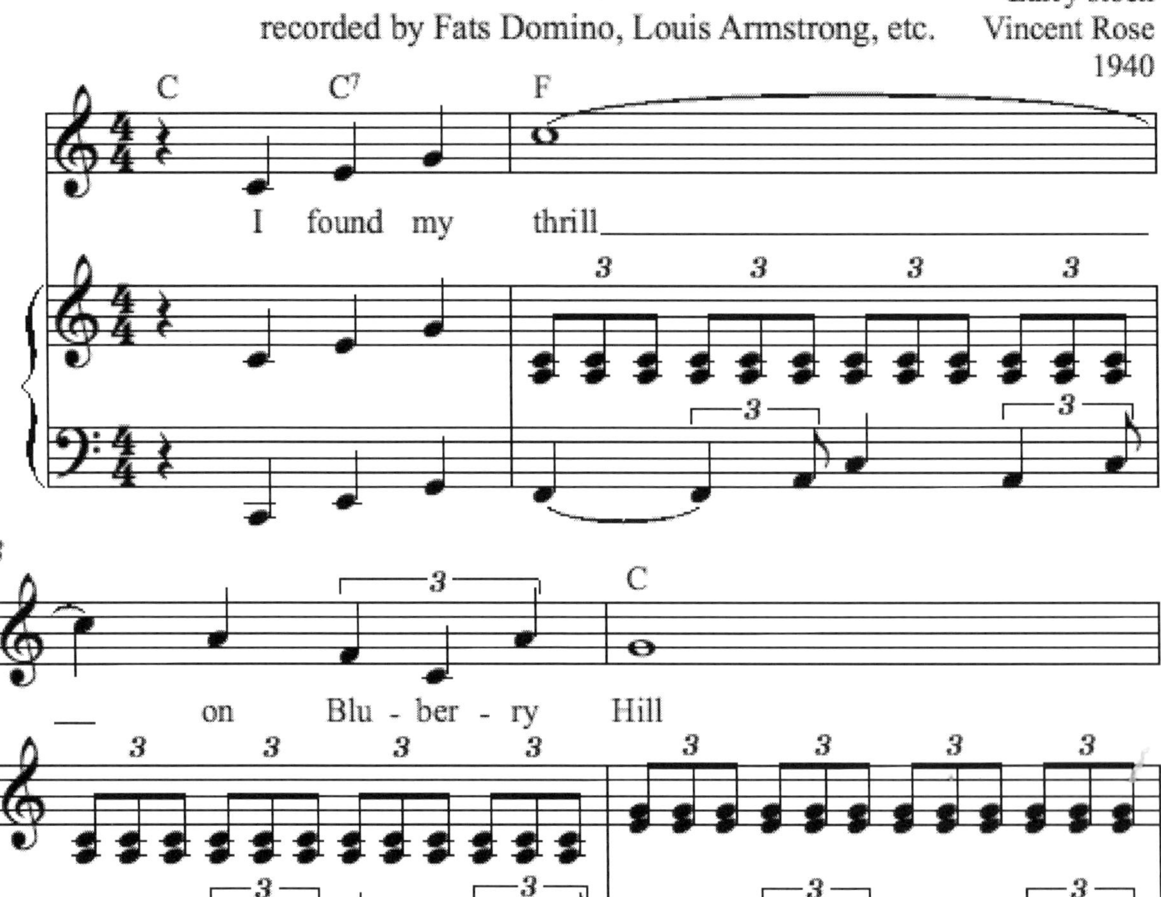

In bar 3, beats 3 and 4, there are triplet quarter notes for the singer's melody while triplet eighths are played in the G clef and a swing rhythm is played in the F clef. It would be no problem to play the piano part <u>or</u> to sing the melody. Every triplet in the piano F-clef is matched with a triplet in the G-clef, and every solo melody triplet quarter note is matched with a triplet in the piano part, but can you do both at once? It took a bit of practice to play and sing it at the same time, but I work solo and it was a request so I had to go home and learn it. A lot of fun things come to you on gigs.

Exercises

Rewrite each of the following two melodies "incorrectly" two ways: with straight eighth notes and with dotted eighths/sixteenths. Refer to Example 18-E above. Write the words "swing beat" over the first bars. Add fake chord symbols above the staves and Roman numerals below. Learn to play them. Be sure the syncopations in the second melody are tied properly. Both tunes end on the keynote. Which of the three versions is easiest to read and perform?

Computer exercise 18.1

Chapter 19
The 12-Bar Blues
Blue Notes
The Blues Scale
The Blues Scale for Guitar
Pentatonic Scales
Playing by Ear

The 12-Bar Blues

The blues style originated with the slaves in the deep south of the U. S. in the 19th Century. We'll concentrate on its structure rather than its sources in history.

The most common form of the blues is a 3 chord piece called the 12-bar blues. It is a simple chord progression that later became more and more complex, but the basic 3-chord progression is still very much alive and in use.

The lyrics of a blues song consisted of a 4-bar phrase, which were repeated in the next 4 bars and then answered in the final 4 bars. The meter was nearly always 4/4 with a swing beat. The lyrics were often made up on the spot. The repetition of the first phrase and the slow tempo gave the performer/composer time to think up a last phrase answer that rhymed with the repeated first phrase. See Example 19-A below.

Example 19-A

The above example is pretty standard for the 12-bar blues. Many Rock 'n' Roll songs use the 12-bar blues form.

Blue Notes

In a major key the blue notes consist of the 5 PNKs not included in the major scale. The 3 PNKs that are the difference between a major and minor key – the lowered 3rd, 6th, and 7th degrees of the scale – plus the lowered 5th scale degree get the most frequent use, less for the lowered 2nd.

If you want to create a blues sound, play the I chord of a major key with the left hand and at the same time play the lowered 3rd of the chord with the right hand. Do the same with the IV, and V chords. Some blue notes and chords in C major are given below in Example 19-B.

Example 19-B

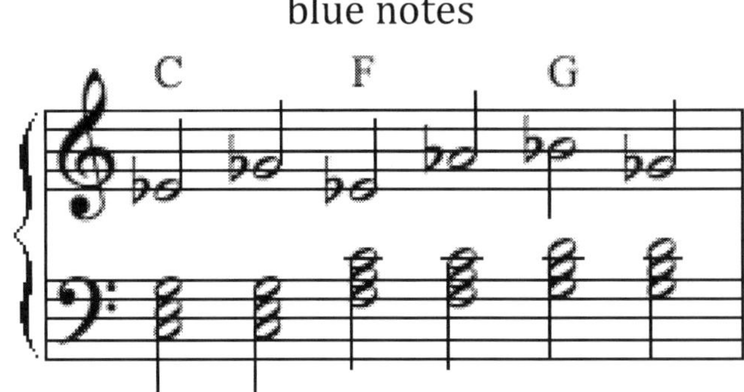

The blue notes can resolve by half step or by skip in either direction. Or not. They are dissonant and the dissonance can be maintained until the rubber band breaks and they lose their connection to the song and become noise. The musician has to decide how much is too much before it happens.

In the Example 19-A (page 171) the blue notes are mostly written as <u>raised</u> 2nd, 5th, and 6th scale degrees rather than <u>lowered</u> 3rd, 6th and 7th scale degrees because of the melodic direction of the following notes, but the blues sound is that of a major triad sounding against a minor (lowered) 3rd.

As an example of how the blues chord progression can be enhanced let's look at bar 11 in Example 19-A. The last three notes over ". . .gon-na do." can be harmonized with A♭7, G7, C. Try it.

Example 19-C

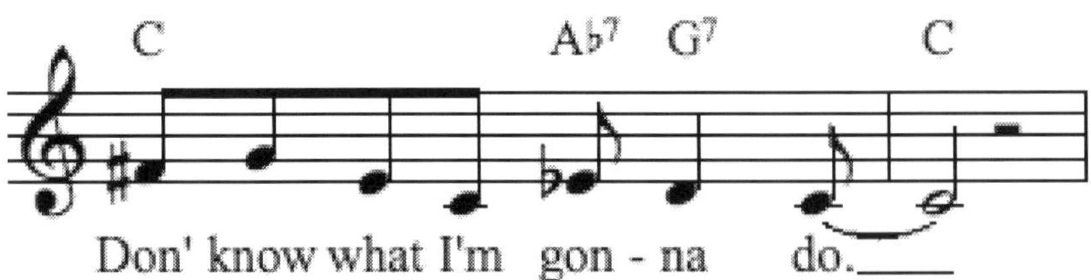

A 7th chord a half step above the dominant PNK (as is the A♭7 here) is discussed in a Chapter 25 where we learn about the Augmented 6th chords.

In Example 19-D which follows, the 12-bar blues progression is notated in the key of C. The Roman numerals will allow you to transpose it to any key.

Example 19-D

12-bar blues

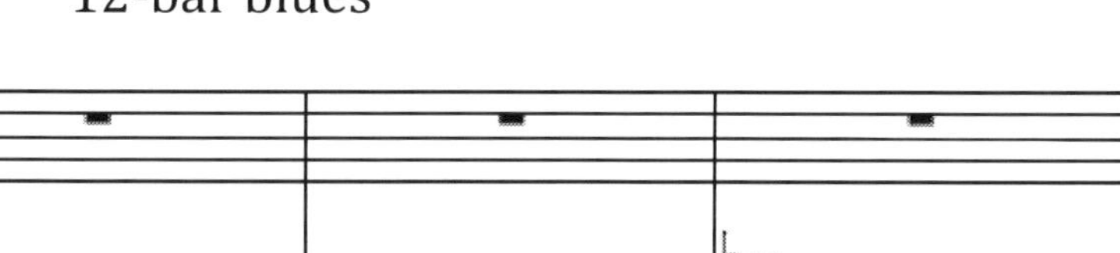

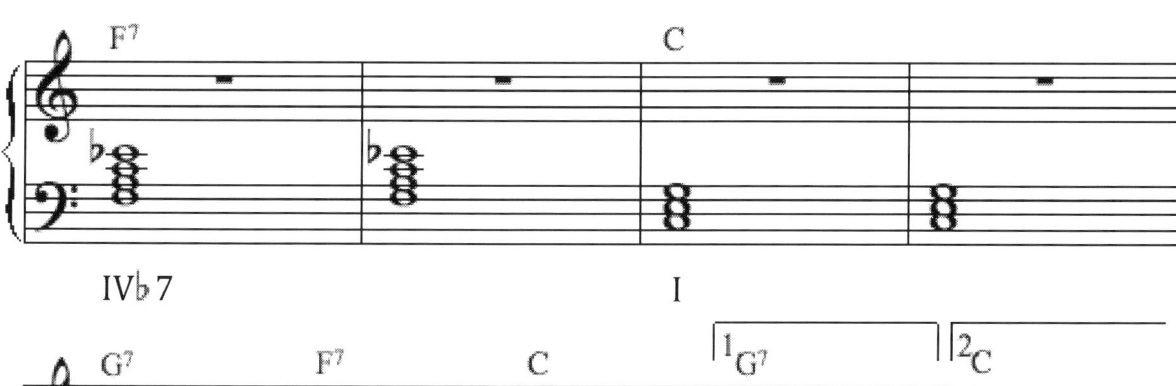

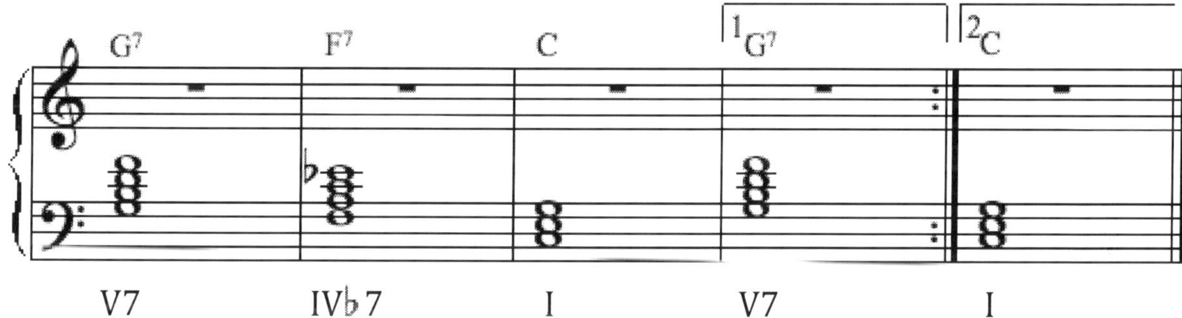

In Examples 19-A and D notice that the IV chord has a 7th added. This PNK is not in the KS, as is indicated in the Roman numerals with the ♭7. This 7th is the lowered 3rd scale degree which is one of the blue notes. It has become pretty standard in the blues to add this 7th to the IV chord. Its origin may have been because it's an easier barre chord on the guitar.

When musicians get together who have never played together before, they often warm up by improvising with the 12-bar blues. Everybody knows how it works and you can hear some really great jazz created on the spot. The more you play it the more improvisation material you'll pick up, especially if you are working with musicians better than you.

In Example 19-E which follows, the chords are realized with a bass riff which includes some NCTs.

Example 19-E

Exercise

A fun way to increase your familiarity with all the major keys is to play the 12-bar blues in every key around the circle.

The Blues Scale

The blues scale is a pentatonic scale, meaning 5 PNKs per octave instead of 7 as in major, minor, and the modes. It is notated below as it would be played with a C major accompaniment. It is fairly easy to create melodies with this scale. It's almost as though you can't play any wrong notes. Using the 12-bar blues as accompaniment you will hear the blue notes loud and clear against the major triads.

Example 19-F

Blues scale in C major.

scale degrees: 1 >3 4 5 >7 1

An easy way to remember the blues scale is to play just the black keys on the piano, using E♭ as tonic. It would be used with an E♭ major accompaniment. See example 19-G below.

Example 19-G

Blues scale in Eb major.

Example 19-G is just a mnemonic aid. You may not find many groups improvising in the key of E♭. The keys of A major, D major, and G major are easier keys for guitar players. The really good musicians will let you pick any key you want, but they won't be stuck with one key all night.

Example 19-H

blues scales

1 >3 4 5 >7 1 1 >3 4 5 >7 1 1 >3 4 5 >7 1

Keep in mind that you are working in a *major* key environment. The blue notes are very expressive dissonances against the major triads. The blues scale could be thought of as an Aeolian scale with a missing supertonic and missing submediant. When improvising with the blues scale a blue note may be resolved into a major scale PNK (as in Example 19-A). Or not.

The Blues Scale for Guitar

The blues scale for guitar is shown below in Example 19-I.

Example 19-I

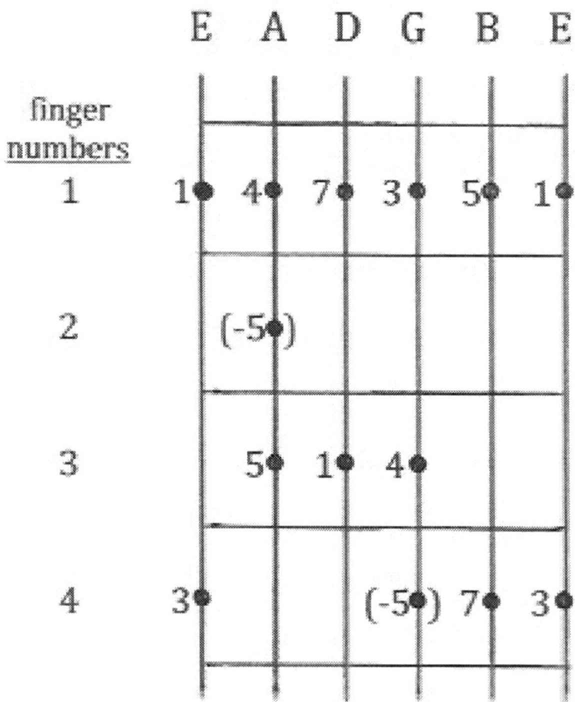

The guitar grid in Example 19-I can be anywhere on the fret board (no open strings). The numbers to the left of the grid are finger numbers and the numbers beside the dots are scale degree numbers. The 1s are tonics, so whatever note you are playing on that fret on that string is the keynote of the piece. The missing 6s and 2s are the missing supertonics and submediants as in the blues scales in Example 19-H. The (-5)s are the lowered dominant PNKs that can also be included in blues improvisation.

Exercise

Play the 12-bar blues progression in every key and add an improvised melody with the right hand using the blues scale. It's more fun, of course, for 2 or more musicians to play together and alternate who plays melody and who plays harmony.

Pentatonic Scales

A **major** scale has the whole/half step pattern:

1 W 2 W 3 H 4 W 5 W 6 W 7 H 1

Two forms of a **pentatonic** scale are:

major:

1 W 2 W 3 W+H 4 W 5 W+H 1

and minor:

1 W+H 2 W 3 W 4 W+H 5 W 1

In notation with C as tonic they look like Example 19-J, below.

Example 19-J

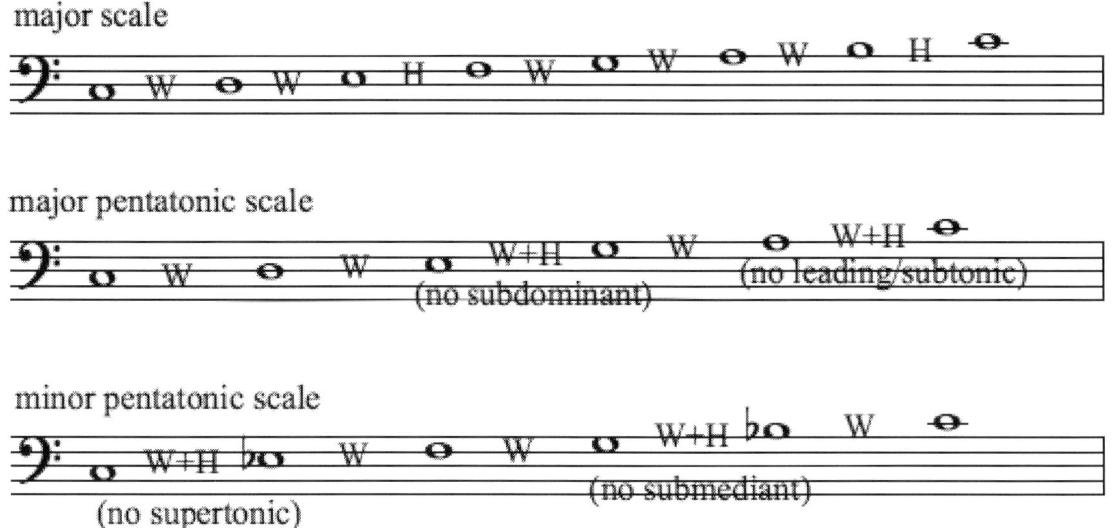

The minor pentatonic scale in Example 19-J is the same as the blues scale in Example 19-F and 19-G. There must be hundreds if not thousands of pentatonic songs, *e. g.*, "Amazing Grace," "Tom Dooley," "Swing Low, Sweet Chariot." If you Google "pentatonic songs" you'll find bunches of them.

Playing by Ear

There is a lot to be said in favor of learning to play by ear. I have expressed it earlier in this book by mentioning that music is sound, not manuscript or a vocation. When Bach was trying out for his gig at the St. Thomas Schule he was given a fugue theme and told to improvise a fugue on the organ for the committee. Many of the instrumental concerti of the Classical period had blank spaces where the performer was expected to improvise a cadenza. Mozart was a master at this.

The blues scale is a great tool for learning to play what you want to hear. It is simple with few choices = few possible mistakes, and has the potential for expansion.

The other side of that coin is composing without referring to an instrument. When you can sit with a blank manuscript and notate the sounds that you hear in your head you have become a literate musician.

Hopefully, you have made the connection between what you see on a score and the sounds that the notes represent. Using a music notation program on a computer is not the same as hand notation if it sounds the pitches as you write them. I am, perhaps, old fashioned since I started composing before the computer programs were invented but I find my creative juices don't flow nearly as well when the sounds instantly come back to me. I can't seem to think ahead of where I am.

Computer exercise 19.1

Exercise

Compose some songs, with or without words, using the major and minor pentatonic scales. Add appropriate chords. Use the I, IV, and V7 or i, iv, and V7 chords first. Then experiment with other chords such as a major triad a half step above tonic as a substitute for V7, or secondary dominants, which are frequently major versions of the minor ii, iii, and vi chords with 7ths added.

One of my students in a music theory class at ASU had a gig playing organ at a strip club in Phoenix. His sister was one of the dancers and they were both very good. During one class we were studying diminished 7th chords and his hand shot up. He announced, "That's an 'and then' chord." The whole class now had a handle whereby they would never fail to recognize by sound a diminished 7th chord. The more references you can attach to one of your musical "tools," the easier your recall will be. Especially if it's funny or weird.

A lot of us have supported our music "addiction" by playing in bars, clubs, and other smoke-filled dens of iniquity. It's a pretty safe occupation. In the western movies and mob stories you'll notice they never shoot the piano player.

Chapter 20 – Rhythm IV

Mixed Rhythms – 2 against 3
Triplets of Different Note Values
Divided and Sub-Divided Triplets
Mixed Rhythms – 3 Against 4
Duplets in Triple or Compound Meters
Mixed Rhythms – Other Combinations
Odd *vs.* Even Tuplets

If you have mastered the feel of triplet beat divisions it's time now to consider music with both even (duplet) beat divisions and triplet beat divisions. Switching back and forth from duplet PNKs to triplet PNKs is going to require some practice. Probably a lot of practice. It is a necessary skill because music in many different styles includes it.

Playing mixed rhythms (aka polyrhythms) – duple and triple divisions at the same time – may sound even more difficult than changing rhythms but it's probably about the same, maybe even easier. You will likely encounter mixed rhythms as often as changing rhythms. This project can be challenging so prepare yourself!

Mixed Rhythms – 2 against 3

Example 20-A below is a combination of triple and duple beat divisions.

Example 20-A

We learned how to calculate lowest common multiples (LCM) in Chapter 14. With mixed rhythms we need the LCM of the two different beat divisions. In Example 20-A the LCM of 2 and 3 is 6. We will divide each beat into sixths but instead of counting 1 2 3 4 5 6 we'll count 1 & 2 & 3 &. The goal is to learn to *feel* the two rhythms simultaneously. It involves several steps.

In Example 20-B below you are to tap the triplets with the right hand on counts 1, 2, 3 and the duplets with the left hand on counts 1, &. Both hands tap together on 1. Notice that the counts are underlined for the tapped notes.

1. Set your metronome to click once for each triplet note in the right hand on counts 1, 2, 3. Start slowly – *ca.* 80-100bpm. The left and right hand tap together on beat 1, then the right hand taps 2, the left hand &, then the right hand 3, with the left & halfway between the right 2 and 3. Count evenly "1 & 2 & 3 &" for each of the 4 beats of the measure. Gradually increase your speed until you can do this comfortably at 150bpm.

Example 20-B

mixed rhythms - triple and duple

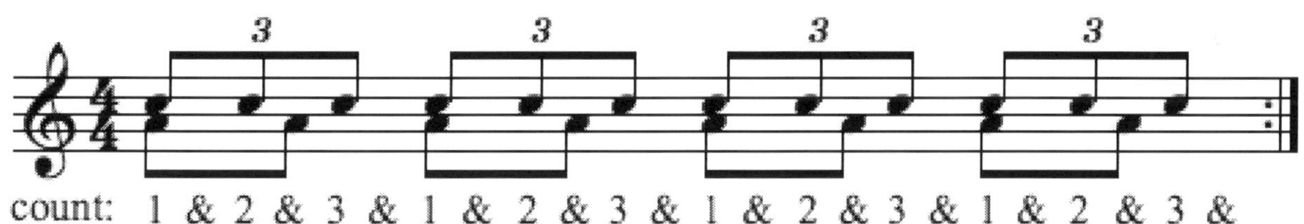

2. You should be feeling the triplets as the primary rhythm. In order to reinforce this, count as in Example 20-C below. To make sure your triplets are even, revert to counting "1 & 2 & 3 &" for each beat as in Example 20-B if you need to. The metronome still clicks once for each triplet.

Example 20-C

mixed rhythms - triple and duple

3. Now we want to feel the duplets become the primary rhythm. While counting and tapping, gradually increase the pressure/ loudness of the duplet taps while decreasing the pressure/ loudness of the triplet taps. Also emphasize vocally the "1"s and the "&"s. See Example 20-D below.

Example 20-D

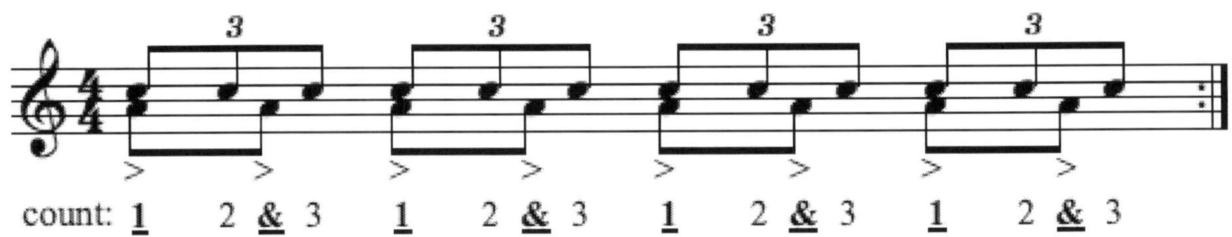

4. Next, drop the "2"s and "3"s entirely.

Example 20-E

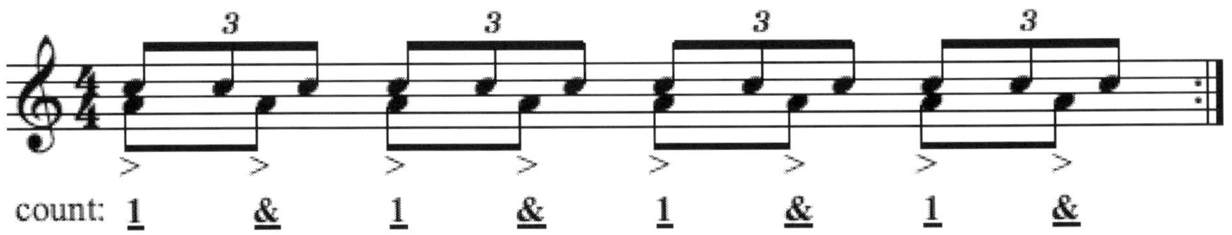

5. Next, replace the "&"s with "2"s.

Example 20-F

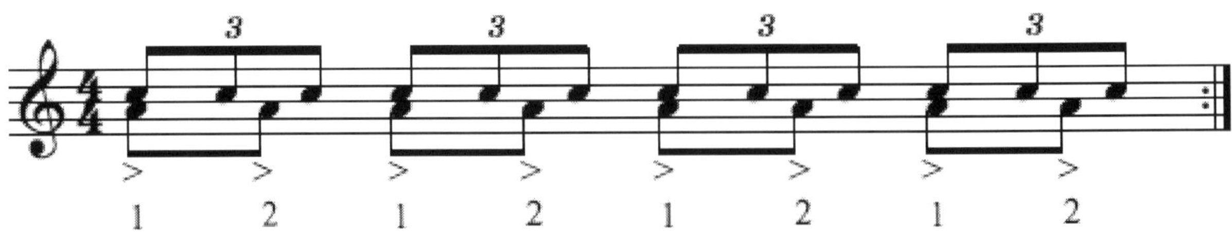

Somewhere in steps 1. through 5. you should feel the duplets become the primary rhythm, even though the metronome is clicking triplets.

6. Finally, slow the metronome to 2/3 speed and count and tap with the metronome beating the 2s.

When you can count and tap Example 20-F as indicated, counting only the "1"s and "2"s with the metronome beating the even duplets, you have probably succeeding in mastering the mixed duple/triple rhythm. At least temporarily. If at any time you feel insecure about your ability to do this, or to check to see if the duplets and triplets are even, don't hesitate to revert back to step 1 and work gradually through the whole process. Each time you do, it will become a more familiar/useful tool in your tool box. If you are going to be a working musician you will for sure need it.

Probably the most common occurrence of 2 against 3 rhythm is triplet quarter notes in X/4 meter (any meter with 4 on the bottom). The triple rhythm is the triplet melody and the duple rhythm is the 2 beats in which the triplets occur. Example 20-G below shows how to apply the LCM of 6 to your counting. The numbers 1 2 3 4 are the metric beats.

Example 20-G

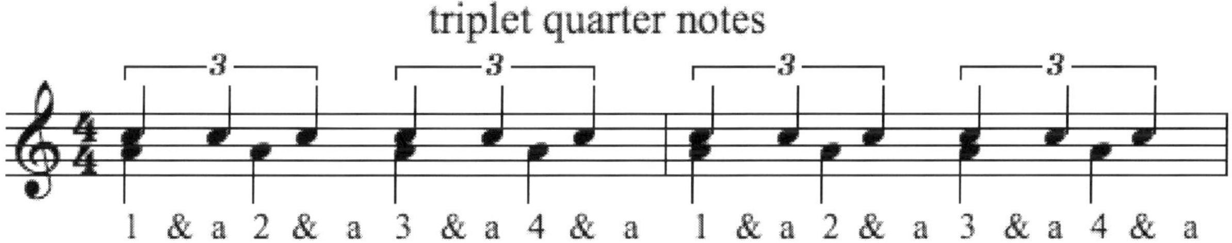

The rhythm section of the band (piano or guitar, bass, and drums) will maintain the duple beats while the soloist sings or plays the triplets. When you can sing or play triplet quarter notes evenly in 4/4 meter you're closer to being ready for a gig.

Example 20-H

Performing changing rhythms can be practiced using the same techniques as above. Start with step 1, with the metronome set to click once for each triplet while counting "1 & 2 & 3 &" for each beat. You will alternate between tapping triplets and duplets. It's best to use just one hand for this operation. When you're playing changing rhythms in a composition they will probably be in the same voice. Proceed through each step until you've mastered the technique. There's a good possibility you can skip some of the steps as long as you're confident you are playing even triplets and even duplets.

An excellent way to practice 2 against 3 is to use large muscles (walking) for the duplets and small muscles (clapping or tapping your fingers) for the triplets. Uneven duplets will become obvious if you're walking the duplets. I used to practice mixed rhythms as I walked from one class to another. BTW, 2 against 3 is just the beginning. We're going to apply the same techniques to others of the infinite set of mixed rhythms. The good news is every time you master a new mixed rhythm the next one becomes less difficult.

Triplets of Different Note Values

Any note value can be changed to triplets. Three triplet PNKs are always equal to two duplet PNKs of the same type. See Example 20-I below.

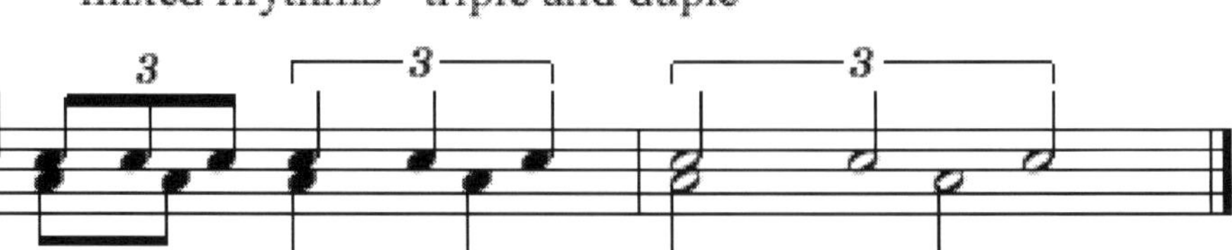

Divided and Sub-Divided Triplets

Notes can be divided and subdivided within a set of triplets. The same rule of one note being equal to two notes of the next smaller division applies –

a 2/3 count quarter note divides into two 1/3 count eighth notes, a 1/3 count eighth note divides into two 1/6 count sixteenth notes, etc.

Example 20-J

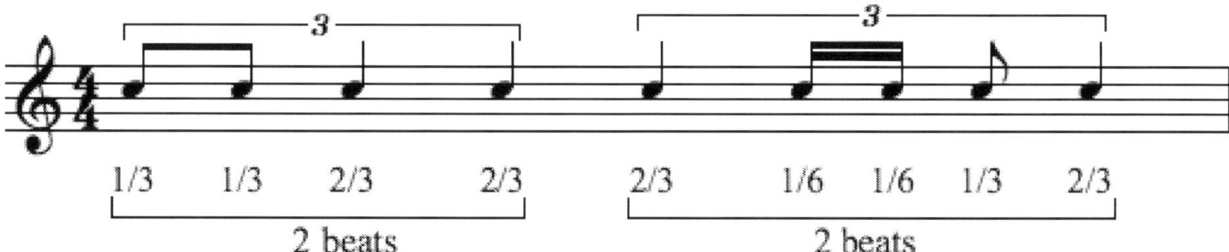

There is no way to give examples of each of the infinite combinations of possible triplet beat divisions and their infinite combinations with duplet beat divisions. By considering the two examples below, a process of working out their relationships and methods of performing them can be developed.

Example 20-K

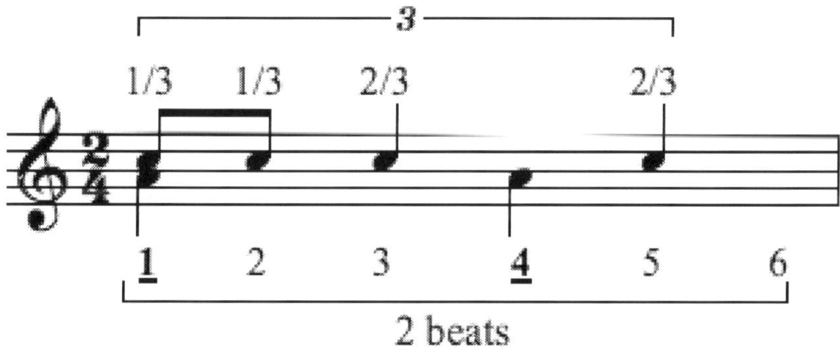

These two beats are relatively simple. There is a triplet note halfway between the 1st and 3rd triplet and a duplet note halfway between the last two triplets. All the notes fit nicely with the 6 (LCM) divisions of the two beats. By emphasizing the metric counts 1 and 2, the two-against-three cross rhythm can be felt.

The two beats in Example 20-L go another step in note divisions which means another step in the LCM. We need to divide these two beats into twelfths, 6 per beat. We could either count from 1 to 6 twice or add & after each of the numbers. Either way works fine.

Example 20-L

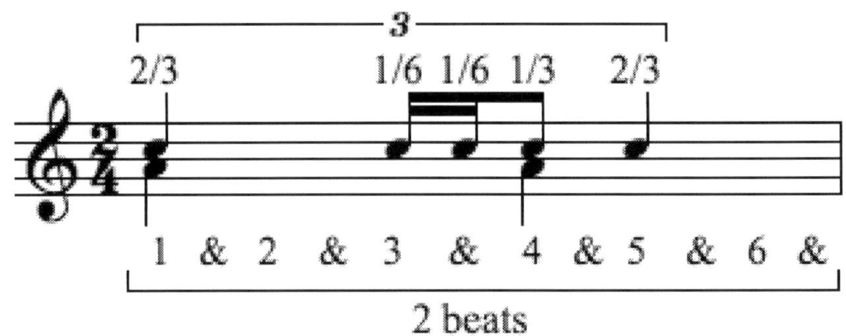

Mixed Rhythms – 3 against 4

In the 5 steps to learning the 2 against 3 rhythm we started with the triplet 3 as the primary rhythm and gradually increased the intensity of the duplet 2 rhythm until the duplets become primary. It is always easier to feel the *faster* rhythm as primary. You will begin to feel both rhythms simultaneously when the *slower* rhythm becomes primary. To learn 3 against 4 we will start with the faster 4 as the primary rhythm.

Example 20-M

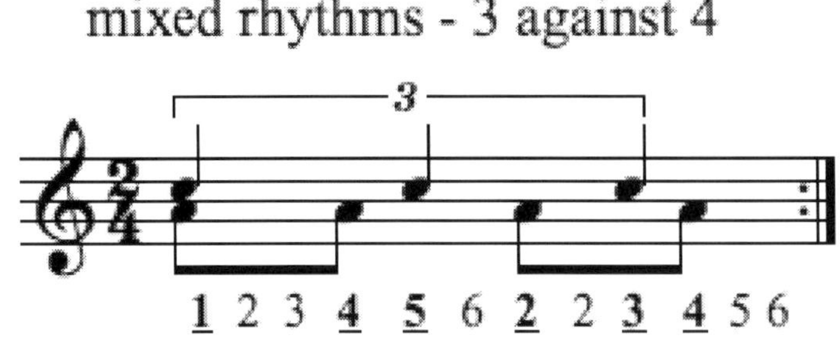

For 3 against 4 the LCM is 12. The numbers on which the notes are tapped are underlined. Set your metronome to click once for each eighth note, which is once for every 3 of the 12 counts. Start slowly – *ca.* 60-72bpm. Tap once with the left hand for each of the duplet eighth notes and tap once with the right hand for each of the triplet quarter notes while counting evenly "**1**, 2, 3, 4, 5, 6, **2**, 2, 3, 4, 5, 6, " for the 2 beats of the measure. Gradually increase your speed until you can do this comfortably at *ca.*108 metric bpm.

The goal, as with the 2 against 3, is to increase the pressure/loudness of the slower triplet quarter notes while decreasing the pressure/loudness of the faster duplet eighth notes until you hear the triplets as the primary rhythm.

When you've gained sufficient confidence you may prefer to do this without the metronome so you can change speeds without having to reset the metronome.

2 against 3 and 3 against 4 occur often enough that a musician should have the skill available at all times as a familiar tool in the tool box. It is understandably impossible to prepare for all the combinations you may encounter, but with the information you have here you should be able to chart and practice and hopefully learn the mixed rhythms that might come your way. The following are 2 examples.

Example 20-N

This first movement of this sonata by Beethoven is often heard in recitals performed incorrectly. It is written as a 3 against 4 rhythm but instead the dotted eighth/sixteenth rhythm in the G clef in bar 1 on beat 4 is often played as a swing rhythm (refer to Example 19-D). *I. e.,* the final sixteenth note receives 1/3 beat and coincides with the last triplet eighth in the F clef. Also the sixteenth note may be incorrectly played as a triplet sixteenth half way between the last triplet eighth and the following beat 1. It is written to be played 1/12th of a beat after the last F clef triplet. See the Example 20-O below.

Example 20-O

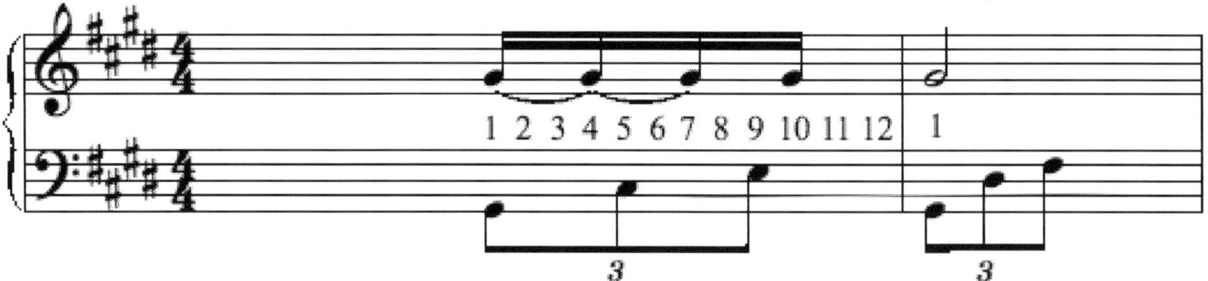

Oh come on! Does 1/12th of a beat really make that much difference? Well, try it and see. Practice it until you can play it smoothly and musically and see for yourself. Play it all three ways, with the final G-clef sixteenth note played (a) with the final F-clef triplet, (b) halfway between the final triplet and the following beat 1, (c) as written – 1/12th beat after the final triplet. For some people that subtle difference can add a great deal of musical meaning to the piece. Chopin once commented that the tuplets in his melodies allowed them to "...soar beyond the shackles of the metric rhythm." I feel a similar effect here. What do you think?

One thing you will discover as you learn more and more about music (or anything else, for that matter) is that you become dissatisfied with sloppy or inaccurate performances. Your appreciation of musical performances becomes more limited. But at the same time your appreciation of a fine performance is enhanced, so it's a trade-off. The mature experienced musician will also become more and more tolerant of the not-so-experienced musicians because he/she will realize how very difficult it is to get there. The loved and respected musician will be tolerant of everyone but her/himself.

If I have students that want to play Beethoven's Moonlight Sonata I start them on the last movement. When they have mastered that they can start on the first movement.

Example 20-P below is an unusual use of triplet whole notes in cut time (2/2 meter).

Example 20-P

exerpt from

Everything's Coming Up Roses

from the Broadway show "Mame"

Stephen Sondheim

Jule Styne

Ev - 'ry - thing's com - ing____ up ro - ses.

Each whole note triplet gets 1 1/3 beats. How do you play/sing that so it fits properly into 2 beats to a measure? Is it 2 against 3 or 3 against 4? Where do you get the numbers for the LCM? There are at least 2 methods that will work using the information given in this chapter.

Duplets in Triple or Compound Meter

The following Example 20-Q is an excerpt from "Claire de Lune" by Debussy. The meter is 9/8 which is felt as three sets of triplets per bar. In 9/8 the accented beats are 1, 4, & 7. In beats 4, 5, and 6 of the first bar and all of the second bar, Debussy wants us to play couplets in place of the triplets, dividing 3 beats into 2 halves. This is indicated by a *2* with a bracket enclosing the 3 beats.

Example 20-Q

The 2 against 3 rhythm here is the 2 duplet PNKs against 3 metric beats. In the first bar, the first of the duplet PNKs is played on the 4th beat and the second is played half way between the 5th and 6th beats. By counting "4 & 5 & 6 &" the first duplet PNK is played on 4 and the second on the & between 5 and 6.

It wasn't necessary to use the duplet *2* sign to indicate the 2 PNKs against the triple rhythm. A dotted eighth note would have achieved the same effect. Each of the dotted eighths receives 1½ beats the same as a duplet eighth. See Example 20-R below.

Example 20-R

Both methods are valid. I think the couplet *2* the way Debussy wrote it is more indicative of what the music *feels* like, with the music "escaping" from the metric restrictions.

Mixed Rhythms – Other Combinations

There are an infinite number of possible combinations of mixed rhythms using 2 whole numbers to compute the LCM. Beyond that there are also LCMs for the infinite rhythmic combinations using 3 or more different whole number beat divisions. Only a very tiny percentage of these would be aurally comprehensible at the current evolution of the human mind. We can, however, formulate a method for analyzing them. A rhythm of 3 against 5 would be computed thus:

1. Determine the LCM of all the beat divisions. If none of the beat divisions of the PNKs are a power of 2, then the bottom number of the meter must also be included as an additional element of the LCM in order to determine where the PNKs are played in the metric context. In 2 against 3 or 3 against 4, the 2 and the 4 are regular even beat divisions. We therefore wouldn't need to consider the power of 2 which is the bottom number of the meter, as an element in our LCM. I have a piano piece in my repertoire in 4/4 meter that has several 3 against 5 PNKs encompassing 2 beats. The LCM must therefore include 2 (metric beats) against 3 (triplet quarter notes) against 5 (quintuplet eighth notes). The LCM of 2, 3, and 5 is 30.

2. Write the numbers from 1 through 30 evenly spaced across a sheet of paper. Mark every 6th number for each of the quintuplet eighth notes (30/5=6), every 10th number for each of the triplet quarter notes (30/3=10), and every 15th number for the 2 metric beats (30/15=2). Add one more 1 after number 30 to show the beginning of the next beat, with all three marks as with the first 1.

Example 20-S

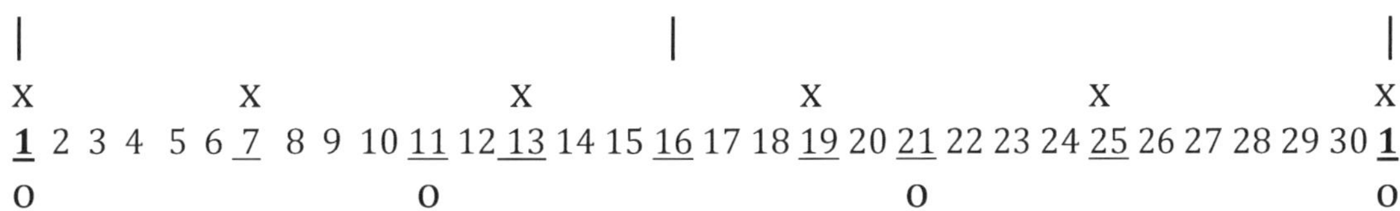

In this example the | represents the metric beats, o represents the quintuplet eighth notes, and x represents the triplet quarter notes. All the numbers where PNKs occur are underlined. You may note that with all mixed rhythms there will be a halfway point – in this case the number 16 – where the first half mirrors the second half. You need the next 1 after 30, where all the elements meet again, to see the mirror.

We now have a picture that shows how to practice this rhythm. As before, we first establish a primary rhythm with the fastest beat division – the quintuplets. Set the metronome at about 92bpm for the quintuplet 8ths. While tapping an even five with the right hand on the x's, tap the o's with the left hand.

The first o goes with the first x.
The second o is just a bit before the third x.
The third o is just a bit after the fourth x.
When you tap the final 1 - with x and o together - it is the same as the first 1, so repeat the set from there.

As you practice this you gradually emphasize the slower triplets until you begin to feel them as even and they become the primary rhythm. It may be difficult to hear whether the triplets are even until you get the quintuplets to ca. 120 bpm. As mentioned earlier, walking the slower triplets and tapping the quintuplets is a very good way to practice. When both beat divisions are even you have accomplished your goal. Check yourself by setting your metronome first for the quintuplets and then for the triplets.

The third element in the LCM – the two metric beats – are not articulated in the piano composition mentioned above. Therefore, as long as the tempo is similar to that of the rest of the piece, it is not a problem. Even if it was articulated it would be fairly easy to place it halfway between the 3rd and 4th quintuplets.

Odd *vs.* Even Tuplets

An odd tuplet number means the tuplets are *shorter* than regular beat divisions, while an even tuplet number means the tuplets are *longer* than regular beat divisions. You may have already figured that out.

Also, when the tuplet number reaches a power of 2, the notes are no longer tuplets but are regular beat divisions of *half the value of the tuplets at their regular* (non-tuplet) *value. I. e.,* if the tuplets are triplet eighth notes at 3 to a beat, 4 notes to a beat would be a regular division represented by sixteenth notes. After 4 sixteenth notes to a beat there would be 5, 6, and 7 sixteenth note tuplets up to 8, the next power of 2. At 8 there would be 8 regular thirty-second notes to a beat, followed by 9 to 15 thirty-second note tuplets etc. See Example 20-T below.

Example 20-T

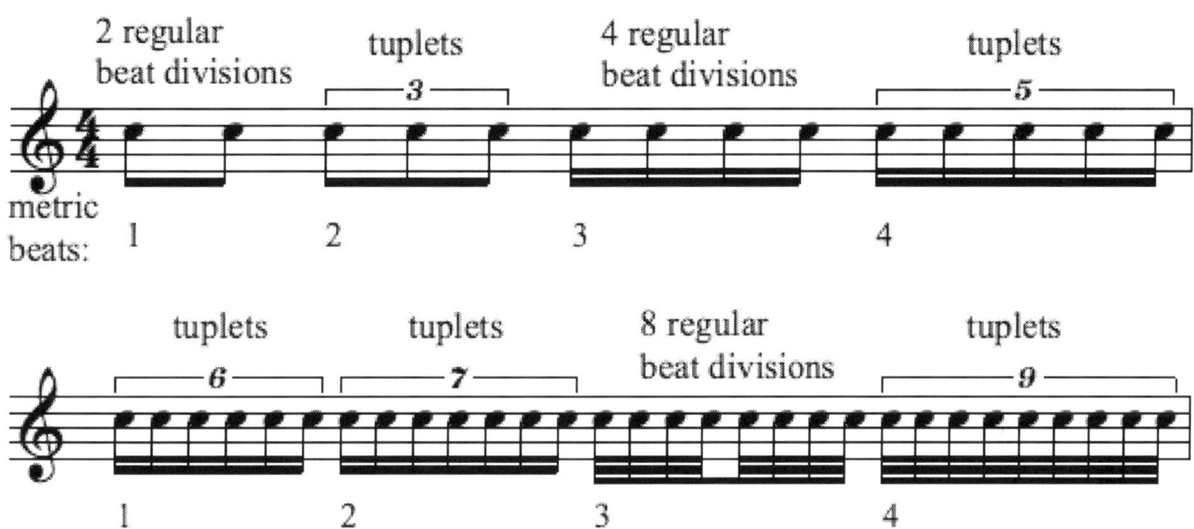

To determine the proper tuplet value for an irregular beat division of 11 tuplets over 2 metric beats in X/4 meter:

1. Determine the next power of 2 below the number of tuplets. The next power of 2 below 11 is 8.

2. Find the value of the regular (non-tuplet) beat division notes it would take to fill the allotted metric beats. It takes 8 regular (non-tuplet) sixteenth notes fill 2 beats in X/4 meter.

3. If it takes 8 regular sixteenth notes to fill 2 beats, it will take 11 tuplet sixteenth notes to fill 2 beats.

After you are confident with 2 against 3 and 3 against 4 experiment with other mixed rhythms. As a performer be aware of the expressive intents of the rhythmic aspects of your music. If you are a composer include rhythm as an important part of your creativity, not just as a novelty but as a truly expressive device.

Computer exercises 20.1 & 20.2

Chapter 21
The Tritone
The Leading Tone
Key Context
Tritones and Key Contexts
New PNKs

The Tritone

The tritone is an augmented 4th or it's inversion, a diminished 5th. The tritone encompasses 3 whole tones (aka whole steps), which is why it is called a tritone. In any major key there is only one tritone which consists of the 4th and 7th scale degrees. All other 4ths and 5ths in a major key are perfect.

1. The tritone includes the last entry in the KS and the natural which would be next in the order of sharps or flats. (Very useful information.)

Computer exercise 21.1

---

2. In a major key the two PNKs of the tritone are the 3rd and 7th of the V7 chord.

Confirm these 2 statements in Example 21-A below by writing the major keynote and notes of the V7 chord on the lines below each tritone.

Example 21-A: tritones

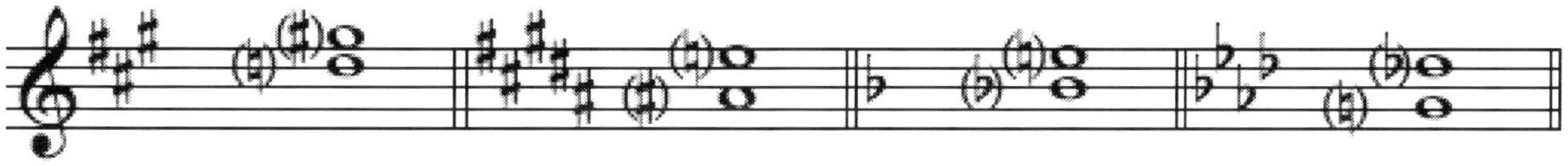

major key: A ______ ______ ______

notes of the
V7 chord: e g# b d ________ ________ ________

Notice that the 2nd tritone (a diminished 5th) and the 3rd tritone (an augmented 4th) are the same pitches spelled enharmonically. The major keynotes are at opposite points on the circle of keys. All tritones can be respelled enharmonically to take you half way around the circle of keys.

The tritone splits the octave in half – an octave is 12 half steps, the tritone is 6 half steps. The tritone is difficult to sing in tune and has been called "The devil in music" for that reason. It is an unstable, dissonant interval that wants to be resolved.

There are 2 half steps in a major scale – from the 3rd to the 4th scale degrees and from the 7th to the 1st scale degrees. The tritone in a major key includes two of those scale degrees – 7 and 4 - and wants to resolve to the other two – 1 and 3 - which are the root and 3rd of the tonic triad. See Example 21-B below.

Example 21-B

In a <u>minor</u> scale the downward resolution of the subdominant scale degree to the 3rd of the minor tonic triad is a whole step. However, the frequent alteration of the *final* tonic triad to a major triad with the raised Picardy 3rd (see Chapter 17) makes that resolution a half step also. Many minor compositions end with a Picardy 3rd. See Example 21-C below.

Example 21-C

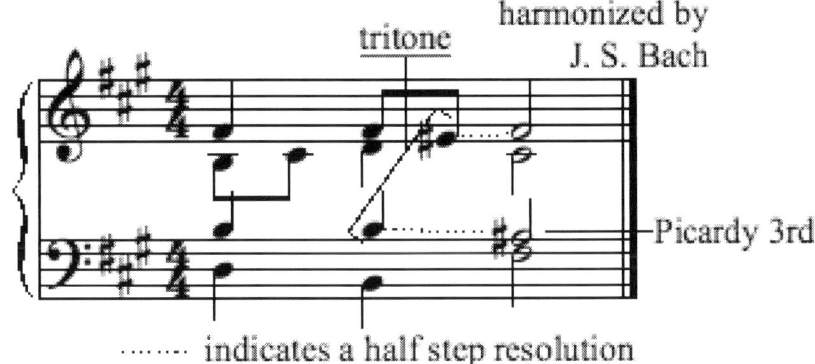

A harmonic minor scale has two tritones – from the 4th scale degree to the raised 7th and from the 2nd scale degree to the not raised 6th. See example 21-D below.

Example 21-D: 2 tritones in G harmonic minor.

When sounded together these two tritones produce a diminished 7th chord with the leading tone as root. (This is discussed in more detail in Chapter 22.)

In its resolution, the root, 3rd, and 7th of the diminished 7th chord can all resolve by half step to the root, 3rd and 5th of the minor tonic chord. In an authentic cadence with a Picardy 3rd in the tonic chord, the root, 5th and 7th can all resolve by half step to the root, 3rd and 5th of the major tonic chord. See Example 21-E below.

Example 21-E

resolution of a diminished
7th chord in minor

G♯o Am G♯o A

Picardy 3rd

A min: viio7 i viio7 I♯3

……indicates half step resolutions

The Leading Tone

Many theory books put strong emphasis on the role of the leading tone to resolve up by half step into tonic. The name "leading tone" itself implies that tendency. From the time of the Baroque period on, composers have routinely raised the 7th degree of the minor scale to provide a leading tone in a minor key just as in major. This reinforces the tonal center of the music.

It is interesting to note that Bach did not always find it necessary to resolve the leading tone up by half step into the tonic, at least not in the same voice. 57 out of 61 of the Bach Chorales end with an authentic cadence (V or V7 to I). Of those 57 authentic cadences, 41 of them have *unresolved* (in the same voice) leading tones – the 3rd of the V chord . The leading tone *does not* progress up by half step to tonic. However, all of the chorales that end with a V7 to I authentic cadence have the subdominant PNK – the 7th of the V7 which is the second PNK of the tritone - resolving down to the 3rd of the final tonic chord as it is "supposed" to.

The V7 chord includes a tritone which makes it want to resolve to I. All the tritones and their resolutions in the example below are in the G clef. The Augmented 4ths all *expand* by half steps and the diminished 5ths all *contract* by half steps into the roots and 3rds of the tonic triads which follow.

Example 21-F

tritones & resolutions

Computer exercise 21.2

Key Context

The term "key signature" implies a tonal center. The key of D minor has a key signature (KS) of 1 flat and the tonal center is D. A "key context" is a set of sharps or flats in the same order as in a KS but often a different number from the KS and often implying a different tonal center from the KS. Key context is a useful concept when dealing with accidentals that change the *context* of the sets of sharps or flats while the KS remains the same.

A key context does not appear on a music score, as does a KS, but is deduced from the KS or the accidentals which represent a departure from the KS. Key context is especially useful when discussing tritones or the modes. The key of A major exists in a key context of 3 sharps. The keys of B Dorian, C♯ Phrygian, D Lydian, E Mixolydian, F♯ Aeolian, and G♯ Locrian also exist in a key context of 3 sharps. Confirm that. (Ref. Chapters 7 and 24.)

Tritones and Key Contexts

A tritone defines a key context. *E. g.,* for a composition in the key of A Major with a KS of 3 sharps, the tritone is G♯ and D♮. G♯ is the 3rd sharp in the order of sharps, thereby signifying *at least* 3 sharps in the key context. D♮ is the next in the order of sharps signifying there are *no more than* 3 sharps in the key context. The tritone G♯ and D♮ = a key context of 3 sharps.

We don't hear key signatures, we hear key contexts. But only if we have heard both PNKs of a tritone. The following excerpt from a Bach Chorale is in the key of A major, but our ears don't know we are in a key context of 3♯s until we get to beat 2 of the first full bar. We have heard the C♯and the D♮ in the pickup PNKs. The C♯ tells us we have at least 2 sharps and the D♮ tells us there are no more than 3 sharps, but until we hear the G♯, the second PNK of the tritone with D♮, we could be in a key context of 2 or 3 sharps.

Example 21-G

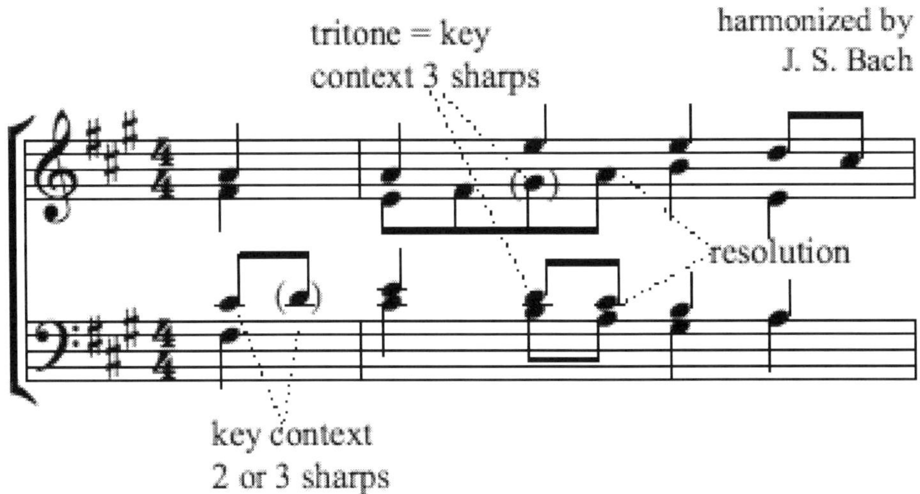

From the Baroque period to the present we find music that can change key contexts quite frequently or maintain the same key context for many bars. The chorale excerpted above changes key contexts 18 times in its 12 bars. The well-known "Ein feste Burg ist unser Gott," aka "A Mighty Fortress Is Our God" is 16 bars long with only 14 changes of key context – 4 changes in the first 8 bars and 10 in the second 8 bars.

New PNKs

Accidentals that occur in major and minor tonal centered music introduce "new PNKs" into a key context. An accidental is any ♯, ♭, or ♮ which is different from the KS and therefore introduces a new tritone and a new key context.

Example 21-H

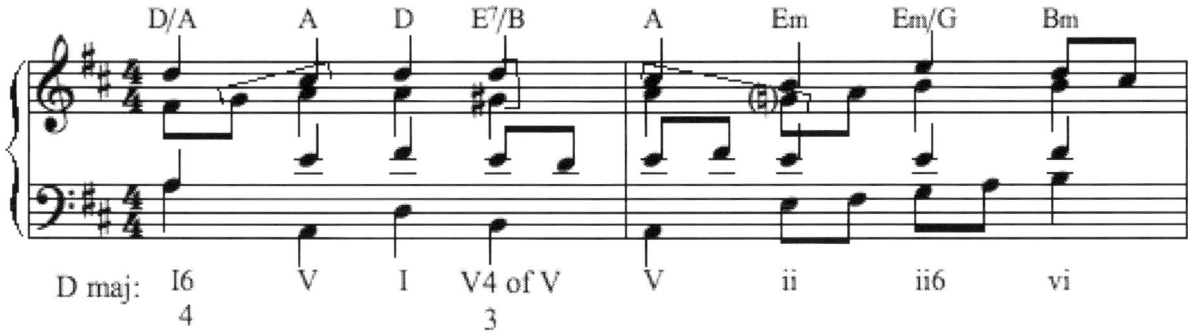

The 3 tritones in the above example are bracketed. The G♮ and C♯ in the first two beats of the first bar create a key context of 2♯. The G♯ in beat 4 of the first bar is a new PNK. Along with the D♮ it forms a tritone and a key context of 3♯. The chord is the V7 chord borrowed from the key of A. Not surprisingly the tonic chord of A major follows. We remain in the key of A major (key context of 3♯) until another new PNK G♮, on beat 2 of bar 2, creates a tritone with C♯ and brings us back to a key context of 2♯.

As stated earlier, a tritone identifies a key context. That key context remains until a new PNK changes it. If the key context is 3 sharps and a C♮ is heard, the C♮ cancels all the sharps following it in the order of sharps, resulting in a new key context of 1 sharp, as in Example 21-I below.

Example 21-I

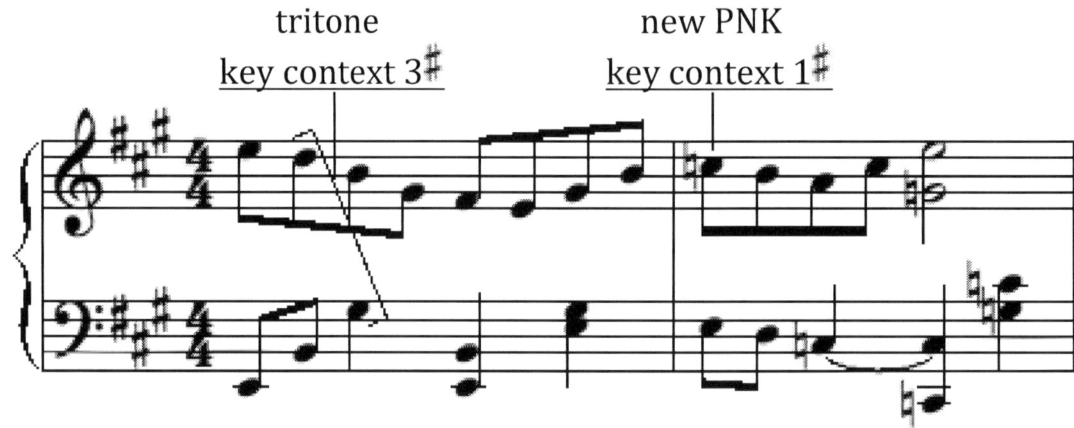

It would be tempting to say that the cadence on the C major chord on beat 3 of bar 2 has established the key of C major with a key context of no sharps or flats, but the G♯ in bar 1 established a key context of 3♯ followed by the C♮ which canceled all the sharps except F. If the next harmony we hear is a G7 chord then no sharps or flats would be confirmed at that point with the new PNK F♮, but a D7 chord with an F♯ would establish a key context of 1♯.

As stated earlier, we don't hear key signatures, we hear key contexts. The key context is not established until we hear both PNKs of a tritone (not necessarily at the same time) *or* a new PNK that doesn't fit the current key context and thereby changing it.

In Example 21-J below there are four chord progressions with new PNKs, new tritones, and changing key contexts. The new PNKs are identified by the accidentals. (Learn to identify the meanings of accidentals in your repertoire as more than just what PNKs to play and/or sing.) The tritones are enclosed in brackets. The first tritone in each bar identifies the key context, which is the same as the KS. Subsequent brackets enclose new tritones. Study each progression to understand and confirm the tritones, new PNKs, and key contexts.

Example 21-J

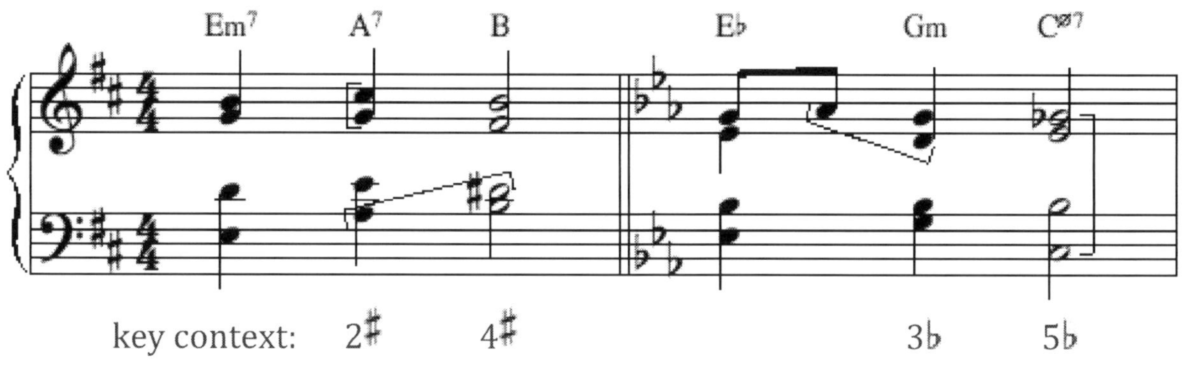

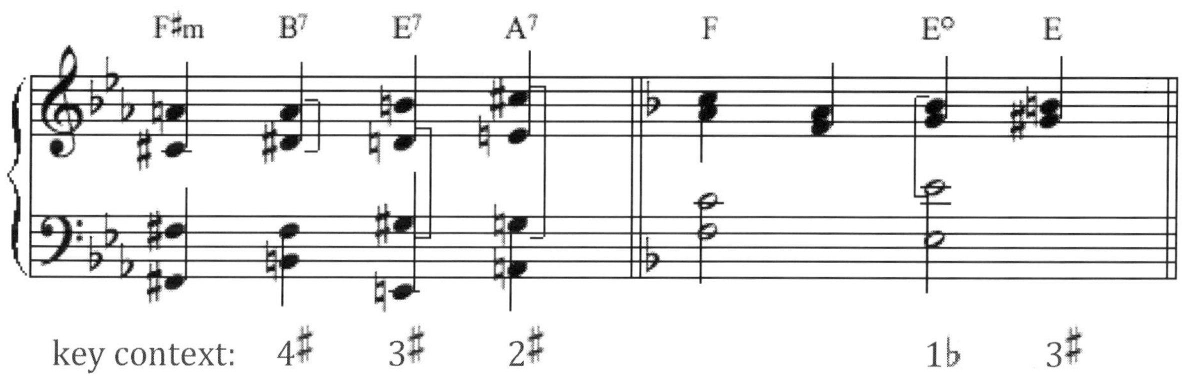

Computer exercise 21.3

Exercise

In your repertoire or in a hymn book identify new PNKs and determine the key contexts. Check for the correct spelling of accidentals. The correct spelling is that which is closest to the preceding key context. A new PNK/accidental A♯ after a key context of 1 sharp would be better spelled as a B♭. From 1 sharp to 5 sharps is a change of 4 steps while 1 sharp to 1 flat is only 2. However, from a melodic standpoint an ascending melody note is usually written with sharps and a descending one with flats. It is possible the two considerations could conflict, which will require an informed choice. Learn to identify the harmonic and melodic meanings of accidentals in your repertoire.

A new PNK does not necessarily introduce a *significant* change of key context. Once again we're dealing with value judgments that can vary with individual listeners. Even so it would probably be safe to say that all the new PNKs of the chromatic passing tones in Example 21-K below are not rhythmically nor dynamically strong enough to effect a change of key context or a new tonal center. The harmonic support in the F-clef clearly maintains the tonal center of D major and a key context of 2 sharps. The effect is similar to the NCTs that don't change the chord but are heard as outside of the chord. We could call them NKCTs – Non Key Context Tones. (But we won't.)

Example 21-K

An interesting series of changing key contexts is in Example 21-L below. It is part of an instrumental interlude for a George and Ira Gershwin jazz song from 1959 titled "The Real American Folk Song."

Example 21-L

In the first 2 bars the notes in the G clef are a series of tritones descending by half steps. Every other tritone is spelled as a diminished 5th followed by an augmented 4th a half step lower. Coupled with the F clef notes each beat consists of a dominant 7th chord with the 5th missing. The chords are in a dominant-to-tonic circle progression – up a 4th, down a 5th. Each chord gives us a new tritone, a new key context, and a new tonal center. Identify the key context for each chord. If there was one more chord what would it be?

Example 21-M below shows this progression moving completely around the circle of major keys.

Example 21-M

Notice that if you move from any chord to 6 chords ahead in the progression you will find the same tritone with one note respelled enharmonically and you will have moved half way around the circle of major keys.

Exercise

Play the progression in Example 21-M at the keyboard, without the notes. At one of the enharmonic keys at 5:00, 6:00 or 7:00 you move from the outside to the inside of the circle and instead of adding one flat with each move you will subtract one sharp. As you play be aware of the changing key contexts and the changing intervals of the tritones.

Chapter 22

Crossed Key Contexts
Augmented Triads and Diminished 7th Chords
Minor Keys and Crossed Key Contexts
Sharpest and Flattest PNKs
Root Definitive Intervals
The Diminished 7th Chord

Crossed Key Contexts

It is possible to have a crossed key context. A crossed key context occurs when you have PNKs sounding at the same time which cannot be accommodated in one key context.

1. Any 2 PNKs sounding together can be notated in a single key context.

2. You never need more than 2 key contexts to accommodate any combination of PNKs.

See if you can confirm those two statements before reading further. We are working with equal temperament, which means that enharmonic spellings of PNKs are considered equivalent C♯ is the same as D♭.

For statement #1: Every possible equal tempered interval – any 2 PNKs - can be notated enharmonically with the PNKs of some major scale, *i. e.*, in one key context. Therefore, any 2 PNKs can be spelled enharmonically to fit into at least 1 and up to 6 key contexts. Example 22-A below gives a few of the *infinite* possible spellings of some intervals and their simplified enharmonic equivalents.

Example 22-A

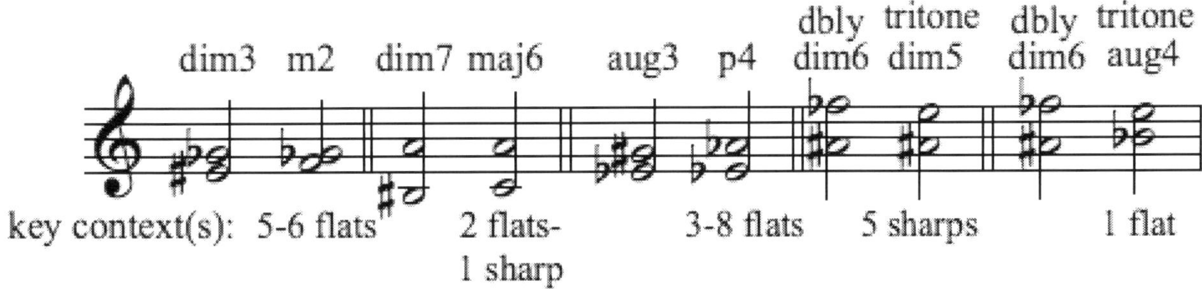

Confirm the possible key contexts of all the second intervals in each bar above. *E. g.,* for the first measure:

> Since F♯ is the first sharp in the order of sharps, the F♮ cannot exist in a key context with sharps. Since F♭ is the seventh flat in the order of flats, the F♮ can exist in a key context of 1 to 6 flats. F♮ can exist in a key context of all♮ or 1 – 6 flats.
>
> Since G♭ is the fifth flat in the order of flats it can exist in a key context of 5 to 7 flats.

The PNKs F♮ and G♭ can exist together only in the key contexts of 5 or 6 flats.

For statement # 2 (page 207): You only need the keys of C major (key context of all♮) and D♭ major (key context of 5♭) to accommodate all 12 PNKs of a chromatic scale. No matter what combination of PNKs are sounding they can all be included in these two key contexts.

The importance of this information is the fact that we tend to comprehend sensory input in its simplest form. I won't take the time and space required to present the pros and cons of that discussion, but I, for one, accept it. When we hear a combination of musical pitches we notice "new PNKs" in their simplest interpretation. We don't hear combinations of pitches in 3 or more different key contexts when their enharmonic equivalents can be interpreted in a simpler setting of 1 or 2 key contexts. It behooves the composer, analyst, and music publisher to notate music in it simplest form, not only for accuracy as to seeing what we hear, but for easier comprehension by the performer. For a very practical example see Example 22-B below taken from a publication.

Example 22-B

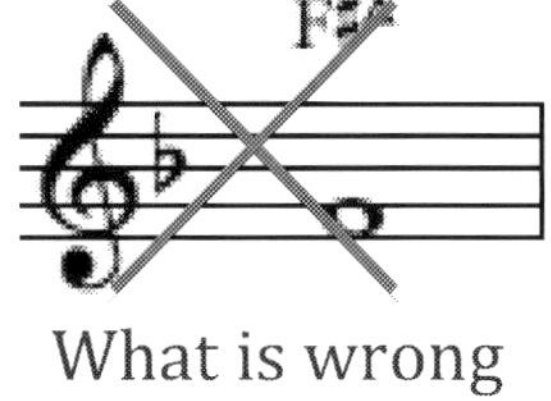

What is wrong
with this picture?

What you see on the left is misspelled as a crossed key context. The melody note is F♮ and the chord is F♯Δ. It will *sound* like an F♯Δ chord with the melody pitch F♮ as the major 7th, but playing it is going to be confusing if you know that an F♯Δ chord has an E♯ for the 7th, not an F♮. You're also trying to justify the F♮ with an F♯ chord root. While you're trying to figure all that out the unstoppable beats have progressed to the next bar. I'm happy to report that this type of mistake is not often found in published music. Don't let it creep into yours.

Augmented Triads and Diminished 7th Chords

There are two fairly common chords that require crossed key contexts - the augmented triad and the diminished 7th chord. You can't notate either of these two chords without an accidental. See Examples 22-C & D below.

Example 22-C

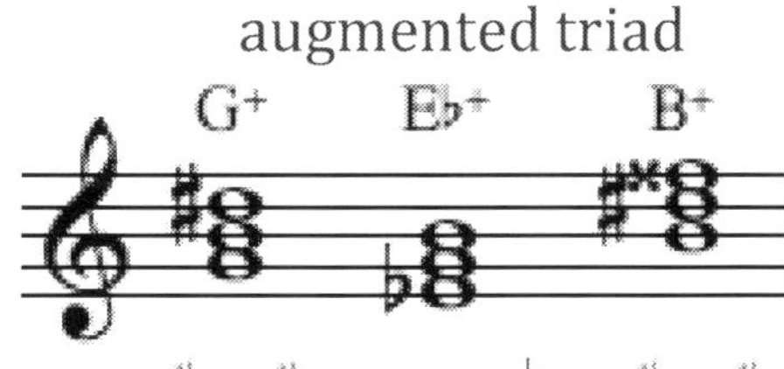

crossed key contexts: 2♯/4♯ 2♭/all♮ 6♯/8♯

In this example the G augmented triad includes D♯. G♯ is number 3 in the order of sharps so the G♮ cannot exist in a key context with more than 2 sharps. D♯ is number 4 in the order of sharps. Therefore these 2 PNKs require a crossed key context of 2♯/4♯. Without the presence of the B♮ the D♯ could be respelled enharmonically as E♭ with a key context of 2 flats which would include both G and E♭, but with the B♮ the E♭ gives a crossed key context of all♮/2♭. With G spelled as F𝄪 the key context is a minimum of 8 sharps and B♮ requires a maximum of 6 sharps.

Example 22-D: diminished 7th chord

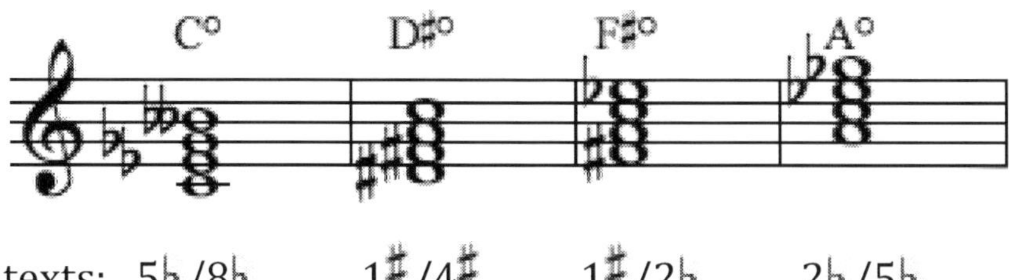

crossed key contexts: 5♭/8♭ 1♯/4♯ 1♯/2♭ 2♭/5♭

The diminished 7th chords in Example 22-D are the same chord respelled enharmonically. The B𝄫 and C♮ require a crossed key context of 5♭/8♭. With the E♭ respelled as D♯ the C♮ gives a crossed key context of 1♯/4♯. With D♯ spelled as E♭ the F♯ and give a crossed key context of 1♯/2♭. With the F♯ respelled enharmonically as G♭, the A♮ gives a crossed key context of 2♭/5♭.

The augmented triad and the diminished 7th chords divide the octave into, 3 and 4 equal parts respectively. The augmented triad divides the octave into 2 major 3rds plus a diminished 4th (enharmonic with a major 3rd), the diminished 7th chord divides the octave into 3 minor 3rds and an augmented 2nd (enharmonic with a minor 3rd.)

> Since: the intervals of these two chords, measured in half steps, are the same, regardless of the inversion of the chords,
>
> therefore: any PNK of the chords can function as the (notated) root,
>
> and therefore: with enharmonic spellings there are only four different augmented triads and only three different diminished 7th chords.

You're probably wishing you had learned that before you practiced each of them around the circle on 12 different roots. Not to worry. Your practice time wasn't wasted. You will need to recognize and play them with all 12 different roots because that's how you'll find them notated in music. These two chords are handy for changing tonal centers to other keys, *i. e.* a modulation. The V+ has a strong urge to resolve to tonic, probably equal to the V7 chord. See Example 22-E below for the enharmonic spelling of one augmented triad progressing to 3 different tonic triads.

Example 22-E

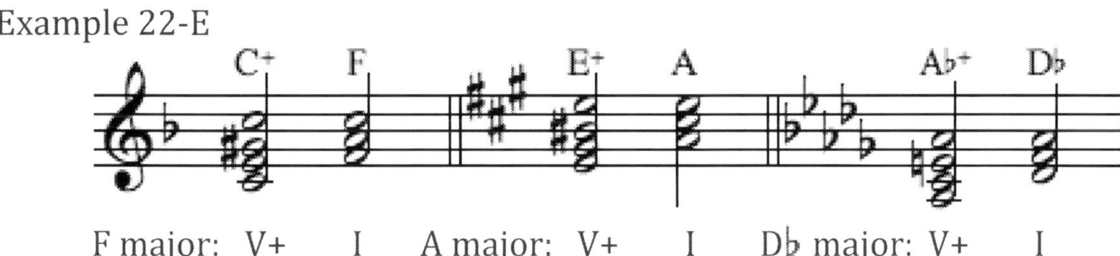

In the key of C major if you alter the I, IV, or V chord to I+, IV+, or V+ to function as secondary dominants, you can progress to 7 other keys of the circle with just one move. The root and third of each of the three enharmonic spellings of the V+, I+, and IV+ triads function as dominant and leading tone of another key. See Example 22-G below.

Example 22-G

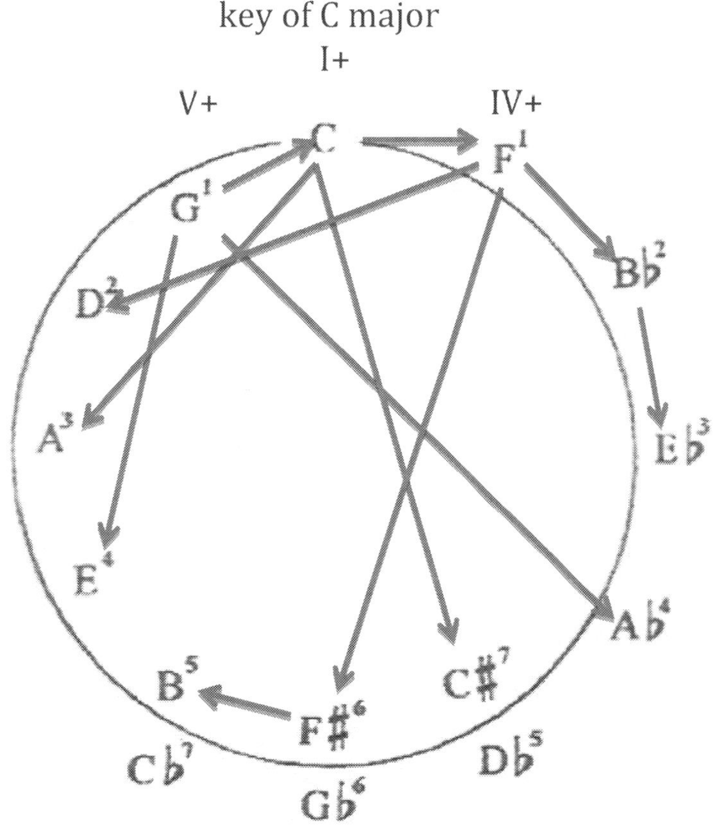

For the two keys that are left – E♭ and B – one more step from their dominants makes them accessible.

It is worth noting that in the major/minor tonal system, the augmented triad occurs only on the mediant of the minor key, with the raised leading tone as the 5th of the chord. If the root of the chord is respelled enharmonically as a raised supertonic instead of the mediant it would become a V+ chord. Regardless of the spelling it resolves well to tonic. When progressing to a minor tonic chord the +5th is a common PNC with the 3rd of the tonic chord. See Example 22-F below.

Example 22-F

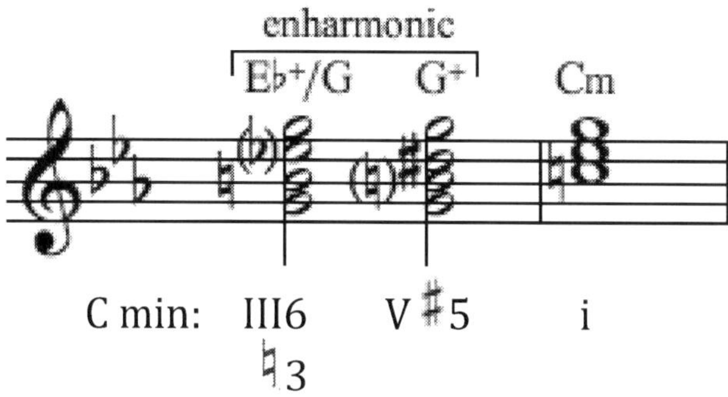

Minor Keys and Crossed Key Contexts

The accidentals in the two minor keys mean they can exist only in a crossed key context. For the harmonic minor the raised 7th scale degree requires a key context of 3 more sharps or 3 fewer flats than the 6th scale degree. For the ascending melodic minor the difference between the 7th and 3rd scale degrees is 2 more sharps or 2 fewer flats. See Example 22-H below.

Example 22-H

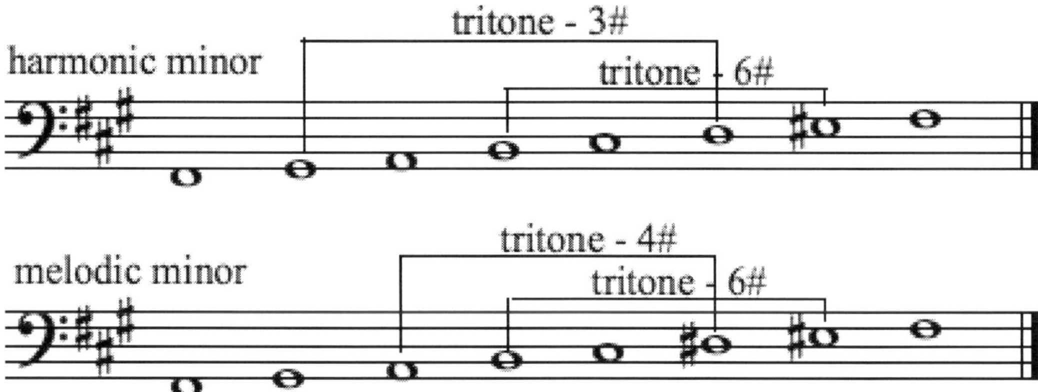

The 2 tritones in the harmonic minor sounded together result in a diminished 7 chord. The 2 tritones in the melodic minor sounded together result in an inverted V7♭5 (aka French augmented 6th chord discussed in Chapter 25).

Sharpest and Flattest PNKs

The "sharpest" PNK in any key – major or minor – is the leading tone of the key with the strongest tendency to resolve up a half step. In a major key it is the last ♯ in the KS or the ♮ which would be next in the order of flats from the last ♭ in the KS. In the crossed key context of a minor key, the raised leading tone will indicate "no more than (<=)" for sharps and "no fewer than (>=)" for flats, which is equivalent to saying "This is the *sharpest* (or *least flat)* PNK in the key." See Example 22-I below.

Example 22-I: Sharpest PNKs/Leading Tones

D maj: B♭maj: E mi: C mi:

The "flattest" PNK in a major key is the subdominant with the strongest tendency to resolve down a half step. Along with the leading tone this flattest PNK and sharpest PNK comprise the tritone, which wants to resolve by half steps to the root and 3rd of the tonic triad.

In a minor key the flattest PNK is somewhat problematical. In the harmonic minor the augmented 2nd between the submediant (the flattest PNK) and the raised leading tone (the sharpest PNK) wants to expand. These 2 PNKs resolve outward by half steps to the root and 5th of the tonic triad. This resolution is felt quite strongly if the submediant is positioned as the flatted 7th of a vii°7 chord or a flatted 9th added to a V7 chord and resolving to the 5th of the tonic chord. See Example 22-J below.

Example 22-J

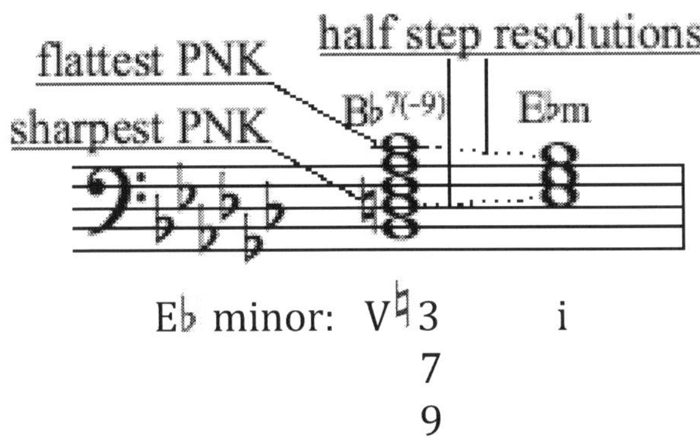

In a melodic minor key the raised submediant means the flattest PNK is now the mediant – the 3rd of the tonic triad – and is not involved in any resolution in a V7 to I progression.

The harmonic tension of the tritone between the subdominant and the raised leading tone would still be felt in the V7 chord of a minor key, even though another PNK is flatter than the subdominant. Also, in a final cadence with a Picardy 3rd in the tonic triad, the subdominant PNK would resolve down by half step to the raised 3rd, just as in a major key.

For most of the borrowed dominants (see Chapter 11) a new sharpest PNK is introduced as the 3rd of the chord and is the leading tone of the borrowed key. In the case of the V7 of IV, a new flattest PNK is the 7th of the V7 and is the subdominant of the borrowed key. See Example 22-K below.

Example 22-K

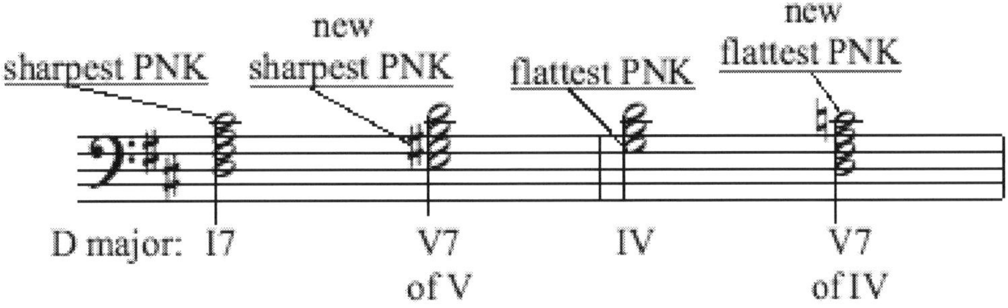

It is not necessary to hear augmented and diminished intervals in a chord, *i. e.*, sounded simultaneously, to feel their harmonic tension. When you are oriented to the environment of a major or minor tonal center the memory of a PNK's urge to resolve may persist until a delayed resolution occurs or the tonal center and/or key context changes.

Example 22-L

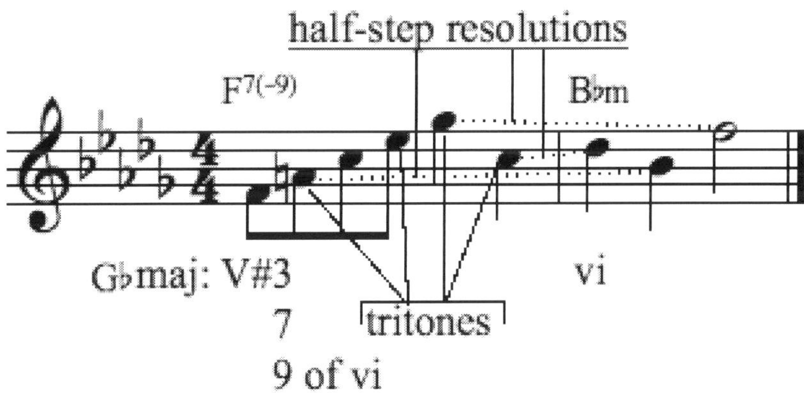

Recognizing these sharpest and flattest PNKs in your repertoire helps you to keep track of key contexts and shifting tonal centers and gives you some powerful material for poignant expression in your music.

Computer exercise 22.1

Root Definitive Intervals

The perfect 5th and its inversion the perfect 4th, are recognized as root definitive intervals (RDI). For the perfect 5th the lower PNK is heard as the root, *i. e.,* the acoustic root. For the perfect 4th the upper PNK is the root.

The overtone series gives support to the concept of RDI. The first 4 partials include the intervals of the perfect 5th and perfect 4th. These 2 intervals have an octave of the fundamental as the root PNK of these RDIs. See Example 22-M below.

Example 22-M

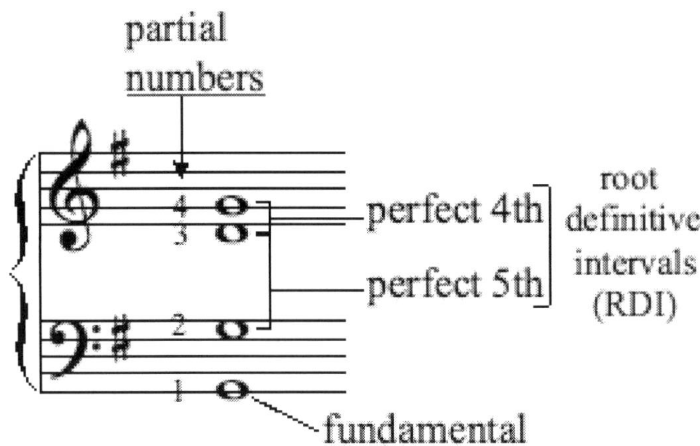

There is no cause/effect *proof* that the fundamental is felt as the root of these intervals *because* it is the fundamental, but it is at least a parallel phenomenon to the feeling of rootness.

When listening to various chords and their inversions it is necessary to identify the root in order to determine quality and positions of the chords. Practice with the RDIs can be a big help in that process. For a major or minor triad in root position the root will be at the bottom of the perfect 5th. For an inverted triad the root will be at the top of the perfect 4th.

A tonal combination can have more than one RDI. In such cases the perfect 5th is considered stronger than the perfect 4th. With two equally strong RDIs, the lowest sounding root will prevail.

The Diminished 7th Chord

The diminished 7th chord has no RDI. However for the convenience of identifying positions/inversions of the diminished 7th chord we refer to its various PNKs as root, 3rd, 5th, and 7th. Without a RDI neither the diminished triad nor the diminished 7th chord play a role in *root* progressions. However the resolution tendencies of the diminished 5ths/augmented 4ths are effective in *chord* and *melodic* progressions.

As stated earlier the augmented triad and the diminished 7th chord divide the octave into equal sections, so that by spelling them enharmonically we can call any of the PNKs the root. Without a harmonic context it is not possible to *hear* whether a diminished 7th chord or an augmented triad are inverted or in root position. Example 22-N below shows 1 diminished 7th chord spelled enharmonically with 4 different roots.

Example 22-N

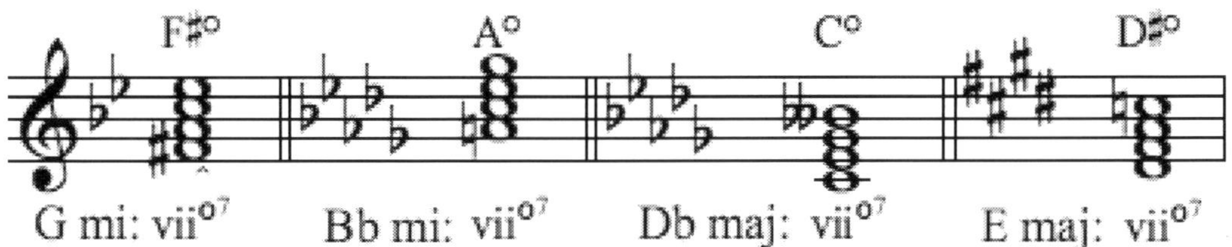

You will find the diminished 7th chord in both major and minor keys. Remember that the diminished 7th chord can exist only in a crossed key context and therefore requires an accidental. For the vii°7 in a minor key the accidental is the raised 7th PNK of the scale which provides the leading tone and is the chord root. For the vii°7 in a major key the accidental is the lowered submediant which is the 7th of the chord.

As stated earlier, with enharmonic spellings there are only 3 different diminished 7th chords. See Example 22-O below.

Example 22-0

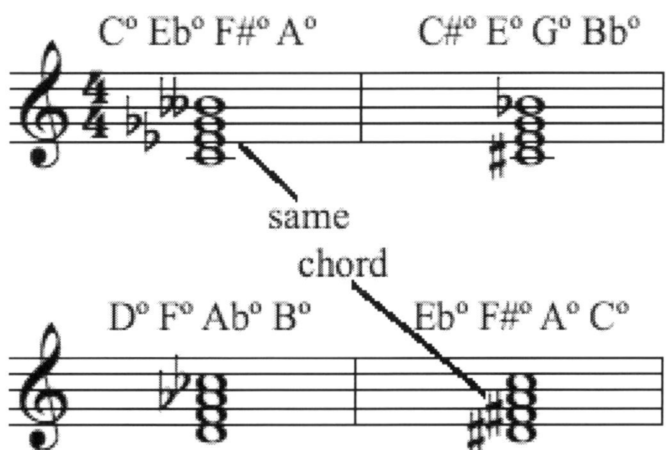

The first three chords in the above example include all 12 PNKs of the chromatic scale. Since any PNK of a diminished 7th chord can function as the root, these 3 chords can serve as all 15 diminished 7th chords and progress to the tonic chords of all 30 major and minor keys.

Exercise

Play each of the 4 augmented triads, considering each PNK in turn as the root, in 3 different V+ to I progressions. Then play all 3 diminished seventh chords and resolve each PNK of the three up a half step to the root of a tonic chord in 4 different vii°7 to I progressions. Then go around the circle playing an augmented triad on the dominant and resolving it to tonic. Then play a diminished 7th chord on the leading tone of each key followed by the tonic chord. Use various inversions for smooth moves. You want to learn the flexibility of these two chords in all keys. The enharmonic spellings of an augmented triad and a diminished 7th chord with their resolutions are given in Example 22-P below.

Example 22-P

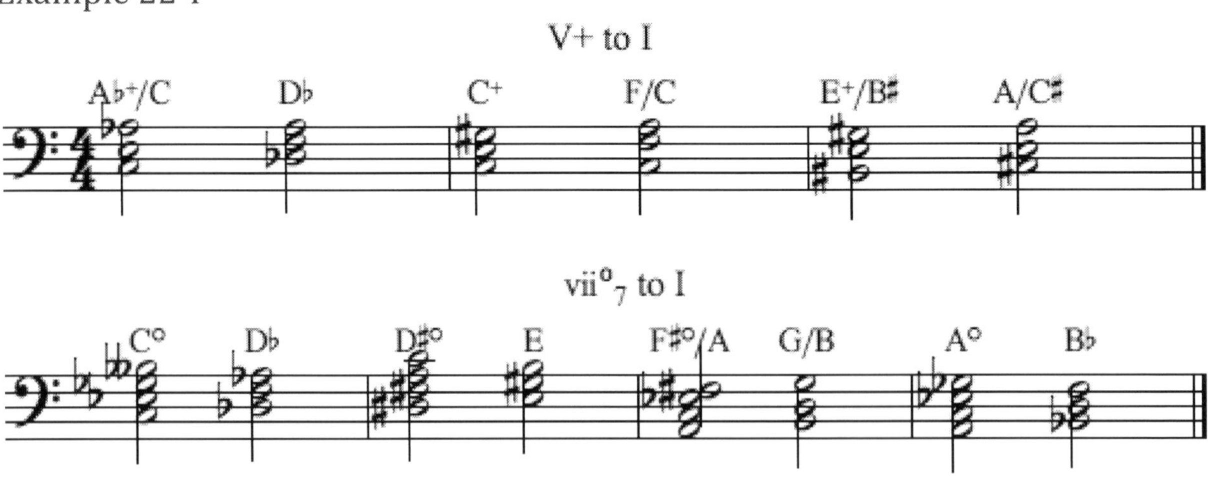

Computer exercises 22.2 & 22.3

Chapter 23
Closely Related Keys
Transposition *vs.* Borrowed Chords
Common Chord Transposition
"Theoretical" Keys

Closely Related Keys

After the Baroque period, composers have produced works that strayed further and further away from a tonal center. As in any art the creators are going to push the envelope. If the envelope is pushed too far so that the recognition of a tonal center is no longer felt, the gravitational pull toward other pitches is lost. The music can lose its sense of harmonic direction. The point at which this loss occurs depends on the experiences of the listener. Just as with the increasing use of dissonance over time, the tolerance for wandering further from the tonal center without losing the feel for that center has increased.

During the Baroque period the limit of distance from the original key of the composition was almost if not entirely restricted to the closely related keys. A major or minor key is closely related to other major or minor keys with a KS not more than one sharp or one flat different. C major is closely related to D minor (1♭), E minor (1♯), F major (1♭), G major (1♯), and A minor (all♮ which is the relative minor).

An easy way to find the keys closely related to a major key is to consider the triads with roots on the first 6 PNKs of the scale. The IV and V chords of a major key are major, and the closely related keys of the subdominant and dominate are also major. The ii, iii, and vi chords of a major key are minor, and the closely related keys of the supertonic, mediant, and submediant are also minor. See Example 23-A below.

Example 23-A

	major scale degree	triad type	key signature
closely	6	mi	(same-relative minor)
	5	maj	+1♯ or -1♭
related	4	maj	+1♭ or -1♯
	3	mi	+1♯ or -1♭
keys	2	mi	+1♭ or -1♯
original key:	1	maj	(original KS)

This principle is applied to the key of E♭ major in Example 23-B below.

Example 23-B

	major scale degree	closely related key	key signature
closely	6	C mi	3♭ (relative minor)
	5	B♭maj	2♭
related	4	A♭maj	4♭
	3	G mi	2♭
keys	2	F mi	4♭
E♭maj	1	E♭ maj	3♭

For minor keys the closely related keys will be the same as for their relative majors. In Example 23-B above, all the keys closely related to C minor are the same as those closely related to E♭ major. Or you could consider the triads on the *descending* minor scale from tonic to mediant (with no accidentals). See Example 23-C below.

Example 23-C

	minor scale degree	triad type	key signature
original key:	1	mi	(original)
closely	7	maj	+1♯/-1♭
	6	maj	+1♭/-1♯
related	5	mi	+1♯/-1♭
	4	mi	+1♭/-1♯
keys	3	maj	(same-relative major)

Computer exercise 23.1

Transposition *vs.* Borrowed Chords

In a composition the reference to a closely related key can be extensive or brief. It can be a transposition lasting several bars or just a single new PNK. See Example 23-D below.

Example 23-D

Erhalt' mein Hertz im Glauben rein

harmonized by
J. S. Bach

The key identifications and brackets under the music in Example 23-D are not chord analysis but indications of the keys/ key contexts.

All the new PNKs in this example are in parentheses. The first new PNK is the D♯ in the second bar in the bass. It adds 1 sharp to the key context and is the leading tone of E major. The half cadence in bar 2, beat 3 and the authentic cadence in bar 4, beat 3 confirm the key of E major. The 3-bar length justifies labeling it a transposition.

The next new PNK - E♯ - on the second half of beat 2 in bar 5 is the leading tone of F♯ minor, the relative minor, and is immediately followed by the F♯ minor tonic chord. The E♯ leading tone is quickly canceled with an E♮, followed by A♯ as the leading tone of B minor which is followed by the B minor tonic triad. It too is soon canceled by an A♮. These are very brief references to these two closely related keys and would not qualify as transpositions. The chords that contain these accidentals which create leading tones are better referred to as <u>borrowed dominants</u>, aka <u>secondary dominants</u>, borrowed from a closely related key. Similarly, two references to the dominant key are the 2 D♯s in the final 2 measures, each quickly followed by a D♮. They are also borrowed dominants rather than transpositions.

How many beats or bars are required to justify a transposition? Another judgment call. A pretty good indicator of a transposition is a cadence. If a new key context lasts until a cadence in the new key, it can probably be called a transposition. On the other hand, if the final cadence chord contained the first appearance of the new PNK/new key context and the next beat cancelled the new PNK I would call that a cadence on a borrowed dominant.

Example 23-E

The C♯ in bar 2 is a new PNK in a key context of all♮. It is the leading tone of the supertonic key of D minor. The chord which follows is the V7 of the dominant key. The 7th of that chord replaces the C♯ with a C♮. With such a short duration of the C♯, the A chord on beat 1 has been labeled as a borrowed dominant - V of ii.

From beat 4 in bar 2 the music stays in the key context of 1♯/G major through bar 4, which probably justifies calling this portion of the piece a transposition. The new PNK F♮ in bar 5, beat 1 returns it to all♮/C Major until the end.

Common Chord Transposition

A transposition often involves a chord which is common to both keys. In bar 4, beat 4 in Example 23-E above, the C chord is common to both G major and C major and has been analyzed in both keys. We hear the key context change when the F♮ sounds in bar 5 beat 1. In bars 1 and 2 however there is no common chord for the transposition from C major to G major before the key context changes.

In any given key context there are 7 different PNKs. There are 5 PNKs outside the key context, *i. e.,* there are 5 possible accidentals outside a KS. That is easy to visualize with the C major scale on the piano. It includes all 7 white keys and none of the 5 black keys. C♯, D♯, F♯, and G♯ are possible leading tones to closely related keys. (Confirm that.) The remaining black key - B♭ - can be found in the V7 of IV chord, progressing to the closely related key of the subdominant. (Confirm that.)

Example 23-F

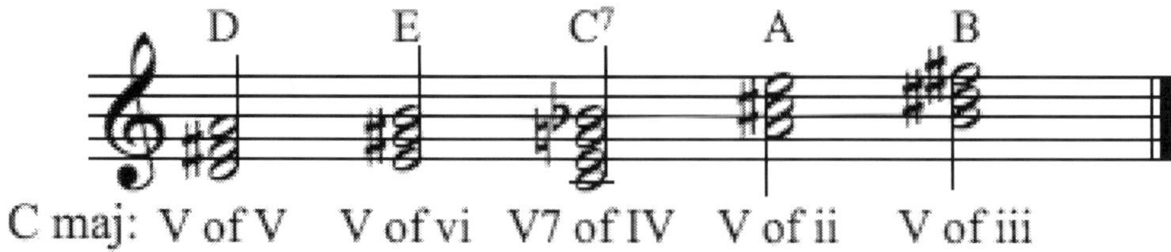

Note that the D♯ and G♯ are more than one sharp away from the key context of C major/all♮. However D♯ and G♯ are not part of the <u>KS</u> of the closely related keys of E minor and A minor, but are the <u>accidental</u>*s* which raise the 7th scale degree to provide a leading tone. The KSs are still only one step away from the original key, a requirement for a closely related key.

In a minor key there can be accidentals which raise scale degrees 3, 4, and 6 to create leading tones to closely related keys. The lowered 2 can be the 7th of the V7 of VI. (Confirm that in keys other than A minor.)

Example 23-G

"Theoretical" Keys

"Theoretical" is in quotes because, despite the term, you may very well encounter key signatures and especially key contexts which include double sharps and double flats. For example if you are performing or composing a piece in the key of C♭ major and there was a section of the piece transposed to the subdominant key, that key would be F♭ major with a key context of 8 flats, which is 7 flats plus a B double flat. When playing scales in theoretical keys just pretend you're playing its enharmonic equivalent. The key of F♭ major is enharmonic with E major.

Parallel keys can also be theoretical keys. One of the characteristics of Cole Porter's music is frequent changes to parallel keys. If your voice range requires your accompaniment to be in the key of G♯ minor you could find yourself playing a section of the song in G♯ major with 8 sharps or D♯ major with 9 sharps. (Think A♭ major or E♭ major.) As stated earlier the circles of keys and chords can be extended in an infinitely continuous spiral through double, triple, quadruple, etc. sharps or flats. It is not uncommon to find chord symbols "off the charts" of the circle of chords. Sooner or later you're sure to find G♯, D♯, F♭, etc. chords. Just think the enharmonic equivalent of the root and play the same chord type. The keys closely related to C♭major, C♯ major, A♭ minor and A♯ minor will include theoretical keys.

Exercise

Analyze some Bach chorales and/or some hymns. Place chord symbols above the staff and Roman numerals below. I find it easier to analyze with chord symbols first to use as a reference. When determining the correct Roman numeral analysis, the chord symbol shows me the root, inversion, chord type, effect of accidentals, and the relationship to adjacent chords, *i.e.*, the chord progression. Mark and identify all NCTs.

Useful tools (in the Baroque style major/minor tonal system):

1. A minor key will always have an accidental.
That is not to say that the 7th scale degree will always be raised, but there will always be raised 7ths in a piece in a minor key. No raised 7th = Aeolian mode.

2. A dominant chord is always major in both major and minor keys.

3. Accidentals other than raised 6th and 7th degrees in minor don't always mean a transposition to a new key. Suspect a borrowed dominant chord first. In later music also consider Neapolitan and augmented 6th chords (Chapter 25).

4. Be sure you know your NCTs and don't try to incorporate them into illogical chord formations.

In addition to hymns and Bach chorales, analyze all the compositions in your repertoire. The real purpose of music theory is to understand why music sounds the way it does. That understanding gives the performer the ability to express the nuances of the composer's intention beyond just playing all the right PNKs at the right time. If you are a composer that understanding will be your tool box full of nuances to indicate to the knowledgeable performer what you want the performer and the audience to feel.

Chapter 24
The Modes

The Modes

Each of the modes (discussed in Chapter 7) has a key context and therefore a tritone consisting of the last entry in the key context and the natural which is next in the order of sharps or flats. Because the tritone in a mode involves different PNKs from a major or minor key, it will not “want” to resolve to the root and/or 3rd of the tonic triad as in a major or minor key. The composers of the Baroque period, in order to effect a stronger tonal center, wrote almost exclusively in the major and minor keys.

Today’s composers utilize the modes and still create tonal centered music. Devices other than the tritone are used to indicate the tonic as the tonal center. When composing or performing a modal piece it is important to be aware of the specific differences between the mode and its relative major or minor key. Three of the modes have just *1 PNK different* from the KS of their parallel (same keynote) minors while two have just *1 PNK different* from the KS of their parallel majors. See Example 24-A below.

Example 24-A

mode	difference from the parallel major or minor KS
Dorian	like minor with <submediant
Phrygian	like minor with >supertonic
Lydian	like major with < subdominant
Mixolydian	like major with >leading tone (subtonic)
Aeolian	like minor with >leading tone (subtonic)

By being aware of the differences you can emphasize the modal feel of the music.

Computer exercises 24.1 & 24.2

With a tonal centered modal piece, that one PNK difference from major or minor KS provides some significant changes in the harmony. Keep in mind that <u>one</u> scale PNK change effects a change in <u>three</u> different triads and <u>four</u>

different 7th chords. In the Phrygian mode the lowered supertonic is quite an expressive PNK. It makes the supertonic triad a major triad with a strong tendency to resolve down a half step into tonic. You can create an entire mid-eastern dance piece using only the tonic and supertonic chords in the Phrygian mode. "Hava Nagila" has a major triad on tonic as well as on the super tonic. The melody exploits the resulting augmented 2nd between the 2nd and 3rd scale degrees.

Example 24-B

You can add the major triad on mediant (bar 2 below) for more flavor.

Example 24-C

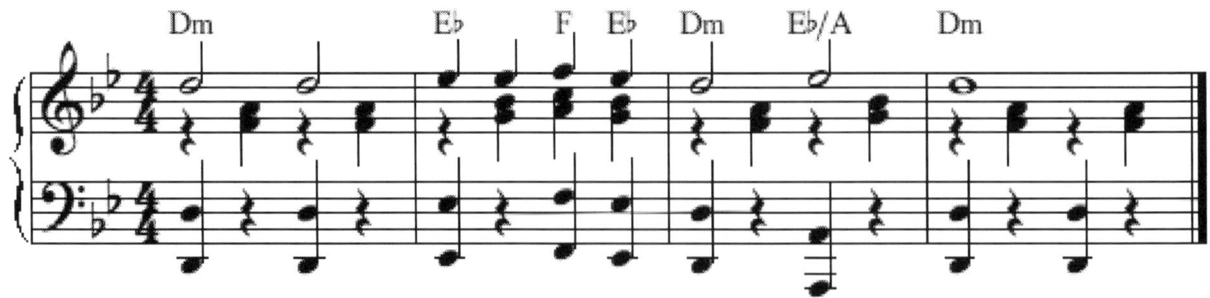

Another aspect of the Phrygian mode is the diminished triad on the dominant PNK. It does *not* have a tendency to resolve to tonic. This lack of dominant function on the v° chord can be replaced by the II chord as in Example 24-B above (bar 5) *or* a combination of a low bass on the dominant

PNK plus a II chord as in Example 24-C above (bar 3) or a low dominant PNK plus a iv chord = v^{11} as in Example 24-D below (bars 2, 3 and 4).

Example 24-D

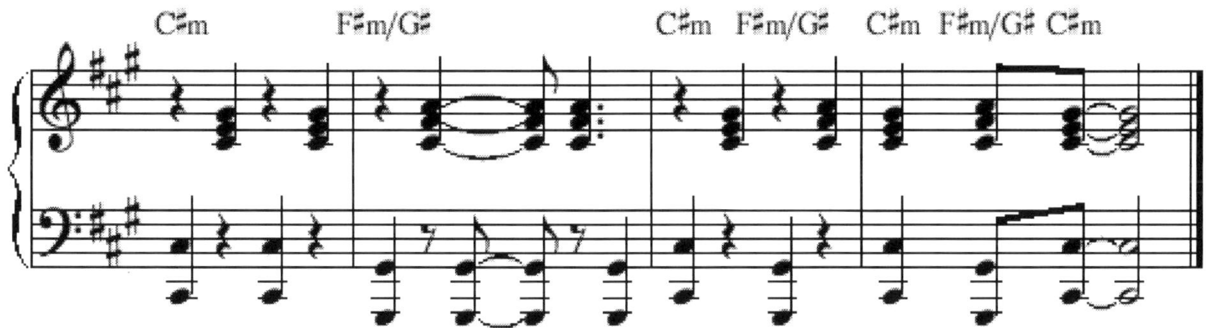

For the Dorian mode the major subdominant chord and the major subtonic chord are very effective modal sounds. In the Dorian, Mixolydian, and Aeolian modes the subtonic chord can be used as a dominant function resolving to tonic. See bar 6 in Example 24-E below.

Example 24-E

excerpt from

O One With God The Father

Jon P. Nicholson

Willaim W. How

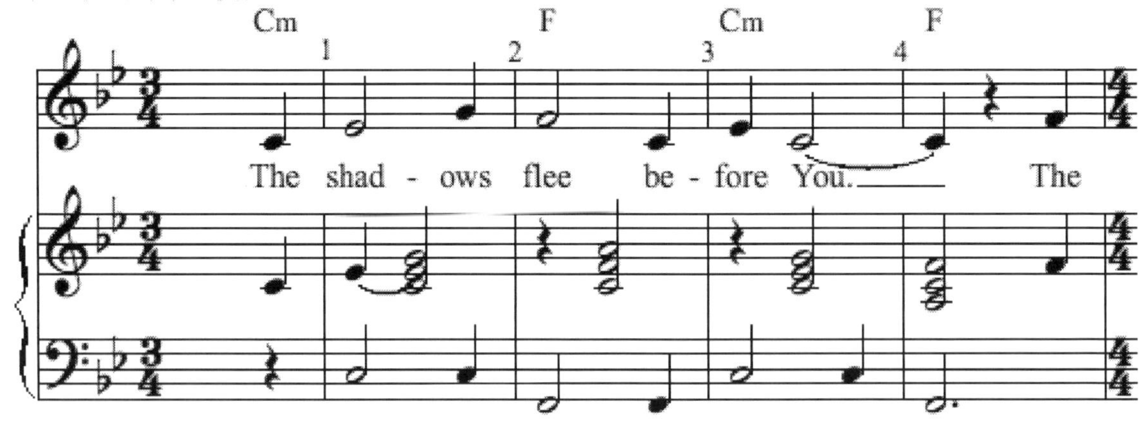

The raised subdominant in the Lydian mode can sound like a mistake but is used quite expressively in mood melodies for movies and TV dramas. See Example 24-F below.

Example 24-F

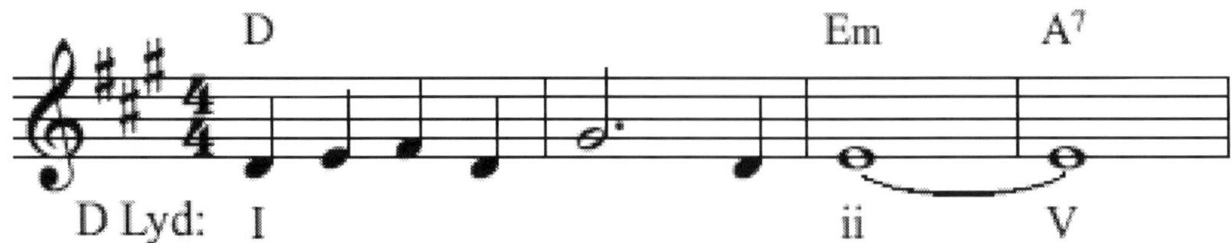

Chapter 25

Augmented 6th Chords
Three Types of Augmented 6th Chords
French Augmented 6th Chords
Resolutions of French Augmented 6th Chords
Neapolitan 6th Chords

Augmented 6th Chords

The structure and historical use of the augmented 6th chords is much more complicated than necessary for understanding their usefulness. They were most often found in a minor key with a crossed key context and analyzed as follows:

1. The 1st inversion of the iv or iv7 chord

2. with a raised root which

3. formed the interval of an augmented 6th with

4. the lowest sounding PNK, which was the 3rd of chord.

5. The augmented 6th interval resolves by expanding to an octave of the dominant PNK.

6. This octave on the dominant PNK was usually the 5th of the tonic triad in second inversion but could also be the root of the dominant chord.

It won't seem so complicated if you will apply each step in the above explanation to Example 25-A below. (The A♭7 fake symbol interprets the F♯ enharmonically as G♭.)

Example 25-A

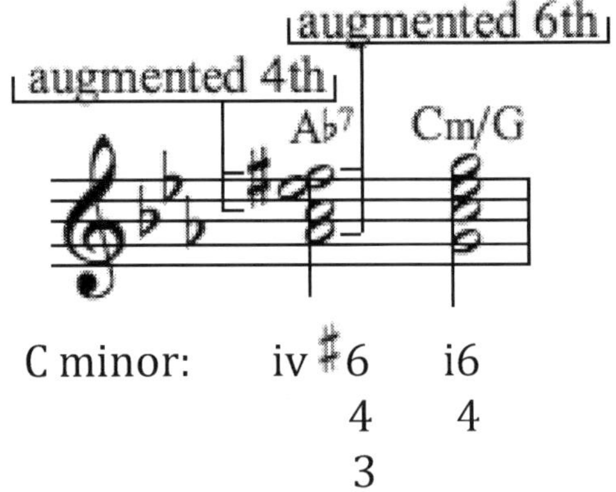

I have trouble imagining a composer going through all those steps to create a chord progression that can be explained in a much simpler manner. All the augmented 6th chords are like a dominant 7th chord with the root a *half step above dominant*. The root progression is down a half step to the dominant chord or to the 5th of the tonic chord in second inversion. It is a very colorful chord progression.

In the above example, do we hear the interval as an augmented 6th with a *crossed key context* or as a V7 chord with the F♯ spelled as a G♭? If we interpret sensory input in its simplest form, the augmented 6th chord will be heard as a V7 sounding in *one key context*. The resolution is a surprise. What we heard as a diminished 5th in a V7 chord resolves instead as an augmented 4th. The surprise is acceptable because the tritone can go either way. It is quite a remarkable surprise because we have resolved to C, nearly half way around the circle of keys from D♭ where we expected to go from an A♭ dominant 7th chord.

The augmented 6th chords in closed position all contain a tritone spelled as an augmented 4th. The augmented 4th wants to expand.

Example 25-B

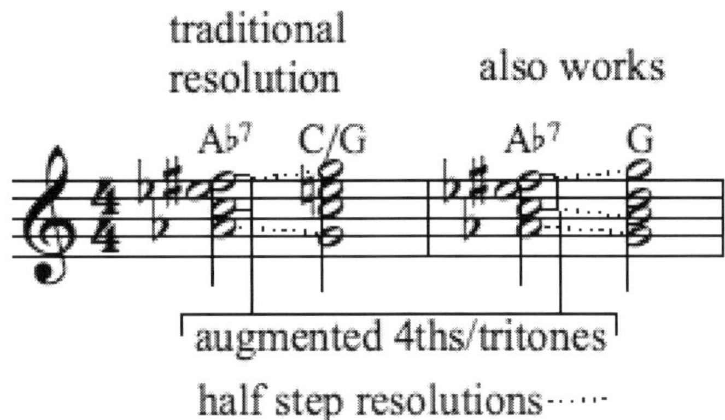

The V7 chord in closed root position contains a diminished 5th. We expect it to contract.

Example 25-C

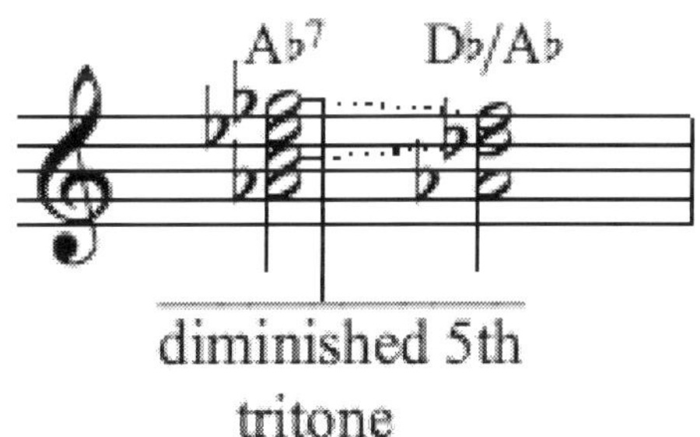

Three Types of Augmented 6th Chords

There are different forms of the augmented 6th chords, but they all include at least 1 tritone. See Example 25-D below.

Example 25-D: Augmented 6th chords

Italian German French

The Italian is like V7 without a 5th. The German is an unaltered V7. The French is V7 with a lowered 5th. (This can help avoid parallel 5ths.)

An augmented 6th chord sounds the same as a dominant 7th but you can hear the difference when they resolve. The root progression of V7 to I is down a perfect 5th or up a perfect 4th – a "circle" progression. The root[4] progression of the augmented 6th chord is down a half step.

Example 25-E: Two German augmented 6th chords with 3 resolutions in C major.

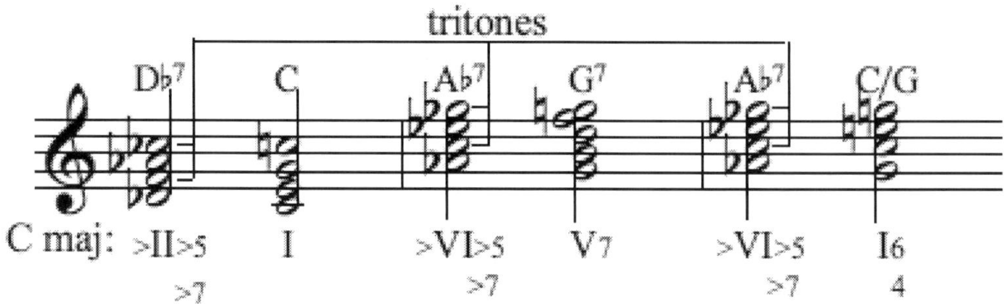

In Example 25-E above, the spelling of the tritones of the D♭7 and the A♭7 chords as diminished 5ths would be incorrect *after you heard them resolve*. They resolve as expanding augmented 4ths. The respelling of the minor 7ths as augmented 6ths justifies their expanding resolutions. The Italian and French augmented 6th chords resolve in the same manner as the German augmented 6th chord in the above example.

You can often substitute an augmented 6th chord for a dominant 7th chord. See the 2 excerpts in Example 25-F below.

Example 25-F

[4] This is the acoustic root (the bass PNK) as defined by the RDI. (See Chapter 22.) In Example 25-D the acoustic root is A♭.

In “Georgia On My Mind” the next to last chord in the original version was B♭7, the dominant 7th of the key. The E7 chord, a half step above the E♭ tonic, gives more of a jazz sound. Notice that the E7 chord would be a German augmented 6th chord if it had been spelled as F♭ A♭ C♭ D. It has the same tritone as the Bb7 - A♭ and D – which resolves the same way into the root and 3rd of the E♭ tonic chord. The traditional use of the augmented 6th chord was a half step above the dominant. As such it served the same function as a secondary dominant with the same tritone.

In the 3rd bar of “Body and Soul” the G7 chord is a German augmented 6th that functions as a substitute V7 of V in B major.

Franz Schubert wrote a beautiful use of the German augmented 6th chord shown in Example 25-G below.

Example 25-G

In the 4th and 5th bars we have the G♭ and D♭7 chords as I and V7 in the key of G♭ major. Then in bars 6 and 7 he respells the D♭7 chord as a B augmented 6th chord (same pitches, different notes), which resolves in bar 8 to the second inversion tonic *and* root position dominant 7th of F minor. It is especially effective with the D♭ octaves in the bass resolving a half step down to the dominant C octaves then finally to the tonic. Schubert has used the same chord, spelled enharmonically, to resolve to 2 tonal centers almost halfway around the circle from each other.

Exercise

To become more familiar with the usefulness of augmented 6th chords in a progression, play each of the V7 chords around the circle and resolve it to the next chord in the circle – a root progression by perfect 5ths. Then play each of the V7 chords again and resolve it across the circle to the chord a half step below the root – a root progression by minor 2nds. Play these 2 progressions for every key on the circle. The first 2 are notated below.

Example 25-H:

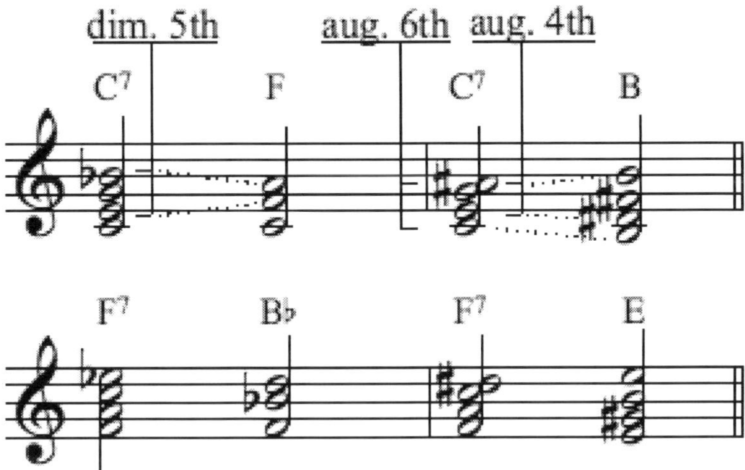

The dotted lines indicate half step resolutions.

The diminished 5th of the first V7 chord resolves inward by half steps to the root and 3rd of the chord of resolution. The augmented 4th of the second V7 chord resolves outward by half steps to the root and 3rd of the chord of resolution. The augmented 6th resolves outward by half steps to an octave doubling the root of the chord of resolution.

French Augmented 6th Chords

The French augmented 6th chord is the only augmented 6th chord with 2 tritones. The 2 tritones overlap by a whole step when the chord is in closed root position.

Example 25-I: French augmented 6th chord

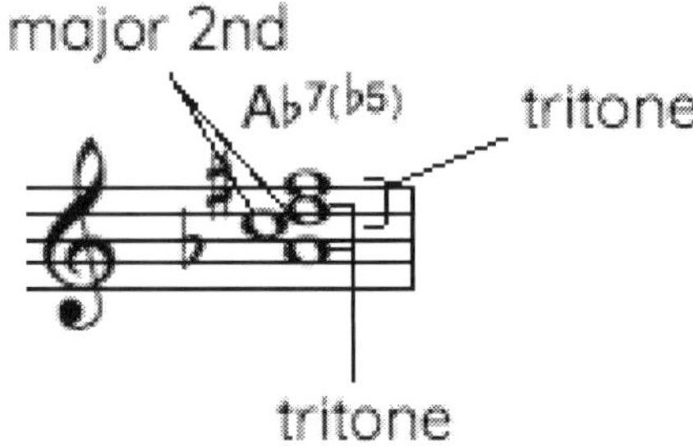

The diminished 7th chord also has two overlapping tritones, but they overlap by a minor 3rd, which splits the octave into 4 equal sections.

Example 25-J: Diminished 7th chord

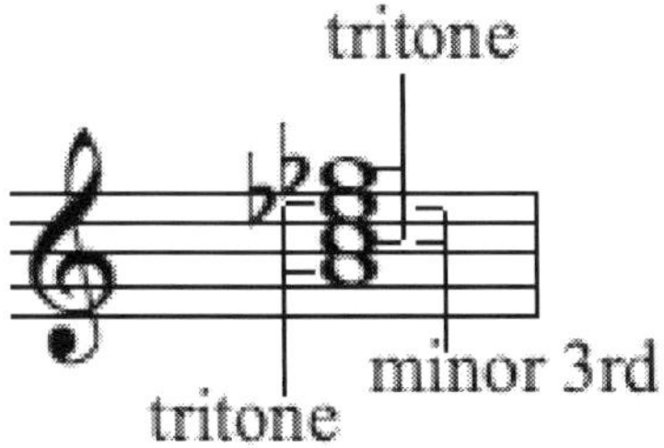

With any PNK of the diminished 7th chord as the lowest sounding note, *i. e.*, in any inversion, the intervals above that note remain the same, which is a stack of minor 3rds. With the French augmented 6th chord, there are 2 possible arrangements – major 3rd, major 2nd, major 3rd - and - major 2nd, major 3rd, major 2nd.

Resolutions of French Augmented 6th Chords

Because the tritones of the French augmented 6th overlap by a whole step rather than a minor 3rd, they don't split the octave equally. It therefore requires 4 French augmented 6th chords – like the first 4 in Example 25-K below - to resolve to every key on the circle, with 4 of the resolutions doubled. With the only 2 remaining French augmented 6th chords - the final 2 chords in Example 25-K - all 12 potential resolutions are doubled.

Example 25-K: Potential resolutions of the 6 French augmented 6th chords.

potential
resolutions: Eb,A,G,Db E,Bb,Ab,D F,B,A,Eb Gb,C,Bb,E Db,F,B,G D,Gb,C,Ab

The 4 resolutions of the 2 enharmonic spellings of the 2 tritones of a French augmented 6th chord are shown in the Example 25-L below. The spelling of each tritone is notated as half notes with half step resolutions to the following quarter notes. The next following quarter notes are the resolutions of the remainder of the chord tones. None of the resolutions exceed a whole step, even to the optional 7ths.

Example 25-L

Play the French augmented 6th chord in Example 25-L above. Then play and listen to the resolutions of each of the augmented and diminished intervals, followed by the remainder of the resolutions.

The German and French augmented 6th chords sound exactly the same as the V7 and V7♭5 chords respectively. As stated earlier, the difference is heard in their resolutions. The root of an augmented 6th chord resolves down a half step. The root of a V7 of V7♭5 resolves down a perfect 5th or up a perfect 4th – a circle progression.

Computer exercises 25.1 & 25.2

Exercise

Play the 6 French augmented 6th chords around the circle with the 4 resolutions of each. This is very good practice for cementing your understanding of tritones, chord progressions, key signatures, intervals, ear training - a big bunch of the tools in your tool box.

Neapolitan 6th Chords

A chord very similar to the augmented 6th chords is the Neapolitan 6 chord. It originated as the first inversion of a major triad on the lowered supertonic in a minor key. Its traditional resolution was to the dominant chord.

Example 25-M

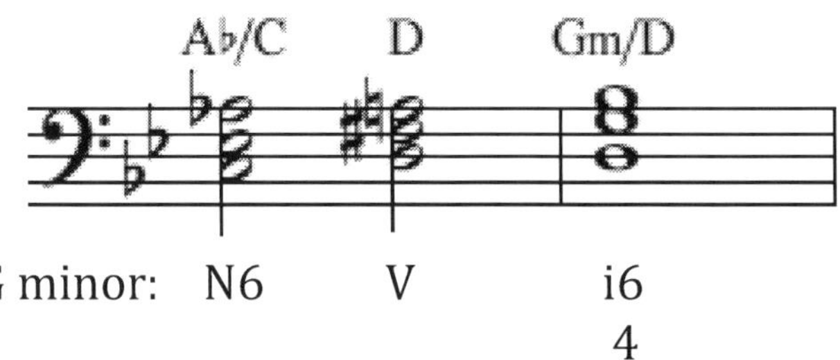

Like the augmented 6th chords, the Neapolitan chord was later used in any inversion, in both major and minor keys. It can also be used as N of V, with the root a half step above dominant. You sometimes will find it referred to as N6 even in other than first inversion. I prefer to indicate position the usual way with N, N6, N6/4.

I think of the N6 as a major triad with the root a half step above tonic or dominant and usually resolving to either tonic or dominant, the same as the augmented 6th chords. Like the augmented 6th chord it can also be used as a borrowed chord progressing to chords other than I or V in the key. See Example 25-N below.

Example 25-N: Neapolitan chord progressions

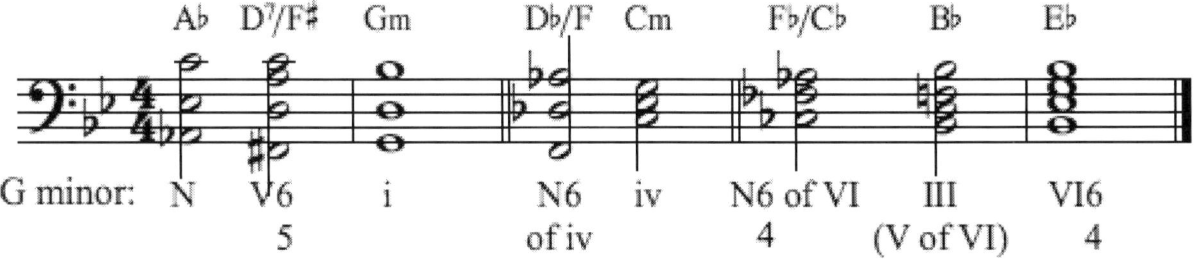

To summarize, the only significant difference between the N and the augmented 6th chords is the difference in sound between a V and a V7 chord, *i.e.,* the absence of a tritone in the V and N chord. The N and the augmented sixth chords serve the same functions.

A college-level music theory text published in 2009 instructs students that the Neapolitan chord is an altered ii chord, thereby making the N6 to V to i (*e.g.,* in F minor, Gb to C to Fm) a circle progression. The circle of keys is a circle of *perfect* 5ths. From the root of a lowered ii to the root of the dominant is a *diminished* 5th. The root of a N6 chord (G♭) is half way around the circle from the V chord (C). I disagree that calling N6 to V makes it a circle progression. Most important for me, I don't think it *sounds* like a circle progression. What do you think?

Chapter 26
Mirror Modes
Mirror Chords

Mirror Modes

I'm not sure yet that an understanding of the mirror modes and scales is useful for a musician. There could be material for contemporary composition and/or some new keyboard technique studies. Other than that it presents some interesting observations of relationships among modes, the topography of the keyboard, and the shape of our hands.

Pairs of modes mirror each other in their half step, whole step sequences as given below.

Example 26-A

mirrors	
Dorian	Dorian (itself)
Phrygian	major
Lydian	Locrian
Mixolydian	Aeolian

You can see it on the keyboard. Starting from D in the middle of the two black keys, if you play an ascending Dorian scale on all white keys you will play the same half step, whole step sequence as you will with the descending Dorian scale.

The modes with all ♮ KS/all white keys that mirror each other in their half step, whole step sequence are shown in Example 26-B below.

Example 26-B

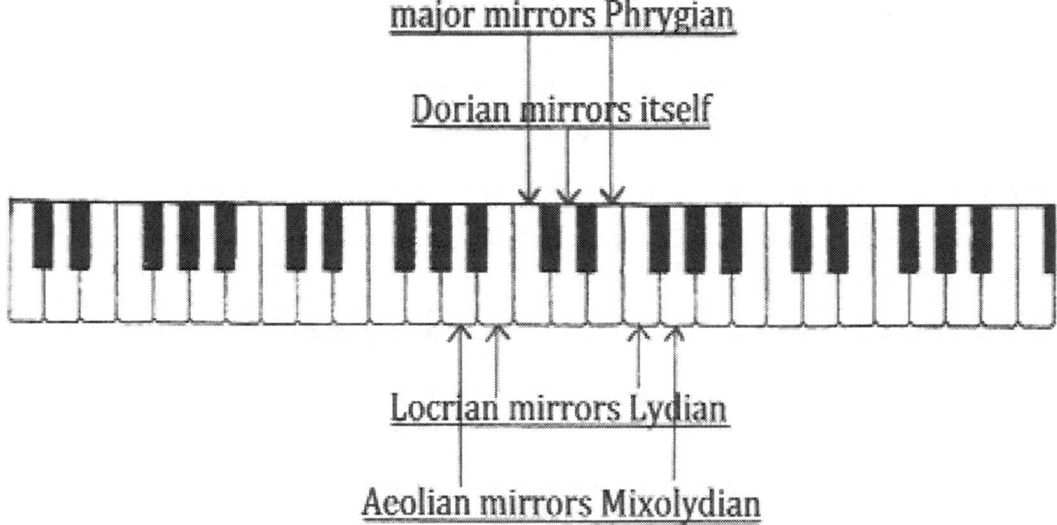

If you play an F Dorian scale with the right hand with a <u>KS of 3♭s,</u> you can mirror the black and white keys and the same consecutive fingering in the left hand if the left hand plays the B Dorian scale with a <u>KS of 3♯s</u> in contrary motion. See Example 26-C below.

Example 26-C

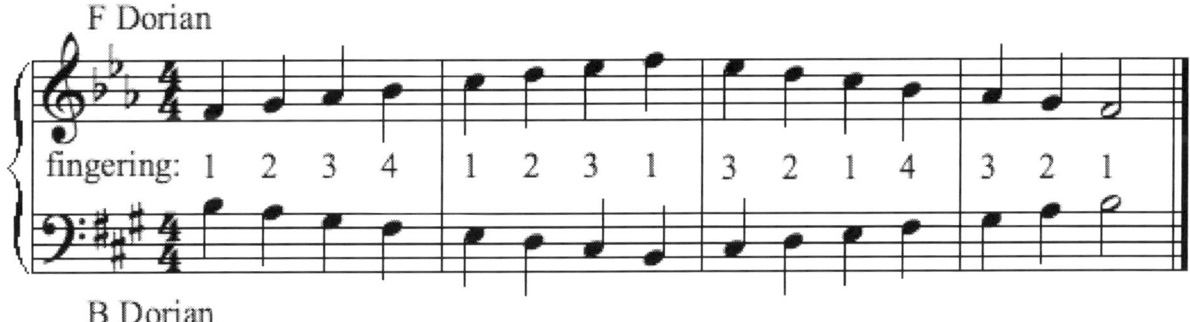

The scales and fingering are also mirrored if you swap the scales/hands.

Example 26-D

The fingering for the scales is based on the system given in Chapter 7 and is the same for both hands when playing these mirrored modes in contrary motion.

The major scale has the same half step, whole step sequence as the Phrygian scale when they are played in contrary motion. Likewise with Locrian/Lydian and Aeolian/ Mixolydian scales. When the tonics of these scales are equidistant from middle D <u>or</u> G♯/A♭, the sequence of black and white keys will be mirrored also, which means the fingering patterns for the scales will be the same for both hands, just as in Example 24-A above for the 2 Dorian scales.

The fingering will be mirrored, in the mirrored modes, when the <u>right hand has the same number of sharps as the left hand has flats and vice versa</u>. It doesn't matter which hand plays which mode *or* which hand plays sharps while the other hand plays flats. A few of the possibilities are given in Example 26-E below.

Example 26-E

R. H. - - -	- - -L. H.
or	
L. H. - - -	- - - R. H.
A Dorian - 1♯	G Dorian - 1♭
B♭ major - 2♭	F♯ Phrygian – 2♯
A Lydian - 4♯	G Locrian - 4♭
D♯ Aeolian - 6♯	D♭ Mixolydian - 6♭

How many different possibilities are there? There are 7 different modes per key context. There are 12 different tonic PNKs not counting the enharmonic keys twice. Each hand will play each of the 7 modes on each of the 12 tonics = 84 different contrary motion scales. The same as if you played all 7 modal scales hands together in every key context or on every tonic.

Why would you do that? Flexibility in technique. You will really learn to feel how the black and white keys fit the way your hands are put together, with the thumbs on opposite sides of your hands. And remember from Chapter 7 that the modal scales were used much more frequently by Mozart and Beethoven than major and minor, and how the fingering system based on key context (you may not have known the term at that time) made scale playing easier.

It could take quite a bit of time and listening experience to *hear* the mirror relationship patterns. Compositions using mirror modes may be a long way from general acceptance. Use your own judgment to calculate the value of spending time writing in mirror modes. A short piano piece is on the following page.

The MirrorrorriM ehT

Mirror Chords

Chords can also be mirrored. See Examples 26-G & 26-H below.

Example 26-G

triad	mirrors
major	minor
diminished	diminished
augmented	augmented

Example 26-H

7th chord	mirrors
dominant 7th	half diminished 7th
minor 7th	minor 7th
major 7th	major 7th
diminished 7th	diminished 7th

Mirrored chords would all be constructed automatically in the mirrored modes.

Made in the USA
Columbia, SC
10 June 2022